Stratford Library Services
1846 - 2003

Dean Robinson

Published by Stratford Public Library, Stratford, Ontario

Production and art by Peter Schlemmer

Cover design by Peter Schlemmer and Dean Robinson

Cover photos
Front: Black and white postcard of the SPL after its new front was added in 1926 (Dr. Don Davis). Back: Colour postcards of the original Carnegie building and the 1926 addition (Stratford-Perth Archives); and sketch of the SPL with the 1975 addition (Norma Bissonnette)

Printed in Canada by Stratford Printing & Graphics, Stratford Ontario

Sue Bonsteel

May 25, 1917-Feb. 6, 2003

When she retired as head librarian at the Stratford Public Library in May 1983, Sue Bonsteel said, "I don't really want to fade off into the sunset."

She talked of her plans to do more travelling, and to increase her involvement with civic, church, and service organizations. True to her word, she did all of that and more.

She was named Stratford's volunteer of the year for 1983 and was a popular member of city council from 1986 through 1988. She did some teaching in Nepal, sailed to Canada's north, and toured in Egypt. She was tireless in her support of Stratford and Area World Aid, the Kiwins and her church, St. John's United. She was tireless in her support of just about anyone who asked her to lend a hand.

She was a humanitarian and an environmentalist, her dedication diminished not a whit by failing eyesight and a struggle with cancer. She had a warm heart and an even warmer sense of humour.

There was no fading in this woman's retirement.

Rather, she continued to make our load a little bit lighter, our days a little bit brighter.

Sue, this one's for you.

SPL

The author and Sue Bonsteel compare notes, July 2002

The American clergyman

and abolitionist, Henry Ward Beecher,

said, "A library is not a luxury

but one of the necessities of life."

On that point he would have drawn

no argument from our grandfather,

R. Thomas Orr, who, in his forthright manner,

made an overture to the Carnegie foundation

that resulted in the building whose centennial

we celebrate on these pages.

We, the Orr family, are proud

of our century-long association

with the Stratford Public Library

and honoured to sponsor

this account of its illustrious history.

Acknowledgements

Researching and recounting the story of more than 150 years of library services in Stratford is a task made lighter with many hands. For the most part, those hands belong to the people listed on this page.

Special thanks to Jane Kirkpatrick, who was talking up this book as many as six years ago; and to Anne Marie Heckman, whose bad luck found her on the receiving end of scores of queries. As the library's go-to person, she squinted through decades of board minutes, many of them handwritten, to unravel or refute.

Her backup on the library staff, past and present, included Cindy Atchison, Joyce Banks, Sue Bonsteel, Ken Clarke, Marion Gibb, Lorraine Greenberg, David Harvie, Winnifred Henderson, Sally Hengeveld, Cathy Perreault, Dorothy Robinson, Irma Sass, Theresa Talsma and Christina Wilson.

There was help, too, from staff at the Stratford-Perth Archives, in particular Cindy Farmer and Kate Jacob, both former employees of the SPL.

And from these significant others: John Banks, Pete Catania, Steve Chandler, Audrey (Crerar) Clark, Cathy Clarke, Dr. Don Davis, Audrey Gale, Brian Hayter, Betsy (Trethewey) Kalmusky, Grant Kropf, Tom Kydd, Betty Larkworthy, Rick Linley, Audrey (Kennedy) Mageau, Sharon Malvern, Phil Marusaik, Bev Neeb, Marg O'Reilly, Anne Orr, Cathy Petryna, Marg Pike, Heather Proctor, Eileen Rae, Marg Ryerson, Barbara Taylor, Charles and Helen Trethewey, Marilyn (Connor) Wells, Reg White, Tom Wilcox and Jack Young.

I am also indebted to my wife Judy, one of the SPL's most faithful patrons, for her reading and re-reading of the manuscript.

Additional sources:

The Beacon Herald. Stratford, Ont.

The Best Gift, A Record of the Carnegie Libraries in Ontario. Margaret Beckman, John Black and Stephen Langmead, Dundurn Press, 1984

The 2000 Canadian Encyclopedia World Edition. McClelland and Stewart Inc., 1999

Centenary of Stratford Public Library. Alexander William Fisher, 1946

Ever Forward, an Adventure in Faith. St. Andrew's Presbyterian Church, Stratford, 1988

Floodtides of Fortune. Adelaide Leitch, City of Stratford, 1980

Free Books for All, The Public Library Movement in Ontario, 1850-1930. Lorne Bruce, Dundurn Press, 1994

Historical Atlas of Perth County 1879, H. Belden and Co. Ross Cumming ed., Port Elgin, 1972

Railway Stratford. Dean Robinson, Boston Mills Press, 1989

Stratford City Gazette. Stratford, Ont.

Stratford Library Services since 1846. Jim Anderson, 1975

Stratford Public Library history. (unpublished) Lillian Morley, 1955

Stratford Times. Stratford, Ont.

Stratford Weekly News. Stratford, Ont.

D.R.
April 2003

Introduction

It may have been men who facilitated its birth, in 1897, but it has been women who have directed the Stratford Public Library for 104 of the 106 years since. Jane Kirkpatrick, the SPL's sixth and current chief librarian, smiles at the mention of that fact.

That the library has had just six chiefs through its first century says something about the commitment of those people and about the trustees who have worked with them to provide a service whose well-being has often been threatened by a shortage of space and money. Indeed, doing more with less has long been part of the job description for those charged with running the SPL.

While their task has often been more daunting than delightful, Kirkpatrick and her predecessor, Sue Bonsteel, have said they would trade their job with no one. They praised the board members with whom they worked. They cited the many volunteers who have given unselfishly to keep the library's programs varied and vibrant. And, they offered thanks for a citizenry that has embraced and defended the library and what it has to offer.

This book is about all of the above.

A work of reflection and celebration, its publication comes at a time when the SPL is again pleading for more space. The building that for a century has been a jewel in the city's core faces another moment of truth. How the moment is met will determine the quantity and the quality of the services the SPL continues to offer.

The plea is not new. And, in step with the library's storied tradition, the corrective response is overdue.

Dean Robinson
April 2003

Contents

"Libraries are not made; they grow."

– Augustine Birrell (1850-1933)

The growing of a library
1846-1902

Numerous are the accounts of pioneers who brought books with them when they emigrated from Britain and continental Europe to take up Canada Company land in the Huron Tract in the 1830s and '40s. Often travel torn and ocean stained, those prized volumes formed the basis for home libraries and sometimes became the first instructional materials for the public and Sunday schools soon established by the settlers.

Those schools and churches gave rise to informal lending rings, but for the residents of Little Thames – eventually renamed Stratford, there was nothing in the way of an organized public library.

That changed in December 1846 with the formation of a mechanics institute, which was based on the model developed in Scotland in the 1820s. Mechanics institutes were voluntary associations of working men wanting to improve themselves through education. They did that by hosting evening lectures, by circulating books and by maintaining reading rooms that offered a variety of periodicals.

The institute's first quarters in Stratford are believed to have been in the log schoolhouse that was built in 1842 on what is now the triangle of land formed by the intersection of St. Andrew and Church streets. In addition to circulating books, its members listened to lecturers and formed discussion groups.

After flourishing for a year or two, the institute in Stratford folded, and remained folded until it was reborn in the fall of 1852 in a room in the new county administration building at Mornington and William streets.

On Aug. 8, 1853, the institute was incorporated, and by the end of that year it boasted 90 volumes, some periodicals and 28 members. Its president was Alexander Barrington Orr, its secretary Samuel L. Roberts. Both men took their turns at delivering lectures, as did Alex McGregor, John James Edmonstoun Linton, Dr. John Hyde, Rev. Thomas MacPherson, William Smith and Charles Julius Mickle.

In his history of the Stratford Public

What was it like in Stratford in 1846?

What was it like in Stratford in 1846, when some of the settlement's literary leaders established a mechanics institute? That's the question Jim Anderson posed near the beginning of his history of the Stratford Public Library, published in 1975. And this is how he answered it: "The population was less than 250. The oldest building was 14 years old, a boy had been half frightened to death by a bear in the bush on Rebecca Street, civic leaders were anticipating the formation of municipal government, and the Canada Company ruled rather heavily under the firm hand of the company agent. He resided on the present courthouse lawn in the middle of the settlement. Anyone predicting a railway through Stratford 10 years hence would have been considered daft.

"Were one to step back into 1846 he would find himself hopelessly lost in a shuffling village. Life was structured around the day's work that had to be done, which differed with each season. Hired people stayed on the job until they were told they could go home. Clocks were curiosities that ministers and teachers, those exhorters of using time wisely, ruled their lives by and hoped the rest of the populace would too. It was years before the town had a curfew bell to ring or churches had chimes or factories had whistles or houses had kitchen clocks, which were loosely synchronized.

"People who worked in business or industry spent most of their daylight hours (at least 10 hours) six days a week under Victorian employers. Shop girls earned 50 cents a day, however long it was, with 25 cents deducted for undue lateness or outside appointments. The employer saw himself as a benefactor to the community's economy and to those members of the community whose lives are ordered by others. There was no insurance for ill health or unemployment, and few had prospects of a pension. The realities of life were sobering.

"It was in this relatively classless setting that a few men with inquisitive minds, some with formal education, shared their interests in a variety of subjects after long days of work. They believed in a semblance of civilization especially in this typical isolated clearing called Stratford. Many people, lost in the endless round of monotonous pioneer subsistence routines and loneliness, were driven to desperate unreality. We owe a debt to the men who brought the mechanics institute here and nursed it. They believed the public good rated higher than individual aspirations and established a pattern of community thinking which in time gave us a remarkable public park, industry relative to existing services, one of the oldest music festivals in Canada and an orderly town plan, to name a few of our present assets."

Library, Jim Anderson said it's a good bet that Linton had a hand in the creation of a mechanics institute in Stratford. The

Edinburgh lawyer, who was also a teacher after settling in what is now Perth County, was a citizen who involved himself in the affairs of the community.

In a newspaper report, the difficulties faced by the institute in those days were said to include the "apathy of working classes to the means provided for their intellectual improvement, and want of proper encouragement from the wealthy and more intelligent residents of town and neighbourhood."

streets. Dr. John Hyde was president of the SRRA that year and in 1861. But in 1861 he was also listed as president of the mechanics institute, which suggests that might have been the year the two organizations amalgamated. At the least, they were sharing a president.

By 1863 the institute had 50 members and from 800 to 1,000 books on its shelves.

The men of the reading room association

In 1975, when Jim Anderson published *Stratford Library Services since 1946*, he included the following list of names, all thought to have been connected to the Stratford Reading Room Association, which was formed in 1859. The asterisk indicates those who were also members of the board of the mechanics institute.

W. N. Hossie *	W. M. Clark *	N. Campbell
C. R. Jarvis *	J. Douglas	J. Fennell
D. T. Bailey	James Kyle *	Dr. John Hyde *
A. McDonald	John Hamilton *	John J. E. Linton *
Gilbert Horne	C. M. Smith	F. A. Atkinson
W. Keily	J. A. Carroll	

But the institute prevailed, even after the Stratford Reading Room Association was formed in August 1859. The association was created independent of the mechanics institute but "with a view to eventually forming a connection with that body," according to a story in the Stratford *Beacon*. The SRRA set up in a room on the second floor of the town hall and charged each of its members an annual fee of $2. Its principals included president Walter Hossie, vice-president Charles R. Jarvis, financial secretary Darwin T. Bailey, general secretary A. McDonald, treasurer Gilbert Horne, and directors W. Keily, William M. Clark and J. Douglas.

In 1860 the town gave the reading room association a grant of $30 when officials moved their operation to the Jarvis block, on the southwest corner of Erie and Ontario

Those shelves were by then in a front room on the main floor of Central Public School, a brick building which stood from 1855 to 1917 on the front lawn of the present SPL. The school board's tireless treasurer, James Steet, was a longtime secretary of the institute.

In 1871 the Grand Trunk Railway moved the equipment and mechanical personnel from its repair shops in Brantford and Toronto to Stratford. With the machinery and men from Toronto came the railway's literary institute, which gave Stratford another library. It was relocated in the railway's office building on Downie Street south of St. Patrick Street. Its librarian for more than three decades was Edward Riley.

One of the GTR Literary Institute's biggest boosters, as well as its president, was John Davis Barnett, a book hound who

The mechanics institutes

Mechanics institutes were the creation of George Birbeck (1776-1841), a British educator who in the early 1800s established courses and lectures for working men in and around Glasgow, Scotland. Out of that initiative was founded the Glasgow Mechanics' Institution in 1823. Soon there were Birbeck-style mechanics institutes throughout Britain.

They began as community-based, voluntary associations of working men seeking self-improvement through education – with evening lectures, lending libraries and periodical reading rooms. Members, it was determined, were to learn the underlying scientific principles of their work as well as the general value of "rational information."

It was a concept that made its way to British North America, and in 1828 a mechanics institute opened in Montreal. Two years later, there was one in York (now Toronto). By 1896 there were 311 such institutes in Ontario, with close to 32,000 members. There were institutes, too, in Nova Scotia and British Columbia.

While they had been started for labourers, anyone could join the mechanics institutes, whose operating budgets were covered by the fees paid by members. After 1835, those fees were buoyed by government grants. It was in that year that an institute was formed in Woodstock.

Another followed in Stratford in 1846, and in nearby Mitchell in 1849.

According to *The 2000 Canadian Encyclopedia World Edition*, those who developed the mechanics institutes in Canada were rarely manual workers. Rather, says TCE, "the institutes were controlled by shopkeepers, doctors, ministers and small manufacturers who sought activities for themselves, and more importantly, the growing number of urban wage-earners.

"The institutes emphasized Victorian discipline and morality while refusing to consider social, economic and political questions. Much debate concerned the reading rooms and libraries which most members frequented for newspapers and popular fiction rather than the works of science, art and religion promoted by institute directors.

"In Ontario, this debate was transferred to communities at large in 1895 when the provincial government used legislation to transform the institutes into public libraries. The mechanics institutes thus reflected important features of 19th-century Canada: the constant anxiety of local leaders about social order and stability; the widespread hope of self-improvement through education; and the increasing popular thirst for reading material."

But, says TCE, internal contradictions, as well as the development of the labour movement, public libraries and adult education prevented the institutes from maintaining a viable identity into the 20th century.

served two terms with the railway in Stratford.

In December 1875 the mechanics institute moved to premises on the second floor of the building at what is now 2 Ontario St. Known then as the Redford block, the red-brick structure sits where Ontario and Huron streets meet, within shouting distance of the institute's former quarters. The building's owner, James Redford, was a supporter of the library and not opposed to making available rooms for reading and lectures. As ownership of that building changed, so did its name, to Macklin and Lloyd.

By then the institute's collection numbered 2,500 volumes, which were available to the public each evening and on Tuesday afternoons. Miss Janet Roberts was the librarian; John M. Moran, a public school inspector, was in charge of evening classes for the instruction of English. Those classes were free for members. Other principals with the institute at that time were David B. Burritt, president; and William R. Knox, secretary-treasurer.

In about 1885 the mechanics institute moved to the Young Men's Liberal Club, a two-storey building on Erie Street, about where the Scotiabank's parking garage is today. In 1892, by which time those quarters were no longer suitable, the library moved to two rooms on the second floor of the Corcoran block (formerly the O'Higgins block) on the southeast corner of Downie and Ontario streets. By then, members were paying a yearly fee of $1, but there was also some financial support from the city. It was during these years that the institute had a catalogue printed. The hours during which its members could use that publication were 2:30 p.m. to 6 p.m. and 7:30 p.m. to 9:30 p.m.

In addition to Hyde and Burritt, presidents of the mechanics institute in Stratford from 1853 through 1890 included A. B. Orr 1853, Robert Moderwell 1857 and 1859, John Idington 1872, John W. James 1873, Charles Herbert Ransom 1874, John Moran 1878, Rev. E. I. Wallace Waits 1880, George Stone 1889 and Rev. Ebenezer Wilkie Panton 1890.

The librarians during that span, besides Janet Roberts, included men named McCall and McKay, Wesley Ebbs, John Hunter 1857,

Thomas Mayne Daly Jr. 1872, Charles J. Mickle 1872, Lawrence Carroll 1874 and 1876, Moran 1889 and Stone 1890.

The mechanics institute in Stratford, wrote Jim Anderson, was supervised by the more successful and influential men of the day, some of whom doubled as librarian when there was a need in that area. In the latter role in the 1870s they learned that a third of the books borrowed were in the category of fiction, but by far the most popular reading matter was Harper's and like magazines of general essays and criticism, and history books.

Louise Jane Johnston is thought to have been the first librarian hired by the Stratford branch of the institute, prior to 1891. She was born in Ancaster in 1859, the second of five children for John and Jane (Lloyd) Johnston. Her father was Scottish, her mother Irish. By 1865 the Johnstons were living in Mitchell, by 1870 in Stratford. Their home in Stratford was at 170 Cambria St., where Louise continued to live with her sister Jessie, a teacher, after their parents had died.

According to Anderson, "The selection of reading material in libraries before 1900 was a very serious matter and the subject of many a boardroom wrangle. The book selection was usually entrusted to an experienced board member of unquestionable taste who prepared the final annual purchase list. This was tendered out to local booksellers and eagerly followed up. If the same person selected titles for a number of years, the collection began to reflect his interests and prejudices.

"In examining old books, one can only wonder how readers kept from falling asleep over much of the subject matter. They must have persisted through zeal. However, in those times when one sat in the backyard to read, it was quiet except for chickens and cows. Books given as prizes at school sometimes equalled the amount spent during the year on consumable supplies. Books were rated highly no matter how stuffy the content, and many of these gifts have survived in a state of unused wear. Canadians by tradition are great givers of books as gifts.

"Newspapers and periodicals were voted on individually each year by board members, and also were subject to preferences. Once a particular Irish newspaper was overlooked at the Grand Trunk library and repercussions rattled through the shops and ended in a showdown at the next meeting. A local source of revenue was the annual auction of periodicals. About 1860, some bound volumes of newspapers were included, which may help to explain the incomplete microfilm set of early papers in Stratford. The *Beacon* and the *Herald* donated or sold almost complete sets of bound papers to the library board, but some of these were destroyed in the 1950s to accommodate the mechanical processes for microfilming.

"In these early times librarians were merely employees hired part time to carry out a long set of rules, keep the floors swept, put the books in order and get books for borrowers who sat and asked for selections from the printed catalogue supplied to all members. Maintaining order and decorum were very important. The librarian in the early years was usually male and was seldom consulted about anything by the board, and was paid wages totalling less than the rent. The busiest time of the week was Saturday night."

In his history of the SPL, Alex Fisher said that prior to 1894 most of the institute's board members were "older men who were probably conservative in their views as to the proper management of a library, which fact developed a certain desire on the part of certain patrons for more modern methods in the purchasing of books and the financing of the institute."

The leaders among those certain patrons, described by Fisher as a "younger element,"

included Phineas McIntosh, Sam Stubbs, R. Thomas Orr, Charles P. Megan and John R. Macdonald. At the annual meeting in 1894 they demanded significant change in the makeup of the board, though they didn't push to oust all its members. Their numeric advantage at the meeting enabled the reformers to have Orr, Macdonald, J. Russell Stuart, James Steele and Thomas Plummer elected to the board. When their successes were challenged because they had not provided the meeting with enough notice of intent, there was a later vote, and it produced like results. Further, Steele was elected the directors' new chairman.

Almost immediately, the reconfigured board went after city council for a grant of $400. The aldermen were unmoved. They cited the institute's small membership – an equally small percentage of the electorate. So the directors tried another tack; they asked the city for $1 per institute member.

When the council agreed to that arrangement, the board cut its membership fee from $1 to 50 cents and went about signing up 800 subscribers. As much as the move caught the aldermen by surprise, they honoured their agreement, and the institute received a grant of $400 from the city.

Not long after that play, board members were back to the council seeking $1,000 and promising to turn their institute into a free library. While that proposition may not have been universally heralded, it was a popular notion with many. J. D. Barnett, the man behind the GTR Literary Institute, was a believer in free libraries, and more than once his pleas to the railway to amalgamate its library with similar services in Stratford had been unsuccessful.

After some political posturing, the mechanics institute was renamed the Stratford Public Library, though its books and reading facilities remained in the Corcoran block. Soon after, the GTR Literary Institute closed voluntarily, and some of its directors gravitated to the SPL board, the

Members of the board of the mechanics institute

Compiled by Jim Anderson in 1975, this is a list of men who served on the board of the mechanics institute. He included it in his publication, Stratford Library Services since 1846. The asterisk indicates those who were also members of the public library board.

John J. E. Linton	John Hamilton	James O'Loane
W. F. McCulloch	W. Strowger	F. M. Workman
S. L. Roberts	G. G. Ewart	John Buchan
A. B. Orr	John A. Scott	William Davidson *
Robert Moderwell	Rev. James George	Dr. L. C. Campbell
William Smith	Rev. Ephraim Patterson	Dr. C. T. Campbell
Dr. John Hyde	Charles James	Dr. W. R. Hamilton
John Idington	J. G. Kirk	Hugh Nichol
Wilfred Haines	Mr. Kahn	D. R. McPherson
J. W. James	J. A. McCulloch	D. McBeth
C. H. Ransom	Thomas Tobin	John Welsh
Worsley Ebbs	T. J. Birch	J. Russell Stuart *
D. B. Burritt *	John Gaudy	Dr. A. Hipple
John M. Moran	James Steet	A. C. Shaw
Rev. E. W. Waits	Mr. Kerr	J. Reid Stewart
George Stone	William Buckingham *	William McBride
Rev. E. W. Panton *	James Wilson	A. H. McDougal
C. J. Macgregor	R. R. Lang	J. A. Loney
Alex McGregor	James Wright	M. H. Ludwig
C. J. Mickle	Joseph Johns	W. H. Harvey
T. M. Daly	P. J. Smithwick	W. J. Holmes
William Imlach	A. Hay	Phineas McIntosh
James Redford	Dr. T. D. Lucas	Samuel Stubbs
P. R. Jarvis	William Whyte	A. P. Megan
John Crisp	Dr. J. A. Robertson	J. R. Macdonald
William Mowat	A. J. O'Higgins	Thomas Plummer
W. M. Clark	W. R. Knox	James Steele *
W. N. Hossie	G. J. Waugh	
James Kyle	John Owen	

first of which was elected on May 18, 1895. It comprised J. Russell Stuart, Harry G. Hopkirk, Rev. David Williams, W. C. Young, R. Thomas Orr, Dr. Edward H. Eidt, Mayor

William Davidson, William Buckingham and J. R. Macdonald. In the following month it was discovered that the board was one member too heavy, so it was rejigged to include Stuart, Davidson, Orr, Eidt, James Steele, Thomas Plummer, George Malcolm and Rev. Ebenezer Wilkie Panton.

It was back in 1882 that the Ontario legislature had provided for the establishment of free libraries, supported financially by a levy of half a mill, assessed on the value of all real and personal property. Toronto Public Library was the largest among the first libraries to choose free status.

On Nov. 4, 1895, J. Davis Barnett joined SPL president J. Russell Stuart and six other members of the library board in pleading the case for a free library at a city council meeting. They took with them a petition signed by 300 ratepayers. Barnett told the meeting he was glad "the (free library) wave had hit Stratford." Rev. David Williams of St. James' Anglican Church said a free library was a necessity because of the public school system. He said it was the duty of the council to see that the public schools were supplied with proper books. He argued that books provided the best education, and without a free library such an education was available only to rich men. Besides looking after the material interests of the citizens, he said, the council's higher duty was to promote culture. After hearing the delegation, the council referred the matter to its finance committee.

It was in February 1897 that the city decided to take over the SPL and transfer its operation to the ground level of the old city hall and market building, where some space had been freed up when the fire department moved to its new building at the corner of Albert and Waterloo streets. The city gave the library board a grant of $600 and hired Becker and Son to make the necessary renovations. With free rooms and some of its other costs now covered by the municipal budget, the library could probably get by nicely with that grant money and whatever it was to get from the provincial government, said SPL president James Steele. The board's assets at that time totalled $4,000.

The library had sought to get into the city hall in the fall of 1896, but the council said it had no money to refurbish the room favoured by the SPL, a room that was being used to store implements.

Finally, on June 11, 1897, the SPL gained "free" status, which meant members no longer paid fees – though they did have to ante up 10 cents a year for what was called a service charge.

Early on Wednesday, Nov. 24, 1897, George Robertson, a city police constable, noticed an unusual red glow in the windows along the west side of the market building. The annual Scottish concert had been staged in the city hall a few hours earlier, but by 1 a.m. the building was empty except for two tramps who had been allowed to sleep in the jail cells. The red glow was the reflection of flames, which soon engulfed the centrepiece of market square. The tramps were awakened and saved, but the building was lost. So was Old Tom, the cat that had lived in the building for about 10 years. Within a month of the fire that took his life, Tom had been stuffed by taxidermist A. Ross and was on display in the clerk's temporary office in the Worth block on Wellington Street.

The library's losses in the fire included between 2,900 and 3,600 of its 4,000 to 5,000 books (reports vary), magazines, the records of the mechanics institute, magazines, and Vol. A of Encyclopedia Britannica. Gone, too, was its shelving and some of its furniture. A table, a reading desk and about a dozen chairs were saved, and the SPL had insured their holdings with Gore Mutual for $2,000. Librarian Louise Johnston and her directors were quick to re-establish their

Periodical fare in 1899

In November 1898, Stratford bookstore proprietors A. Hayward Alexander and J. Herbert Kenner submitted their tenders to the SPL for its 1899 supply of periodicals. This is how the two submissions compared.

In 1926, Alexander began a 10-year term as a member of the SPL board.

Weeky magazines	A. Hayward Alexander	J. Herbert Kenner
Black and White	$8.50	$8.00
Graphic	$8.25	$8.00
Harper's Weekly	$3.50	$3.20
Illustrated London News	$5.60	$5.40
London Times	$3.50	$3.00
Musical Courier	$3.40	$3.25
Outlook	$2.95	$3.00
Punch	$3.65	$3.30
Scotsman	$2.75	$2.50
Monthly magazines		
Frank Leslie	$0.95	$0.90
Birds	$1.40	$1.25
Harper's Round Table	$0.95	$0.80
Atlantic Monthly	$3.50	$3.20
Boys Own	$1.70	$1.25
Bookman	$1.90	$1.63
Century	$3.75	$3.20
Canadian	$2.00	$1.50
Contemporary	$4.15	$4.00
Fortnightly	$4.15	$4.00
Forum	$2.90	$2.75
Ladies Home Journal	$0.95	$0.75
Munsey's	$0.95	$0.90
McClure's	$0.95	$0.80
Outing	$2.55	$2.40
Pall Mall	$2.85	$2.50
Popular Science	$4.75	$4.00
Scribner's	$2.75	$2.50
Strand	$1.10	$0.90
St. Nicholas	$2.80	$2.50
19th Century	$4.15	$4.00
Daily newspapers		
The Globe	$4.00	$3.25
The Mail	$4.00	$3.25

operation in the Corcoran block, where she was instrumental in rebuilding their collection, in part with the donation of books from patrons.

Board members James D. Barnett and J. Russell Stuart were among those donors, as were Newton A. Bosworth, Mrs. J. Sicklesteele, Katherine Rankin, George G. Ewart, Charles J. Macgregor, J. Reid Stewart, Miss Alice Beatty, Miss E. Smith, Hugh Nichol, Daniel R. McPherson, Mrs. E. Patterson, James P. Woods, Alex F. MacLaren, a Mrs. Palmer and a Mrs. Perry.

By January 1898 the directors had ordered about 2,200 books. In March they decided to move from their by-then cramped Downie Street digs to rooms in the Macklin block at 2 Ontario St., the address of the mechanics institute two decades earlier, but more recently the home of the Young Men's Christian Association. The rental fee for the library was set at $6 a month.

Regardless of location, the directors were serious about the system they had in place for the borrowing of books, and just as earnest in fining those neglectful about returning them. More than one client was deprived of their privileges.

It was also in 1898 that the Ontario legislature discontinued its support of mechanics institutes in favour of public libraries. In addition to $212.50 from the provincial government, the SPL in 1898 received $800 in municipal money. That year, the library had 3,210 books on its shelves, 1,293 of them fiction. Its book loans totalled 23,465. Among its financial expenditures were $2,348.70 for new books; $222.15 for rent, lighting and heat; $190 for salaries; $123.28 for periodicals; and $25 for typing book lists. On the other side of the ledger, its receipts included $70.50 in memberships; $47.83 in fines; and $40.10 from the sale of magazines. It ended 1898 with a bank balance of $266.15.

Meanwhile, the city fathers were fumbling their way through the designing and building of a new city hall, which, yet unfinished, hosted its first council meeting on Jan. 8, 1900. Library officials used Feb. 26 to make their move into the fresh facility, but this time they set up in three rooms, two of them just east of the main front door and the third, for reference material, in the basement. The two levels were connected with a spiral staircase.

In 1900 the library's hours of operation stretched from 9:30 a.m. to 9:30 p.m., and the books circulated totalled more than 30,000. For $25 the board bought 20 volumes of the Stratford *Herald*.

In April 1900, from 31 applicants, the same board needed several votes to choose Mrs. J. W. Robertson as its assistant librarian. The directors also drafted and printed new rules and regulations, which took effect on May 1, 1900. In them was reference to an Ontario statute that called for a $10 penalty against anyone who marked, defaced, clipped or mutilated a paper, book or periodical.

In July the board hired Gertrude Cook at $4 a week to provide vacation relief for Miss Johnston.

In November 1900, the provincial inspector of libraries, Samuel P. May, declared the SPL to be one of the best in Ontario. That was the month the board gave its 1,400 or so patrons access to the shelves that held its fiction collection, but there continued to be no such access to non-fiction books and all reading material in the juvenile section.

In March 1901 the Stratford directors approved the disbursement of $2 for membership in the Ontario Library Association, which had been founded in the previous year. After some debate, they also banned advertising material from their reading room. And they approved the training of a Miss Ridgedale to act as librarian in relief. In May 1902, Miss May Cook was hired and trained for the same role.

John Davis Barnett

One of the most interesting and influential men connected to the railway scene in Stratford was John Davis Barnett, who, as a 17-year-old, arrived in Montreal from his native London, England, in 1866.

He was just as influential in the development of the Stratford Public Library.

Born into a family of railway engineers, Barnett joined a group of workers who were dispatched to Canada to work for the British-backed Grand Trunk Railway. His father had already taught him the basics of drafting and in Montreal the young Barnett

was soon put in charge of the GTR's drafting room. That provided him with the opportunity to draw plans for the first coal-fired locomotive to be built in Canada. In a life that produced many accomplishments, he remained particularly proud of his involvement with that phase of Canadian railway history.

Studious and well-read, Barnett quickly became a master mechanic, and from 1880 to 1884 he held that position at the repair shops in Stratford. In 1888 he returned to Stratford to supervise the GTR's expanded operation. While he gave a lot of himself to the shops, he was equally dedicated to the city. Rail work aside, his most passionate interest was books, collecting them and reading them. An ardent traveller, Barnett brought home books from wherever he went. And the result was an addition to that home, a white frame building at 29 Douro St. Now stuccoed and since 1985 distinguished with a historical marker, the house was jammed with books. In a front room off the hall was a special collection by and about Shakespeare, a subject for which Barnett held a special interest. Its 1,500 volumes made up one of the finest Shakespearean collections in the world. Barnett's overall library eventually numbered about 42,000 bound volumes and more than 1,000 indexed envelopes containing unbound papers, pamphlets, booklets, maps, pictures, prints and other illustrative matter. A shed behind the house contained another five tons of uncatalogued material.

Barnett was a driving force behind the Grand Trunk's employees' library – the GTR Literary Institute – which was started in Toronto but moved to Stratford in 1871. In 1889, when the GTR closed its Great Western Railway repair shops in Hamilton, the library connected to that operation was

Board members of the GTR Literary Institute

The following are men who served on the board of the Grand Trunk Railway Literary Institute after it was relocated in Stratford in 1871. The list was compiled by Jim Anderson in 1975 and it appears in his publication, *Stratford Library Services since 1846*. The asterisk indicates those who were also members of the Stratford Public Library board.

J. Davis Barnett *	W. Coulter	A. Anderson
Robert Boag	Chris Iles	Thomas Honey
C. McLellan	J. Abey	A. L. Lyle
William H. Trethewey *	M. McLaughlin	S. J. Mallion
Joseph Baxter	G. I. Pugh	J. McGrath
John Cross	L. Ballard	J. Malone
Maurice J. Dillon	A. Elder	E. Mitchell
Sampson Gill	R. R. Neild	D. McNichol
Edward Mullins	James Markey *	C. Trombley
Thomas Patterson	A. Patton	R. T. Dass
George Nornabell	R. Beatty	A. McArdle
George Carpenter	James L. Armstrong	C. McCarthy
John C. Ryan	J. H. Cook	J. Plank
J. B. Hill	H. Walton	J. Robertson
Andrew Pillar	A. W. Davis	Harry Burgess
Albert E. Neil	John Dunne	M. H. Westbrook
J. F. Holland	James Battley	James Herriot
George J. Lazarus	J. Whitney	F. J. Jones
George Collis	Robert Patterson	John Ridgedale *
W. H. Carruthers	Benson E. Johnston	

also moved to Stratford. Originally, the library quarters in Stratford were part of the railway offices on Downie Street, but they were transferred to the new YMCA soon after it was opened in 1904. The library was available only to GTR employees, and when workers complained they were too dirty at day's end to use the facilities, the 1896 library board, with Barnett as president, installed baths. At its annual meeting in 1897 the board's baths room account showed income of $44.25 from 785 baths. Members had hoped for higher numbers.

Though established primarily as a technical and scientific institute, better than 80 per cent of the library's business was in fiction. Loans in science and art were less than five per cent. Nevertheless, Barnett supported the library with donations of time and books. In similar fashion he served the city's library, and he was instrumental in establishing Stratford's first free library, in 1897. A member of the Stratford Public Library board for 20 years, he was its chairman in 1899 and 1900, and its secretary-treasurer from 1905 through 1918, when he left town.

A sought-after speaker on any number of subjects, Barnett frequently submitted articles and book reviews to the Stratford

Herald. Also, he made his private library available to researchers.

Initially, he said he would leave his book collection to McGill University in Montreal, but he changed his mind and donated it to the much younger and struggling University of Western Ontario in nearby London. In 1918 he moved to London to oversee the collection's re-establishment at UWO. His gift became the foundation of that university's library. The rare volumes were preserved and safely stored, but many of the others, carrying the bookplate of John Davis Barnett, remain among the stacks. A portrait of the donor by Mary Healey today hangs in the special collections room. Among the many honours bestowed on Barnett was a doctorate of laws from UWO in 1919. He spent the final three years of his life ill and bed-ridden, but taking comfort in knowing his efforts were contributing to scholarship at the university. He died on March 21, 1926, at the age of 76, and was buried in London's Woodland Cemetery.

The house of books

John Davis Barnett used to joke about how his house at 29 Douro St. was held up by the stacks of books he had accumulated.

The books are long gone, but the house remains, marked since Oct. 5, 1985, by a rock and a plaque on the front lawn. On the plaque, which was made by a Chicago company, is text written by Stratford's first official archivist, Jim Anderson, and a photograph of the man whose passion was books. The photo was provided by the University of Western Ontario in London, and fieldstone to which the plaque is attached was donated by Roy Baumbach of Gadshill.

Designating the house in such fashion was a project undertaken by the Avon Valley Historical Society and the 1983-84 history club at Juliet Senior Public School.

The Saturday ceremony at which the marker was unveiled was chaired by Sue Bonsteel, chief librarian at the Stratford Public Library. Also on hand were members of the Juliet history club; Marg McGreevy, chair of the Avon Valley Historical Society; Ted Blowes, Stratford mayor; Douglas V. Gonder, retired vice-president of the Canadian National Railway; Elizabeth Miller of UWO, president of the Canadian Library Association; and Jan Mullock, a member of the Local Architectural Conservation Advisory Committee.

After the formalities, there was a reception in the council chambers at City Hall.

DEAN ROBINSON

The Barnett house and plaque on Douro Street, November 1988

Posing beside a wall of the burned-out Stratford City Hall in the winter of 1897-98. Library officials moved their operation to the Corcoran Block, and the municipal offices were relocated temporarily in the Worth Block.

The Carnegie connection
1900-1903

As handsome as their quarters were in the new city hall, the directors of the Stratford Public Library knew their days there were numbered, mostly because they needed more room. That had been a concern of theirs for some time.

Indeed, early in 1900, when the need for a dedicated SPL building came up during a chance meeting on the street of board chair R. Thomas Orr and banker William Mowat, Mowat asked Orr if he'd thought about directing a request for money to Andrew Carnegie. No doubt both men viewed such a petition as a longshot, but that didn't stop Orr from writing to the American industrialist. And his efforts paid off, as he found out in a letter from Carnegie's

personal secretary James Bertram. On Dec. 14, 1901, Bertram wrote from New York:

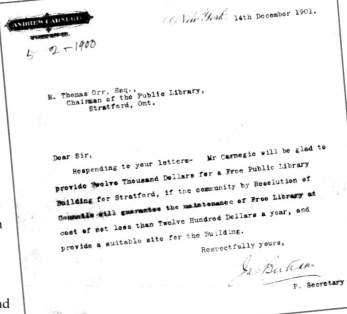

New York 14th December 1901.

5-2-1900

R. Thomas Orr, Esq.,
Chairman of the Public Library,
Stratford, Ont.

Dear Sir,

Responding to your letters- Mr Carnegie will be glad to provide Twelve Thousand Dollars for a Free Public Library Building for Stratford, if the community by Resolution of Council will guarantee the maintenance of Free Library at cost of not less than Twelve Hundred Dollars a year, and provide a suitable site for the Building.

Respectfully yours,

Jas Bertram
P. Secretary

Ten days later, on Christmas Eve, Orr officially presented the news to his colleagues. After considerable discussion, the board unanimously passed a motion forwarded by William J. Ferguson and seconded by John Davis Barnett to accept the "spirit of the proposition" subject to the approval of city council.

It's not likely that any of the library board members expected the firestorm that followed. Not all, particularly those in the labour movement, were eager to accept Carnegie's donation. They argued that the steel magnate had made his millions off the backs of undervalued and underpaid employees.

Rev. Arthur H. Gowing of Trinity Methodist Church on Waterloo Street called the offer "blood money, accumulated at the sacrifice of the working man," and said Carnegie would do better by directing his goodwill to the widows and orphans of workers who were shot and killed while picketing during the infamous strike against his steel works in Homestead, Pa., in 1892.

The Scottish-born Carnegie had further enraged his Canadian critics by suggesting their country had no future except under the wing of its neighbour to the south. That did not sit well with Rev. Gowing, who proclaimed he "would touch money from no man who would aim to pull down the British flag from over the Dominion, to replace it with the Stars and Stripes."

While not wholly endorsed perhaps, Gowing's stand struck a favourable chord with many in Stratford, a city liberally sprinkled with British street names and those not unfamiliar with the plight of labour.

On Dec. 27, 1901, an editorial in the *Beacon* said that council "would act wisely in accepting the very generous offer of Mr. Andrew Carnegie of $12,000 for a new library. Such an offer may not again present itself in many years, and in view of the growing demands of the library, acceptance would be a wise provision against inroads on the city treasury in the near future. The premises in the city hall building that would be vacated could be utilized for other purposes to the advantage of the city. The offer should be all the more appreciated in that it calls for no conditions which will add to the expenditure or the cost of maintenance, that is if the triangle on Erie Street is utilized as a building site. The cost of maintaining the present library approximates $1,200 per annum, and this is the maximum expenditure required under Mr. Carnegie's deed of gift.

"Such a building as is proposed would be a valuable contribution to our already handsome public structures. Located on Erie Street, it would be convenient to the post office and in the very heart of the city. Indeed, this spot would be an ideal site for such a structure.

"The *Beacon* is not enamoured with the begging spirit, and would not have been a party to an official application to Mr. Carnegie, but as the offer came practically unsolicited, along with his other grants to similar institutions in the Anglo-Saxon world, we should like to see it accepted in an appreciative spirit in keeping with the generous and praiseworthy motive which prompted it."

From pub to pulpit, the Carnegie matter quickly became a hot topic in the city. William Battershall wanted the council to call a public meeting at which he be allowed to debate Rev. Gowing. In issuing the challenge, Battershall called Carnegie a great benefactor. There was no debate as such, but on Jan. 20 the Stratford aldermen formally addressed the Carnegie issue at their regularly scheduled meeting. Present were three members of the library board, namely its secretary James Steele, Dr. James A. Devlin and William J. Ferguson. In defending their decision to accept the $12,000, they made it clear that Tom Orr had not "begged" Carnegie for any money; he

had merely outlined "the local circumstances."

Most vocal in his support of the library's move was Ald. William Davidson, who said he thought there were enough "public-spirited persons in Stratford to subscribe a sufficient amount to provide a site." In other words, he didn't think the Carnegie proposal would cost the city even a building lot. In the end, the aldermen did the predictable – they referred the question to one of their sub-committees, specifically the finance committee, chaired by Ald. Davidson.

That prompted the *Beacon* to forecast the council's quick endorsement of the library board's course of action, though it did not agree with Davidson's campaign idea. "If the site on the Erie Street triangle is not suitable, or objection is raised to its being used for building purposes by the property owners in the vicinity, then the city should purchase a site," said the paper in an editorial. "If the matter is left to subscription, we are afraid not much progress will be made, and the undertaking may fall through."

On Jan. 24 the *Beacon* spoke out against "our good friends of the trades and labour council," in particular their reference to blood money. "We are afraid they are going far afield for a grievance," said the paper. "The millions which Mr. Carnegie made as a manufacturer, and which he is now freely distributing for worthy objects, are no more 'blood money' than the millions accumulated by the thousands of other manufacturers who are using the products of other men's labour to indulge their appetites for luxury and escaping adverse criticism. It is because Mr. Carnegie has chosen to distribute his great wealth for the benefit of the very class of people who most freely criticize him that he is thus abused – for in the building of public libraries he is benefiting the working classes most, as they constitute the great majority of those who use them. The trades and labour council could with better grace let up on Mr. Carnegie and divert their shafts of criticism to the millionaires in both America and Europe who are using their wealth in riotous living instead of devoting a portion of it to good works as Mr. Carnegie is doing."

Five days later, the newspaper carried a letter to the editor from T. H. Lennox, a teacher who lived on Daly Avenue. "It is greatly to Mr. Carnegie's credit that he is making such excellent use of his wealth," wrote Lennox. "By endowing institutions of learning and of scientific research , he is conferring vastly more benefit upon his fellow men than if he distributed the profits of his business amongst his own workmen. As things are constituted, moneyed men have a function to perform in society. They can and do carry out schemes for the benefit of the race and the advancement of civilization which poorer men cannot and governments will not do. It is safe to say that if Mr. Carnegie's offer be rejected, no citizen of Stratford now living will ever see a library building put up."

There were letters, too, about possible sites for a library. In the Stratford *Herald* on Feb. 8, 1902, Fred J. Corrie, proprietor of the Queen's Hotel, said he thought the island in the Erie and Ontario streets intersection was unsuitable because "road traffic must pass both sides of the building, thereby causing a continuous uproar." He preferred the grounds below the post office – where the city's war memorial now sits – and suggested surrounding the building with a park, walkways, benches, trees and a bandstand. "There would be a nice view of the lake (Victoria), the music from the band concerts would ring nearly all over the city, the library would be undisturbed by traffic, and the park sight from the windows of the library would be a scene of grandeur," wrote Corrie, who parlayed his interest in civic matters into a seat on city council in 1908.

That letter brought response from Samuel S. Fuller, whose letter appeared on Feb. 12 in the *Herald*. As the city's postmaster, Fuller had more than a passing interest in the site favoured by Corrie, and that interest was not newly fashioned. He wrote: "In the spring of 1896, and again in the spring of 1897, I presented a largely signed petition to the city council in favour of buying the lot on Erie Street and north of York Street down to Lake Victoria, and west as far as Beattie and Co.'s warehouse, and on which stands Mr. E. G. Smith's livery stable, and make said lot a fine central park in conjunction

with Erie and the other unused streets below the post office. Had the city council at that time acted upon either petition, we would now have already prepared a beautiful spot to place the new library building on, laid out with lawns, walks, flower beds and shade with fine growing trees."

On Valentine's Day 1902, it was reported that the Hon. Thomas Ballantyne, one of the letter writers who had weighed in on the side of accepting Carnegie's money, had offered to the city a lot he owned at the rear of Knox Presbyterian Church on Waterloo Street. If it proved suitable for a library, there would be no cost to the municipality. It was a welcome gesture from the former speaker of the Ontario legislature, but the property was deemed to be too small.

In March the trades and labour council waded back into the fray to say it was not opposing the grant because it was "blood money," but because a new library would mean an increase in taxes and compound the financial demands on the working man. The library's present accommodation was sufficient, said the labour council.

At the end of March 1902, when delegates gathered at McMaster University in Toronto for the second annual convention of the Ontario Library Association, there was ample discussion of the Carnegie money. On a list of 13 centres in the province that by then had accepted a grant was Stratford.

But it wasn't until a week later, on April 7, that the council in Stratford voted to accept that grant. And not without considerable discussion. The finance committee came to the meeting with a lengthy recommendation, which included the purchase of land on St. Andrew Street – east of St. Andrew's Presbyterian Church on the corner of St. Andrew and Birmingham streets, and west of Central Public School on the corner of St. Andrew and Church streets.

In his history of the library, Alex Fisher

said two other addresses were on the city's short list of sites, one of them on the northwest corner of Albert and Waterloo streets, where the Stratford armoury was built in 1905. The other was in the same neighbourhood, on the southeast corner of Albert and Waterloo streets, where today there is a chiropractic office.

The politicians, however, opted for property owned by St. Andrew's, whose trustees were asking $800 for their land, though there was reason to think it could be purchased for less. As well, on that site was a cottage that could be sold to reduce the monetary outlay. The finance committee endorsed the acceptance of up to $15,000 from Carnegie, but restricted the city's annual operating commitment to $1,200, which was 10 per cent of the original grant proposal. If the grant were $15,000, the library board would be on the hook for the remaining $300 in operating funds each year, said the committee.

The population in Stratford in 1902 was 10,741, and its expenditures $220,972, of which $800 was earmarked for its public library.

When aldermen Barnett and Davidson sought council's adoption of the recommendation to take the Carnegie money, Ald. Thomas Savage and John D. Hamilton forwarded an amendment that called for the question to be put before the ratepayers. When it came down to a vote, Savage and Hamilton were joined by Elijah K. Barnsdale and Henry Pauli. Those who voted against the amendment, and thus for the original recommendation, were Barnett, Davidson, William Daly, Dr. Edward H. Eidt and James Trow. Absent was Ald. John L. Bradshaw.

So it was, by a vote of five to four, and after more than three months of lively debate, that Stratford came to have a Carnegie-funded library. Its application was one of eight to be approved in Ontario in the first year the grants were available. As well, Stratford's was the second Carnegie-funded library to open in Ontario, five days after one in Chatham, Ont.

When the library board convened on April 8, the night after the vote of council, it named J. Russell Stuart, James Steele and O'Loane to a committee charged with working with the city's finance committee to buy the necessary land and erect the building.

There was a bit of a snag with the land, in that it had been a burial site for St. Andrew's church in the 1800s. James Sharman said eight members of his family had been buried there, and that his father had been given a deed to the family plot. Sharman was assured that the remains of all those still buried on the site would be carefully exhumed and placed in plots in Avondale Cemetery. Since Avondale had been opened in 1871, bodies had been disinterred from the St. Andrew's property on an ongoing basis: five in 1873, one in 1875, seven in 1877, one in 1879, three in 1880, 41 in 1885, three in 1886, five in 1887 and one in 1896.

As it happened, transferring the dead was easier than transferring the deed. City solicitor John Idington was reluctant to pass title of the land in question to the library because there was more than a little confusion as to who owned it – St. Andrew's church or heirs of William Bell of North Easthope Township. The church asked Alex Caven, William Hepburn and William Taylor to represent its interests. The matter was eventually sorted out, and in September 1902 the city gave the SPL directors $800 to buy the property – which measured about 52 feet by 104 feet, but not before the library was asked to investigate other possible sites. Idington had not favoured the St. Andrew Street location because of its proximity to the hubbub of Central Public School.

In May 1902 the city delegated the mayor, James Stamp, and Ald. J. Davis Barnett, who was also secretary of the library board, to work with J. Russell Stuart on the design of the new library. The architect they chose was James Russell of Stratford. They also entertained suggestions from librarian Louise Johnston in terms of the interior layout and needs.

Their building, they decided, would be of red pressed brick with Credit Valley brown stone and terra cotta trim. The foundation was to be built of stone from the quarry in St. Marys.

Early in July it was reported in the press that Carnegie had agreed to increase his Stratford grant to $15,000, though in his history of the library, Alex Fisher said there was no record in the board minutes of how, when or why the amount was upped.

At the end of that month, the building committee accepted a bid of $11,172 from William Daly, a city alderman, for the construction of the library. That price excluded the plumbing and heating requirements, which were to be met by Joseph Myers and Co. for $1,190, and an allotment of $1,800 for beautification of the grounds. When the tenders were originally let, they exceeded $15,000, so the committee pared off some of the brown trim, dropped one of two furnaces, and ordered the exterior steps – a couple of dozen of them – to be made of wood rather than concrete. The subcontractors included John Read and Co., electrical wiring, $145; Edwin C. Edmonds, brick and mason work; William Ireland, plastering, $390; and Ruston Bros., millwork.

While work crews busied themselves on St. Andrew Street, it was business as usual for library officials during their last few months in the new city hall. They hired Richard Wilton as their janitor, but that arrangement lasted just a few months, and in July 1903 he was replaced by Albert Murr, who held the same job at St. Andrew's church.

On July 27 the *Herald* used space on its front page to describe the SPL building:

"The new Carnegie library is nearing completion and could be occupied in two weeks' time should the board see fit. The library board, however, does not meet until Aug. 7, and it is expected that definite steps will be taken then. When seen by the *Herald*, one of the prominent members of the board stated that he thought the building would not be occupied until the cold weather comes, as the present location was very satisfactory. No new books will be ordered at present, but some of the old ones will be classified.

"The new library building is built of red brick and is two storeys in height, with large double windows. A double set of cement steps leads to a platform, at the entrance. Immediately on entering is a hall, off which entrance may be had to either the library, top floor, or basement. The interior is handsomely finished.

"On entering the library, which is situated immediately in front, desks are handy on which will be found catalogues. Two wickets are installed for the convenience of the librarian, and it is through these that all books must be passed. The face work on the counters is very pretty. The library is capable of holding 10,000 books and is very commodious.

"To the right of the entrance is the large public reading room, occupying the west wing of the building. Tables will be placed here for magazines and other literature, while paper racks have been placed along the east side of the room. The room is well lighted and heated. A place has been provided for hanging up wraps and will be a great convenience.

"To the left of the main entrance is another reading room, but of smaller dimensions. This is set aside for the children and is called the children's reading room. Both rooms are in view of the librarian, who can thus see that order is preserved.

"Leaving the main floor and going

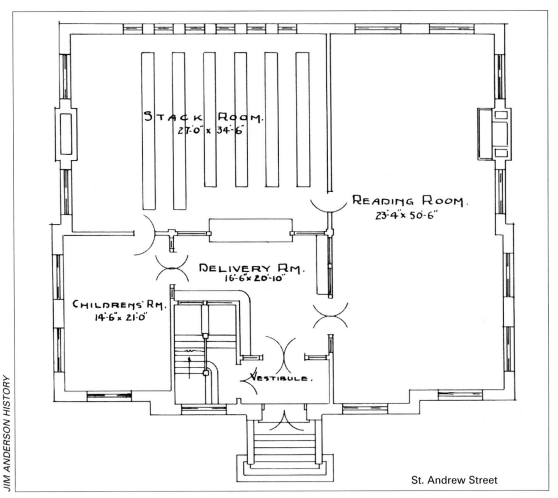

Layout of the main floor of the SPL, 1903

upstairs, the large assembly hall, immediately in front of the stairs, is the next attraction. It occupies the south half of the second flat and is well lighted. Outside the assembly hall is a long corridor off which all entrances to rooms are found.

"Facing on the north, and partly on the west sides of the building, on this floor, is a large room set aside for society meetings. Several societies have made applications, including a statistical society. The room is very comfortable for such purposes. To the left of the corridor is another room, which will be used as a boardroom, where all meetings will be held after Aug. 7.

"Returning downstairs, the visitor is directed to the basement, where a commodious dwelling has been prepared. The caretaker and family will make their home in this part of the building. A large corridor runs down the east wing of the building, and facing it are three bedrooms, a kitchen, a parlour and a large sitting room. To the right is another large room, which will be used as a storeroom and pantry. The boiler room leads off the latter room, and it is in this room that steam is made for the heating of the building.

"The floors in the building are built of hardwood, with the exception of the boiler

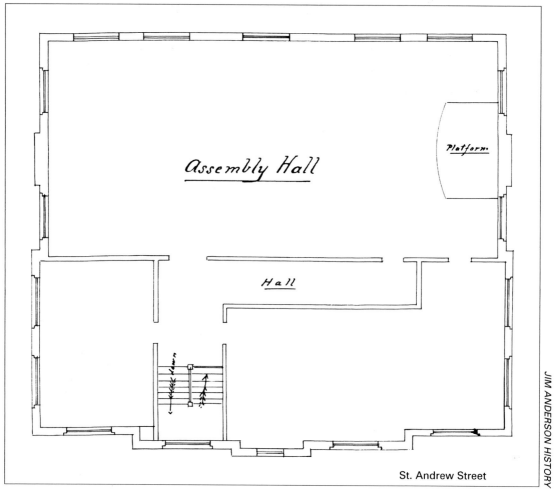

Assembly Hall

Platform.

Hall

St. Andrew Street

Floor plan for the second storey of the SPL, 1903

room which is cement. All rooms are well lighted, large double windows having been put in instead of the singles ones. There are almost 150 electric lights in the building. Steam radiators are placed in each room and supply abundant heat."

Functional space in the new building totalled 3,286 square feet, or about a third of a square foot for every person in the city. At the same time, that per capita figure for the library in St. Marys was 0.74, for Sarnia 0.64 and for Chatham 0.40.

On Aug. 7, 1903, the Stratford board members decided to be operational at their new address by Oct. 1. To that end they closed their rooms in City Hall on Sept. 16, and the move took place over the following two days.

On Thursday, Sept. 19, the SPL building was opened for business. There was no official ceremony, no fanfare – testament perhaps to the divided mood of the ratepayers over the acceptance of Carnegie money. Even the local papers chose to ignore the opening of the city's newest public building, to which the name of its benefactor was nowhere attached. By contrast, when Ottawa opened its new library in 1906, Andrew Carnegie was at the ceremony.

The man behind the money

"Only in popular education can man erect the structure of an enduring civilization."

Andrew Carnegie

The son of a craft weaver, Andrew Carnegie (1835-1919) was drawn to libraries as a youngster.

His father, William, was a founder of the first circulating library in their native Dunfermline, Fife, Scotland. The senior Carnegie pooled his books with those of two fellow weavers, and they formed the Tradesman's Library.

When the Carnegies immigrated to the United States in 1848, the junior Carnegie's formal education ended. His first job in his adopted land was as a bobbin boy in a cotton mill in Allegheny, Penn., for $1.20 a week. In the following year he became a messenger in a Pittsburgh telegraph office and learned telegraphy.

It was then, in 1850, that he and other apprentices made the acquaintance of Col. James Anderson, the man who came to be known as the founder of free libraries in western Pennsylvania.

Not only did Anderson make his 400 well-worn volumes available to working boys, but he acted as their librarian on Saturday afternoons. In no small way was Andrew Carnegie affected by the lead of Anderson.

"Books which it would have been impossible for me to obtain elsewhere were, by his wise generosity, placed within my reach, and to him I owe a taste for literature which I would not exchange for all the millions that were ever amassed by man," wrote Carnegie in his autobiography.

When the Anderson collection was expanded and named the Mechanics and Apprentices Library, Carnegie successfully campaigned for the abolition of all fees for its use.

His skills as a telegrapher earned Carnegie a job with the Pennsylvania Railroad, as the private secretary to Thomas Alexander Scott. Through a series of promotions, Carnegie became superintendent of the Pittsburgh division of the railway. He also invested in the Pullman Palace Car Co. and in oil lands near Oil City, Penn., and his fortune began to grow.

During the American Civil War, Carnegie served under Scott, who was in charge of military transportation and the government's telegraph service. When the war ended, Carnegie left the railway to establish a company that made iron railway bridges. That led to his founding of a steel mill. He was innovative and successful, and by 1899 the Carnegie Steel Co. controlled about 25 per cent of the American iron and steel production. In 1901 Carnegie sold his company to the J.P. Morgan for $480 million and set about disposing of more of his fortune.

By then, Carnegie was as well known as a philanthropist as he was a steel magnate. At age 33, after his annual income had reached $50,000, he declared, "Beyond this never earn, make no effort to increase fortune, but spend the surplus each year for benevolent purposes."

To that end, he gave away more than $350 million to educational, cultural, and peace institutions, many of which bear his name. His first public gift was in 1873 for baths in his Scottish birthplace. His largest single gift, $125 million, was used in 1911 to establish the Carnegie Corp. of New York, a foundation to "promote the advancement and diffusion of knowledge and understanding among the people of the

United States." That goal was later amended to include countries that are or were members of the Commonwealth of Nations.

Carnegie's love of books and his appreciation of libraries no doubt were catalysts for one of the corporation's first efforts – the establishment of free public libraries throughout the English-speaking world. Reflecting in his autobiography, Carnegie wrote, "It was from my own early experience that I decided there was no use to which money could be applied so productive of good to boys and girls who have good within them and ability and ambition to develop it, as the founding of a public library in a community which is willing to support it as a municipal institution."

Through 1917, Carnegie disbursed more than $56 million U.S. (about $875 million U.S. by 2003 standards) for the construction of 2,509 free public library buildings worldwide. The bulk of that money, more than $41 million, was used for 1,681 buildings in the United States. A further $11.8 million went to Great Britain and Ireland. Third on the list was Canada, recipient of $2,556,660, for 125 library buildings. Most of those 125 – 111 – went up in Ontario, funded in large part by $1,866,745 from the Carnegie corporation.

"No millionaire will go far wrong in his search for one of the best forms for the use of his surplus who chooses to establish a free library in any community that is willing to maintain and develop it," reasoned Carnegie. With that in mind, he created some fundamental criteria for those wanting his money to build libraries.

First, the municipality had to make available a suitable site. It also had to promise to provide – through taxation – at

A portrait of Andrew Carnegie, 1884-87, painted by James Archer

least 10 per cent of the total grant for annual operating expenses. And third, the library had to be free to its citizens; society or association libraries which charged membership fees received no Carnegie money – at least not until they did away with such fees.

The availability of the Carnegie money did much to increase the number and broaden the appeal of free libraries.

As of 1908, communities were required to forward building plans before grants were authorized. Applications were handled by his personal secretary, James Bertram, who insisted on dealing with elected officials and library trustees rather than volunteers.

The Town of Collingwood was the first Canadian municipality to apply for a

Carnegie library grant, but it was the City of Windsor that first received one, on Feb. 13, 1901. Collingwood's request was approved on Aug. 16, 1901; Guelph received approval on Oct. 17, 1901, Ottawa on Nov. 6, 1901.

Money for Stratford and Sault Ste. Marie, $15,000 each, was granted on Dec. 14, 1901. The last two recipients in that first year were Cornwall, Dec. 21, and St. Catharines, Dec. 31. Of the eight Carnegie libraries built with money granted in 1901, all but the one in Stratford have been destroyed.

"The Carnegie program of library building undoubtedly stimulated and forced the library movement," writes Lorne Bruce in his 1994 book *Free Books for All, The Public Library Movement in Ontario, 1850-1930.* "Free library service and the popular use of books grew steadily during the Carnegie years. The public perception of the library changed at the same time new library methods, building techniques, architectural concepts were introduced. Trustees, librarians, and architects

experimented with open access; shelving arrangements which accommodated books classified according to the decimal system; less imposing circulation counters which used more efficient charging systems; children's sections; and improved floor layouts which reduced the number of halls and passageways. The emphasis in library design evolved from a priority on storage to user convenience and preference. As a result, the public library's service programs garnered increased public respect; its institutional base in the community was strengthened; its ranks were swelled with new recruits; its goals were redefined with the object of catering to the convenience and perceived needs of users. The Carnegie boom of the first two decades of the 20th century helped create a shared vision of the library as a busy centre of community intellectual life."

What all the citizens of Ontario didn't share, however, was a kindly view of the man behind the Carnegie money. The U.S.

Preserving the past

In 1903, as well as being secretary-treasurer of the Stratford Public Library, R. Thomas Orr was president of the Perth County Historical Association.

It was during that year that he joined SPL chairman J. Russell Stuart and fellow board members James Steele and Dr. James A. Devlin on a committee to study the feasibility of establishing a museum or collection of historical material.

In all likelihood, their mission grew out of a gesture by William M. O'Beirne, who donated all the files from his Stratford *Beacon* from 1855 to 1903 to the historical association on the condition they be stored in the fireproof basement

of the new library. At the time, O'Beirne was secretary of that association.

The library board put shelves in its basement to accommodate those files as well as subsequent copies of Stratford newspapers. And Tom Orr began filling a second-floor room with a variety of items that continue to illuminate the city and county's past from their places in either the Stratford-Perth Archives or the Stratford-Perth Museum.

It was his collection and material from the Perth County Historical Association that became the nucleus of the Perth County Archives when it was created on Jan. 13, 1972.

industrialist had done little to endear himself to Canadians when he claimed that their country's ties with Britain would ultimately give way to a future decided by the United States. "What book, what invention, what statue or picture, what anything has a colony ever produced, or what man has grown up in any colony who has become known beyond his own local district?" asked Carnegie rhetorically. "Canada has no future except as part of the United States."

SPL at the Carnegie world meet

In August 2002, when Glasgow, Scotland, hosted the 68th International Federation of Library Associations general conference, the theme was "Libraries for life: democracy diversity delivery."

DUNFERMLINE *Carnegie Library*

The World's First Carnegie Library

But, in the homeland of Andrew Carnegie, the conference also hosted something called a Carnegie world meet.

The organizers invited administrators and governors of the 2,500 Carnegie libraries still operating around the world – among them five in Perth County – to come together for the first time. They designated a lounge where those librarians could meet and talk about their common heritage.

There was also a lecture series on topics related to Carnegie libraries, and visits to Carnegie's birthplace, the Carnegie Trust, and Dunfermline Public Library, the first Carnegie library.

The first pictures of a Carnegie library to be mounted on the walls of the lounge were of the Stratford Public Library. They were put there by the SPL's systems administrator David Harvie. He also made available postcards of the SPL.

"I felt it (the conference) was a very worthwhile experience, meeting colleagues from around the world," says Harvie. "It was interesting to note that SPL faces many of the exact same challenges that other libraries across the world are facing."

He was the first SPL employee to attend an IFLA conference. The next such gathering is planned for Berlin.

Awkward adolescence
1904-1924

In 1904 the SPL was again praised by the superintendent of libraries. In his report to the Department of Education, he said, "I can only reiterate what I said last year, that it is one of the best conducted and cheapest library buildings in the province, with Carnegie funds. They have an excellent library board of practical men who take an interest in all details of management. The citizens are to be congratulated on the success of the free library." Exactly what the superintendent meant by the word "cheapest" is anyone's guess.

In October of that year, the practical men wanted a Miss Sharman to become their librarian in relief, but when that didn't work out, the job fell to Miss E. Addie Dingman.

In 1905 the library had 7,516 books and 48 periodicals on its shelves, and its circulation was 38,185. By then the SPL was quickly outgrowing its new facilities, and the directors elected to return to the financial well that they had come to know in 1901. In April 1906, board member J.

Russell Stuart wrote to the Carnegie foundation seeking funds to enlarge the Stratford library. Stuart had been the board chairman when the initial Carnegie money had been granted, so he well knew the relationship shared by the two organizations. It's not likely, then, that he was surprised to receive this response from Carnegie staff: "The (Stratford) board would gladly have qualified (back in 1901 and 1902) under the terms of your offer for a grant of $18,000 but for the illiberal attitude of the municipal council, largely controlled at that time by a fanatical labor element, which made this impossible."

It was also in 1906 that the city held an "old boys" reunion, which served to remind the directors of the library of their cash-strapped lot. Their decorative celebration of the event was limited to a few flowers and shrubs on the pedestal caps by the front steps. A shortage of operating funds had long plagued the library board, and early in the 1900s there were no signs of that situation easing.

The north-facing front of the SPL after the original double set of entrance steps had been replaced by a single set.

That year, the SPL's grant from the provincial government was $250. From the municipality, whose population in 1906 was 9,959, the library received $1,200. Stratford's population in 1901, at the time of the Carnegie grant offer, was 11,000.

In 1908 the board gave Miss C. Hepburn permission to study as an assistant librarian. In the same year, Mrs. J. W. Robertson resigned her position as assistant librarian and was replaced by Miss Margaret Macklin, whose wage was $14 a month. When she resigned early in 1910, she was replaced by Miss Susie J. Hamilton. When Miss Hamilton resigned after about 10 days, she was replaced by Miss Elizabeth Hay.

Also in 1908, Isaac W. Steinhoff and Thomas Ballantyne approached the board on behalf of the school trustees, wanting to rent one of the upper rooms in the library

The trustees needed some schoolroom space and a deal was struck for $11 a month. It was the first time, but not the last that elementary school classes would be held in the library.

Still in 1908, in an effort to increase patronage, the board offered full privileges of its library to any resident of Perth County, if the county council would support the library with a grant of $100 a year. The county rejected the offer.

In 1909 the board increased the annual salary of its chief librarian, Louise Johnston, to $350, and retained two assistants, each at $16 a month.

In January 1910, the SPL hosted the first of several annual get-togethers for librarians in Huron, Grey and Perth counties. Called institutes, most of them over the next several years were held in Stratford.

Also in 1910, the SPL board resurrected its expansion plans and talked of putting an addition on the east side of its building, to form an ell. The directors wanted to expand their stack room and fit it with steel shelving. As well, they wanted to add a front porch and make the main entrance safer, enlarge and finish the children's rooms, put a public bathroom in the basement, and double the heating capacity so the auditorium would be available for lectures during the winter months.

To finance their plans, they asked the city for a grant of $1,800 and went back yet again to the Carnegie foundation, this time for $13,000. Upon the latter's suggestion, plans and cost estimates compiled by architect Thomas James Hepburn were forwarded to New York in 1911. While Stratford city council said no to the library's request, the Carnegie people asked for even more information. Its spirits buoyed by that followup, the SPL dispatched treasurer J. Davis Barnett to the Big Apple. Barnett returned thinking money to cover at least part of the construction might be forthcoming, but he was wrong.

On behalf of Carnegie, James Bertram pulled no punches (and used no spell checker) in sending this response to Barnett:

On referring back to the correspondence, we find that you were the party who originally was the recipient on behalf of the city of Mr. Carnegie's gift of $12,000 for a library bilding. When he agreed to increase the amount to $15,000 he had a rite to expect that care would be taken that a library bilding complete and redy to occupy would be secured. There seems to hav been mismanagement, however, from the start, inasmuch as in your letter of Dec. 8, 1910, you propose to spend another gift from Mr. Carnegie partly to finish the inside rough walls and furnishing the top floor auditorium, etc.

You propose in your program providing a public bath and fittings and apparently the provision of living accommodation. Mr. Carnegie provided money for a public library bilding, not a public bath bilding or a dwelling . . . A janitor normally has one room, if he has any. In the additional part there are three rooms added, markt janitor, nine in all. Surely some explanation is needed here . . .

In the revised plan you show a stack room about three times the size of the reading room, which is absurd. In a stack room 76 feet by 52 could be shelved many many thousands more of

books than Stratford could hope to purchase in many years . . .

Disappointed but not dissuaded, Barnett tried to justify the Stratford proposal. He explained that a large stack room was necessary because it was open to the public. Then he addressed the matter of the accommodations in the basement:

As to the janitor's place – he has always lived in the basement, and when you remember the ordinary rigour of our climate, and the fact that we are on the topside of the watershed between the great lakes, more than 900 feet above Lake Ontario, there is justification for the caretaker's living on the premises . . . The suggested addition to the basement under the new stack rooms was made so that every room used would have natural light and ventilation, leaving the old blindrooms vacant. The difference in cost between leaving the basement as an earth-floored cellar, or utilizing it for sanitary living is $528.

Bertram was unmoved, and no more Carnegie money was directed to the Stratford Public Library.

In March 1911, Reta Jeffries was hired as an assistant librarian. In May of that year the library bought the 11th edition of Encyclopedia Britannica. In July the directors bumped the assistant librarian's monthly pay to $18 from $16. But that wasn't enough to keep Miss Hay, who resigned in October and was replaced by Jennie V. Daly, who introduced a weekly story hour to the library's children's program.

In June 1912, Addie Dingman asked for and was granted a six-week leave of absence. In November of that year the board raised the chief librarian's monthly wage to $37.50. In the following month, Miss Dingman resigned.

At the board's annual meeting in January 1913, teacher Lydia Dent became the library's first female director. Three years

Rules, regs and rewards in 1914

In 1914, the hours of operation for the Stratford Public Library were "from 10 a.m. to 9 p.m. and the reading room from 10 a.m. to half past 9 p.m. every weekday, except statutory, civic or special holiday at discretion of the board and during July and August when special hours will be fixed by the board."

In part, the SPL's 30 rules and regulations for that year specified that "any well-behaved person may have the use of papers, magazines or books in the reading room. But anyone disorderly, or unclean, or living in a health placarded house, may be debarred all privileges, at the discretion of the staff.

"Silence in the rooms is imperative, and none may there talk, lounge, eat, sleep, smoke, chew, spit, or make such a misuse of the place as shall inconvenience others. Dogs or any live pets are excluded.

"All books or papers damaged by users shall be renewed or made good, by those in fault.

"Mutilators are liable (under an Ontario Act) to a $10 fine for each offence; and anyone giving such information as will convict a mutilator shall be given a five-dollar reward.

"Each book may be retained 14 days, and once renewed for the same period except it be labelled 'seven-day book,' when it will not be renewed or reissued to the same person within 24 hours. Juvenile books must be kept three days.

"If the book is not returned within four weeks of the day of issue, a notice will be delivered by messenger who is empowered to bring the book back, collect the fines (two cents a day) and an additional 25 cents. If this rule is not complied with, collection will be made through the local courts.

"All fines must be paid to the officer on duty and the card dated before books will be reissued; if not paid, the card will be taken up and use of the library refused until full payment is made.

"If the health officer shall place contagious disease notice upon any house in which there is a library book, the book and card must be handed to him for disinfection and the borrower will get his card from the library after the health officer removes the house notice."

later, she was named its chair.

In 1914 the trustees made some more noise about enlarging their building, but nothing came of it. There was noise, too, from the city's superintendent of buildings, who found the library's wiring and gas installation to be less than safe. After checking out the building, George F. Heideman told the SPL directors to turn on their gas service "under no circumstances."

His suggestions for updating the wiring included a heavier service in the overloaded janitor's quarters and lining the present distribution box with eight inches of asbestos.

In May 1914, Miss Daly was given a one-month leave of absence to take a course.

By 1915 the library had 13,911 books in its collection. Its circulation was up to 53,520, and its grant from the city at $2,300.

In March 1916 the board hired Miss Jean McTavish as an assistant librarian at 75 cents a day. She resigned in August 1917, by which time the city's grant was up to $2,600.

In September 1918, J. Davis Barnett resigned after 20 years on the library board, the last 14 as its secretary-treasurer. He also left Stratford, to live in London and oversee the transfer of most of his book collection to

SPL book stamp from the 1920s

the University of Western Ontario. He donated about 200 books and stacks of sheet music to SPL, but they were eventually sent to London at the request of UWO.

In 1919 the city's grant was $3,000, and in 1920 it went to $3,400. It was in 1920 that the provincial government extensively revised its libraries act, a piece of legislation that called for municipalities to support their libraries on a per capita basis. By then, Stratford's population was approaching 16,000.

In February 1919, Miss Ruth Moore was hired as librarian in relief. She resigned in September 1920. In November 1919 the directors hired Miss Valerie Todd as assistant librarian. In October 1920 they appointed Miss Edna Leckie as a relief librarian, but she gave up the job after about two months.

Unlike Miss Leckie, the SPL's next hire, in February 1921, was no short hitter. After Lois Thompson signed on as a librarian, for $40 a month, she stayed for almost 49 years.

It was also in 1921 that Ontario libraries took part in the first Canadian Book Week.

In 1921, as well, Stratford gave its library title to the site of the adjacent Central

school, which became available after the building was closed in 1917 and taken down.

In September 1922 a Miss Hess was hired as an assistant librarian and paid $1.50 a day. Two months later a Miss Scott was taken on in the same capacity, but she cited poor health when she resigned in February 1923.

It was in 1922 that the board members decided to advertise for the return of about 100 books that had gone missing from the SPL stacks in the previous four years. In light of their cramped conditions and need for expansion, they also took one last stab at getting more money from Andrew Carnegie. This is how Alex Fisher summarized the attempt in his history of the library: "The result was negative. In some quarters there was a disposition to think Mr. (J. Davis) Barnett had been too meticulous in advising Mr. Carnegie, when he interviewed some years previously, as to the uses to which the library had been put.

"For a very short period (in 1908) a room upstairs in the library had been rented to the school board and upon learning this Mr. Carnegie had vetoed the grant. This objection should have been anticipated as it easily could have been overcome. About this time a number of library boards were found to have failed to obey the letter and spirit of their undertaking to the Carnegie Foundation in using rooms in their libraries for 'lock-ups' and in other unwarranted ways. Mr. Carnegie explained that his donations were for libraries only, unless otherwise specified. Then, might it not have been possible that someone had sent copies of Stratford papers containing reports of city council meetings to the multi-millionaire?"

In October 1923 the board appointed a Miss Kappelle as an assistant librarian. In June 1924 it hired Samuel Andrews as janitor, to replace Albert Murr, whose resignation took effect on July 1 of that year.

Thanks Mr. Barnett

Sept. 20, 1918

To Mr. J. D. Barnett Esq.

Upon your retirement from the Stratford Public Library board after 21 years service, we desire to express to you our sincere regret that your removal from the city necessitates your retirement from the board and to express our very great appreciation of your work for the Stratford Public Library during those years.

As the head of the old GTR Institute, your influence in forming the free public library in the year 1896 was very great, and you naturally became a leader in the work of the newly formed library.

Always tolerant of other people's wishes and opinions, your work in selecting books was of great value to the library, and our shelves bear a broader literature because of you.

Always in touch with progressive library work all over America and Great Britain, you were a pioneer in removing barriers which had been raised in the past between readers and books, and consequently today Stratford Public Library is one of the most liberal in its rules relating to the circulation of books and the admission of the reader to the book itself.

As secretary of the board for 16 years, you have painstakingly cared for the material interests of the library and have performed those duties to the very great pleasure of the board and officials. Always courteous and businesslike, it was rarely that friction crept into the business of the board.

The removal of your very fine private library to a sphere of greater usefulness is a loss to our City of Stratford, but we hope that under your care it will fulfill that mission which we know is dear to your heart.

Our wish is that you may be long spared to do the work you love, and we assure you that the Stratford Public Library board, as well as our readers, will always retain a warm spot in their heart for you.

Signed on behalf of the Stratford Public Library board, Stratford, Sept. 20, 1918.

J. W. Emery	J. H. Smith	James Steele
Chairman	Secretary	for committee

The Public Library Institute

On Jan. 19, 1910, the Stratford Public Library hosted the first Public Library Institute for the counties of Huron, Bruce and Grey. The gathering was the brainchild of the Ontario Library Association and Walter R. Nursey, the province's inspector of public libraries.

In the notice of the meeting, prospective delegates were asked to "note how thoroughly practical the topics are and how closely they are connected with the problems of the smaller library. All the papers are open for the fullest discussion and it is hoped that all present will feel free to take part in the discussion. The travelling expenses of one representative from each library in the district will be paid by the government, the name of the representative to be forwarded to Mr. J. Davis Barnett, Public Library, Stratford, who is in charge of the local arrangements."

The notice then suggested how it might be advantageous for public libraries in the three counties to be represented at the institute:

"The clauses of the new Public Libraries Act bearing on the matter are here quoted in full:

26. I. (c). The minister may pay the travelling and other necessary expenses of one delegate from each board in attending a meeting of the Institute.

II. If a board, after having received notice of the date for holding a meeting of the library institute does not send a delegate to such meeting the minister may withhold a sum not exceeding $5 from the next government grant payable to the board.

You will note from the above clauses that the expenses of your representative will be paid, and that part of your grant is liable to be forfeited if your representative does not attend. We confidently expect, therefore, to have every library in the district represented."

Forty-eight delegates signed in for the daylong session. They represented 30 of the 44 public libraries in the three-county area. In addition to Barnett, the SPL colours were carried by James Smith, R. Thomas Orr, Rev. D. J. Egan, Howard Barker, Dr. James Devlin and librarian Louise Johnston.

After a tour of the SPL facilities, the delegates were welcomed to the city by Mayor William S. Dingman, and Smith and Barnett from the host library board.

They then listened to addresses by OLA president Alexander David Hardy, a judge from Brantford, and by the government inspector, Nursey.

After adjourning for a noon meal at the Albion Hotel, the delegates returned to the library, where W. Brydone of Clinton had been scheduled to talk about "government aid to libraries." But he couldn't make it on this day, so his address was presented by Dr. J. W. Shaw, also of Clinton.

Then, Rev. W. H. Johnston of Chesterfield in Oxford County talked about "the small library's problems." His speech was followed by a discussion, and by a session on "the best methods of selecting and purchasing books" by William O. Carson of London, the man who from 1916 to 1929 followed Nursey as the Ontario inspector of libraries.

Proceedings wound down at about 4:30 p.m. so many of the attendees could get to the Grand Trunk station and catch home-bound trains to as far away as Port Elgin, Walkerton and Wingham.

Before they did, however, the delegates agreed to call on the provincial government to "prepare and publish for free distribution a model Canadian public library book list, say of 5,000 volumes . . . as a help to the smaller libraries in their selection of shelf literature," and to make more money available to smaller libraries – more than they qualified for under the grant conditions of the day.

On Feb. 24, 1911, 40 or so delegates reconvened in the SPL for the first renewal of the Stratford district institute, of which J. Davis Barnett had been named president and James Smith secretary. The latter position was assumed by Miss Johnston in 1913.

At their meeting in 1911 the delegates discussed library financing, open access, fiction, annotated bulletins, reading circles, literary societies and children's departments.

On Feb. 23, 1912, bad weather postponed most of the trains into Stratford, so the third meeting of the institute was not held until March 15. About 30 delegates showed up, and they talked about attracting readers, advertising the services and benefits of a public library, getting increased funding from city and county councils, and the "difficulties of young librarians." They also decided their libraries "ought to be open on Saturday afternoon and evening to keep young men out of the bar room."

On Nov. 14 and 15, 1912, the Public Library Institute, Stratford District, staged what it called the fourth annual meeting of the Stratford Library Association. The lineup of speakers was predictable, as was the array of subject matter, but the program included an evening session on the 14th.

There was also a less-than-subtle reminder about expenses on the notice to delegates:

Summary of Attendance at Public Library Institutes

District.	Date.	Place.	1911-1912. Libraries represented.	1911-1912. Libraries not represented.	1911-1912. Total.	1910-1911. Libraries represented.	1910-1911. Libraries not represented.	1910-1911. Total.	1909-1910. Libraries represented.	1909-1910. Libraries not represented.	1909-1910. Total.
Brantford..	July 17, 1911	Dundas	29	5	34	18	17	35	22	15	37
Chatham ..	July 18, 1911	Sarnia........	25	12	37	19	18	37	16	23	39
Western. .	July 21, 1911	Fort William..	5	1	6	....	....	....	....	....	....
Northern..	July 25, 1911	North Bay....	11	11	22	....	....	....	....	....	....
Georgian ..	July 27, 1911	Barrie........	16	6	22	10	12	22	10	11	21
Niagara....	Oct. 24, 1911	Port Colborne	18	7	25	17	8	25	9	16	25
Eastern....	Oct. 27, 1911	Ottawa	32	23	55	26	30	56	23	39	62
York.......	Dec. 1, 1911	Weston	18	5	23	8	14	22	....	....	....
London....	Feb. 28, 1912	London	16	4	20	21	13	34	25	5	30
Guelph....	Mar. 1, 1912	Galt.........	21	11	32	22	10	32	25	9	34
Lindsay..	Mar. 5, 1912	Oshawa ...	20	17	37	20	17	37	20	18	38
Belleville.	Mar. 7, 1912	Napanee......	18	8	26	19	7	26	16	11	27
Orangeville	Mar. 12, 1912	Hanover......	15	15	30	18	12	30	20	14	34
Stratford ..	Mar. 15, 1912	Stratford......	28	17	45	26	17	43	30	14	44
	Duplicates....		272	142	414	221	175	399	216	175	391
			....	....	....	3	....	....	3	....	....
			272	142	414	221	175	399	213	175	388

122 Libraries represented at Institutes 3 consecutive years.

46 Libraries represented at Institutes 2 consecutive years.

171 Libraries represented at Institutes one year.

75 Librarians not represented at Institutes, any of these 3 Institutes.

339 out of 414 Libraries have been represented at one or more Institutes, and of the other 75 Libraries 24 are reported by Inspector as defunct or dormant.

PUBLIC LIBRARY INSTITUTE
STRATFORD DISTRICT

Under the Direction of the Ontario Library Association.

PROGRAMME

of the

Fourth Annual Meeting of the Stratford District Library Association

to be held in the

Public Library

in the City of

STRATFORD

On Thursday and Friday, November 14th and 15th, 1912

Commencing at the hour of 10 o'clock a.m.

OFFICERS OF THE STRATFORD DISTRICT
PRESIDENT: J. Davis Barnett, Stratford.
VICE-PRESIDENT: Rev. W. A. Amos, Atwood.
SECRETARY: J. H. Smith, B.A., I.P.S., Stratford.

EXECUTIVE COMMITTEE: William Elliott, Mitchell; W. H. Kerr, Brussels; J. H. Fowler, Goderich; W. F. Bald, B.A., I.P.S., Port Elgin; James Warren, Walkerton.

O. L. A. LIBRARY INSTITUTE COMMITTEE
A. W. Cameron, Woodstock.   W. O. Carson, London
E. A. Hardy, Toronto.   David Williams, Collingwood.
Norman Gurd, Sarnia.   Miss B. Mabel Dunham, Berlin.

The Public Library Institute program for November 1912

INSTRUCTIONS
Re: expenses of delegates

In view of the many mistakes made during the past four years by delegates in matters of vouchers, attention is called to the following instructions. These instructions must *be observed to the* letter, or the audit office will refuse to pay the accounts.

In submitting statement of expenses, the following particulars are positively required by the provincial auditor in every case:

1. Original vouchers for all Pullman or sleeper fares, no matter what the amount, and for each and every item of expenditure of *one dollar and over*, excepting ordinary return railway fare.
   Note: Railway fare must, however, be accurately given. An error of 10 cents may delay payment of all the accounts of the institute.

2. The items requiring vouchers are: boat fares, Pullman or sleeper fares, meals on train or boat, hotel and board bills, cabs, livery hire, omnibus or other conveyance, odd meals.
   Note: Delegates from libraries not on railway lines, please note that livery bills must have vouchers dated and receipted.

3. Hotel or board bills must be receipted and show the number of days and the rate per day, and the dates.

4. All charges of one dollar or over for which vouchers are not produced will be struck off the statements before presentation to the auditor.

NOTE: These instructions must be observed or expenses will not be paid.

If in spite of above instructions any delegates should submit undated hotel bills, or livery bills, or make any other error in vouchers, any such error must be corrected at once, and corrected voucher sent to the inspector of public libraries, Department of Education, Toronto, within 10 days of close of the institute, or the amount of the voucher will not be paid.

NOTE: See back page of circular letter for sample of form of statement to be filled out by delegate.

A year later, on Nov. 13 and 14, 1913, Stratford hosted what was called the "sixth annual meeting of the Eastern District Library Institute."

In the following year, on Nov. 12 and 13, the venue changed to Walkerton. On Nov. 11, 1915, 35 libraries were represented at the seventh annual meeting, in St. Marys. Now back to a one-day format, there were sessions in the morning, afternoon and evening.

The eighth gathering was in Stratford, on Nov. 9, 1916, by which time William O. Carson of London had replaced Walter Nursey as Ontario's inspector of libraries.

Again, there were three sessions, possibly the institute's last. There are no further entries in the SPL's library institute minutes book.

Living in the library

Most of the people who have looked after the Stratford Public Library have lived the job. More accurately, they have lived at the job, specifically in the basement of the century-old building.

The SPL's first custodian of record was William Ashmore, who held the job from at least 1897 through April 1900. He was followed in 1902 or 1903 by Richard Wilton, who tendered his resignation in July 1903.

His successor was Albert Murr, who had been working with the Grand Trunk Railway in Stratford. He and his family became the first to live in the basement apartment of the Carnegie building when it was opened in 1903. Officially, their residence was 18 Church St.

Albert and his wife Catherine had two children, Walter and Viola. Walter moved to Toronto after the First World War and worked for the Canadian National Railway. Viola married Harry Young and lived in her parents' house on Birmingham Street. Their son Jack was born after his grandparents had left the library, but he recalls his grandfather being an ambitious man. "He didn't have a lazy bone in his body. I remember he used to help out on a farm (Gordon Riehl's) just out of town. He'd go out there and work when he had the time. He was a great guy."

It was the Murrs who donated a small glass case of stuffed squirrels to the children's department of the library.

Albert resigned as custodian on May 20, 1924, and returned to railway work, this time in the machine shop of the CNR's repair operations in Stratford. His resignation was effective July 1, which gave him and his family time to find new living accommodations.

Their departure from the library brought to a head a longstanding issue concerning a bathtub. It seems that back in 1907 the Murrs had asked the board to put a bathtub in their apartment. The directors were slow on the uptake, and though the matter resurfaced regularly, there was no compliance on their part.

By May 1915, Albert had had a tub installed and was seeking recompense from his landlord-employer. Again, the directors didn't see it his way. In August 1915 they said he had not received prior approval for the upgrade, so they were not obliged to cover its costs. From the Murrs' point of view, that was not an appropriate response, but one they were forced to abide.

The dispute was reborn when they told the board they were taking the bathtub with them. In June of that year the directors, their mood changed, agreed "that the management committee should have the power to make arrangements with Mr. Murr to leave the bathtub in the library." An agreement was reached, but the SPL board minutes do not offer details. So, sans tub, the Murrs moved to Birmingham Street.

The wage for Albert's successor at the library was $12 a month, in addition to the rent-free basement apartment. Samuel Andrews was hired on June 17, 1924, but in 1926 he took a similar position with the Stratford YMCA and moved to 82 Huntingdon Ave.

It was in 1926 that the library was enlarged with its new front. At the same time, the janitor's quarters were remodelled.

Andrews was replaced at the library by Hugh McMillan, who left his job as a storeman with the CNR and moved to the SPL from 139 Church St. It would appear he was assisted with his janitorial duties by his wife Annie, because it was she who resigned from the job in July 1928.

The McMillans were followed by William Kirkham, hired on Sept. 18, 1928. In addition to the apartment, he was to get free "light, water and heat, except for cooking." He submitted his resignation a year later, on Sept. 17, 1929, and when he did, the board gave him $15 to help cover moving-out expenses.

The library's next live-ins were the Crerars: Fred C., his wife Mabel, and their children Perc, Marjorie, Russ and Audrey. Fred was hired on Oct. 15, 1929, and he and his family moved from 19 Daly Ave. The kids were a little farther from Hamlet Public School but closer to Central Secondary.

"Things were tough at the CNR at that time," recalls Audrey (Mrs. Howard Clark), the lone survivor of the six. "My dad had been laid off and this job opened up. He thought this was an opportunity to live rent-free. Then he got back with the CNR. At different times they had layoffs back then, but he was with the CNR until he retired." For its caretaker, the library was still paying $12 a month, in addition to the gratis accommodations.

Not long after the Crerars' move to the library, Perc left for university in Toronto, where he became a pharmacist, and Marjorie took a secretarial job in the assessment department at City Hall. She later married Howard Ballard and moved to Dunnville.

So Russ and, to a lesser extent, Audrey became their parents' helpers in caring for the library. "It was quite a job," says Audrey. "There was no stoker or anything on the furnace. They used to get 50 ton of coal, and Dad would shovel that 50 ton of coal over the winter. The snow had to be shovelled; there were two long walks, one out to Church Street and one out to St. Andrew's Street. There was a big lawn to cut by hand, with a push mower.

"Dad used to put the storm windows on, go up the ladder with those old windows spring and fall. It was quite a job, really. A lot of the cleaning was done on Sunday because the library was open Saturday night. There was an old electric floor polisher. I'd go up and dust when I got a little bigger. My brother Russ used to get up early and go out and help shovel snow before Dad went to work. I didn't do an awful lot around there, but Russ did. Last thing at night they had to make sure the windows were shut and the place was locked up. And when the library roof leaked they had to get up and put a pail here and a pail there. There were all kinds of problems from time to time. It was a job that tied us down, but Dad had a good friend that used to help him out if he wanted to take two or

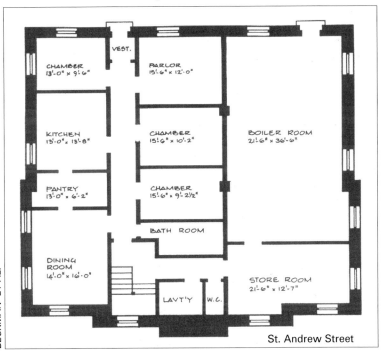

The basement plan for the original library. It featured a three-bedroom apartment for the SPL's janitor and his family.

three days off for a holiday in the summer."

Russ eventually worked as a clothier, first in Brown's department store in Stratford, then in London.

Audrey was three when her home became the SPL, and she was there for 22 years, until she married. "I enjoyed living at the library," she says. "We had quite a large living room, three bedrooms, a bit of a den, a kitchen and a dining room. It was a big apartment. It was warm and comfortable with all kinds of room. We lived rent-free and had our heat for nothing. If times got tough and there was a layoff at work, we still had a roof over our heads.

"I had access to all the books I needed. It (the library) wasn't open Sunday so I could go up there where it was quiet if I was studying for an exam, and nobody bothered me. There was a historical room in the basement. It was the archives, where they kept all the old newspapers. If I had a school project, I'd get back in there on a Sunday and dig up information."

Her neighbourhood friends included the Yeandles and the Browns, who lived in the courthouse and Masonic Temple, respectively, where their parents were also fulfilling custodial roles.

Those who lived in the library had a separate entrance on the south side of the building, where half a dozen steps took them down to the apartment. "We didn't have a lot to do with the staff," says Audrey. "There was Jennie Daly, Lois Thompson, Winnifred Henderson and Jean MacDougall. The four of them pretty well did the job at that time."

In 1957 Fred retired as a boilermaker at the CNR and as, as of June 30 of that year, as the SPL's custodian. He and Mabel, an avid reader, moved to newly built apartments for seniors on Britannia Street at Churchill Circle. He died in 1962, she in 1966.

Fred's place at the library was taken by Walter Philip (Butch) Kelterborn, who kept the job until his death. By 1966 his annual

salary (plus accommodation) was $500. In January of that year, it was bumped to $1,200.

"I remember Butch would come up (from the family's living quarters in the basement) about five or 10 minutes before we closed, with his pail and mop," says former SPL staffer Dorothy Robinson. "And he would stand around, just to let everybody know he wanted to get started. He also liked to talk about his time as a hockey player."

Indeed, the St. Jacobs-born left-winger had plenty to talk about when it came to hockey. Most memorable were his two seasons of junior, 1918-19 and 1919-20, with centre Howie Morenz as a linemate. In the latter of those two, he and Morenz teamed with Frank Carson, and the Stratford Midgets made it to the Memorial Cup final before losing to the Toronto Canoe Club Paddlers.

Morenz and Carson went on to the National Hockey League. Kelterborn, who played with teams in Hamilton, Niagara Falls, Buffalo and Houghton, Mich., was 70 when he died on Feb. 6, 1971, after six weeks in Stratford General Hospital.

In the following month, SPL board chair Chris Swanston and trustee Dan Devlin hired Russell Marlow as their new caretaker, in part on the strength of his licence to work with natural gas installations.

Russ was working for Superior Propane when he saw the ad for library custodian. It said the living accommodations had recently been redecorated and the salary was negotiable. He had been looking to end long days on the road and bring some relief to his back, which he had broken in a job-related accident in 1967.

So he, his wife Shirley, and their daughters Sonia, Yvonne and Cathy, all teenagers, moved from Falstaff Street and took up residence in the SPL. That was a condition of the job, he says, because the library could reduce its insurance premiums if someone were living in the building.

On at least one occasion, the Marlows weren't the only people in the library after hours. In the 1970s, a middle-aged man working quietly in the room that housed the microfilm machine, was inadvertently left in the building by those charged with closing up at the end of the night shift. Not wanting to set off alarms, the man used a library telephone to call the police. They in turn notified the Marlows, and Russ went upstairs and let the man out.

SPL

Custodian Russ Marlow, 1980

The custodian's job at the SPL has changed with the times. The gas-fired Progress boiler made the place easier to heat. Heavy storm windows gave way to aluminum replacements which, recalls Russ, "didn't fit too well." Don Drown was contracted to cut the lawn. And Andrew McCreadie was hired in a relief capacity.

But the roof still leaked, mostly, says Russ, because "with the amount of roofing that had been done, the (roof) drains were half full of pitch." When they backed up, the water worked its way inside.

So did bats, which lived mostly in the attic, where there wasn't a finished floor. "I remember one time sitting down to use a typewriter, and there was a bat sitting by the keyboard," says Theresa Talsma. "Irma (Sass) comes in, picks it up by its wings and takes it outside."

While bats have caused a stir through the years, they have been far less damaging to the library than raccoons, which took to climbing down the unused – and uncapped – half of the chimney after the renovations in 1974-75.

Library administrator Jane Kirkpatrick has vivid memories of one living above Brian McKone's desk in the audio-visual department. "We knew there was something

up there, in the crawl space in the lower floor," she says. "Finally we called animal control, and they put a trap in Brian's office, up in the ceiling. They caught the raccoon, but it went berserk in the trap, and its defecation came down through the ceiling tiles and onto Brian's desk. It took a week, I think, to fumigate the place. They figure the raccoon had come down the old chimney. It had been living in the library for weeks. In fact, there was a family of them. Just recently, we caught a squirrel in the Chalmers room."

Former staff member Lorraine Greenberg remembers another raccoon invading the library through an opening in the concrete by the front steps.

The Marlows' stay in the library lasted less than four years. Before construction began on the addition in 1974-75, they moved to Downie Street, and a colourful chapter in the history of the library came to an end. Their living quarters in the SPL were reborn as audio-visual and children's departments.

But Russ continued as caretaker until 1994, when he retired. Since then, the job has belonged to Perry Wilson, who had worked with Russ for a couple of years.

public Library, Stratford, Ont. Canada.

Stratford's Carnegie library, soon after it was built in 1903. The double set of steps off St. Andrew Street was eventually replaced by a single set.

A new front, a touch of dignity
1925-1930

By October 1925, enlarging their building was priority No. 1 for the library directors. And, as Alex Fisher put it, "preparations for an addition to the library matured." The board prevailed upon Stratford architect James Simpson Russell for some plans, and in April 1926 it accepted the low-bid tender of $19,003 from city builder and contractor John L. Youngs for that addition. Then, board chairman A. Hayward Alexander, secretary William E. Goodwin and members James Steele and R. Thomas Orr were empowered to represent the library's interests through the period of construction.

By then the city's annual grant to the library was up to $9,500. But that was for operating expenses. To finance the addition to the east end of the building, the city took out a 20-year debenture for $22,500. That was the eventual price tag with extras that included architect's fees ($700), linoleum, blinds and painting. As planned, the city's loan was paid off within 20 years.

In the spring of 1926, chief librarian

Louise Johnston and her staff invited patrons to take home as many books as they would like for the summer. It was their way of keeping the books away from the dusty world created by construction crews.

Charles Trethewey, a kid growing up on Nile Street, recalls hauling home a wagonload of books. "We could take as many as we wanted," he says. "It was great. I remember filling my wagon. I don't remember taking them back, but I'm sure we did."

SPL board member R. Thomas Orr insisted the basement in the addition include a fireproof space for his growing collection of historical documents and assorted other archival items. And library staff members were consulted about the layout of the new space into which their work would flow.

When the library reopened for business on Thursday, Nov. 25, 1926, it was 1,200 square feet larger and facing east. That is, its impressive new front was across the east end of the original building. The Stratford

B. 114. Public Library, Stratford, Ont.

A westerly view of SPL with its 1926 addition and new entrance

Beacon Herald said the makeover "fills a long-felt need for something that would adequately lend a touch of dignity and impressiveness as well as beauty to such a public institution. The old building, while it served the purpose, could not be classed as an imposing structure by any means, but with the magnificent new entrance of the very finest type of architecture, the building has taken on a new and much more pleasing appearance.

"The new front is of classic design and built of red pressed brick with artificial stone trimming. The old building has been changed somewhat in design to conform with the new work, giving a very dignified appearance, something which has been lacking in the old building.

"In fact the building has been remodelled to such an extent that it is hardly recognizable. An addition 20 feet by 60 feet has been built, facing Ontario Street. The entrance with its unsightly and dangerous flight of steps has been removed and a new entrance provided in the addition. This entrance is only seven steps above the level of the ground and gives entrance to the vestibule, where five steps more bring one to the main floor.

"The vestibule itself is floored with red quarry tile, and the steps are of slate. This gives a fine effect against the oak wainscotting on the walls. The stairs to the upper floor are in this vestibule. They are of oak with hard maple treads. Large double doors give entrance from the vestibule to the main floor, and it is here that the patrons of the old library will be agreeably surprised.

"The ground floor of the old building has been opened out into one large room with a very fine beamed ceiling. The walls and ceilings are done in rough plaster, tinted. The floor is covered with a dark green shade battleship linoleum. Handsome electric fixtures provide a good flood of light and carry out the general effect of pleasantness.

"The delivery desk is placed directly facing the entrance, and it has good display shelves at the left with a workroom alongside, making it very convenient for the attendants. The private office of the librarian is on the main floor also, and it is so placed as to give her oversight over practically the whole floor.

"The stack room runs along the south side of the building now, with the reading room along the north side. The stack room has been greatly enlarged and will provide ample accommodations for some years to come, the shelf space having been almost doubled. Another feature that will commend itself to library patrons will be the fact that the shelves have been made lower, making it much easier to reach books on the higher shelves. These are well lighted and ventilated and are model rooms in every respect.

"The historical rooms are in the basement of the new addition. There are two of them, both absolutely fireproof, and here are kept many important historical records. One of these is shelved to hold the files of the daily paper from its first issue, Jan. 1, 1855, to the present date.

"On the upper floor a room has been provided for the use of the staff, also a boardroom. The balance of the building is left as it was, except that the children's room has been redecorated and linoleum laid on the floor.

"The janitor's quarters have also been remodelled and redecorated and new plumbing fixtures put in. The heating plant has been rearranged, and an additional furnace installed, thus insuring the proper

heating of the building even in the coldest weather."

To varying extents, most of the interior had been rearranged, which resulted in the hiding of the main-floor fireplace. It was on the west wall near the southwest corner of the building, and was obscured from view by shelving. In about 1960 the fireplace was removed when a fire door was installed nearby. Signs of the old chimney are still visible in the library roof.

Unlike the opening of the building in 1903, which went mostly unnoticed, there was some ceremony when the addition was unveiled in 1926. In the evening of Thursday, Nov. 25, the board hosted an official opening, for which members of the public were invited to assemble in the children's room on the second floor. There, board member James Steele emceed a program that included words of praise from Mayor David R. Marshall; Fred Landon, the University of Western Ontario's first director of libraries; Richard Crouch, chief librarian at London Public Library; and William O. Carson, the inspector of libraries for Ontario. The last of those expressed warm approval of the economic efficiency with which the SPL was operated, and for the manner in which the citizens of Stratford had come to use their library. He

Thanks Mr. Orr

On Feb. 19, 1929, the SPL board members adopted this motion of thanks for their retiring colleague, R. Thomas Orr (Oct. 28, 1870 - March 11, 1957):

That the Stratford Public Library board desire to express their appreciation of the very great service that Mr. R. T. Orr has given to our public library during the many years he has served on the board.

As always, he was in the van to make the library of more value to our citizens and for the past 35 years gave unstintingly in the effort to raise our library from a small mechanics institute serving a few dozen people to the big institution it is today, serving thousands of our citizens. We regret Mr. Orr's retirement from the board, but we the comrades in the work take this opportunity to say that his work has been deeply valued by us.

said annual circulation was up to six books per capita, double what it had been a decade earlier.

With the impressive addition came a recurring problem, but only when it rained. The newly leaking roof was a source of frustration for staff and board over the next several decades. Samuel Andrews soon excused himself from the problem when he resigned as janitor. He was replaced by the husband and wife team of Hugh and Annie McMillan. When they took their leave in July 1928, the board hired William Kirkham to live in the basement and look after the library and its leaky roof.

It was also in 1928 that the board took a serious look, perhaps its first serious look, at opening its library for a few hours on Sunday afternoons. But the nays carried the day, and it remained a six-days-a-week operation.

Kirkham's role as janitor lasted a year, until Sept. 17, 1929. He was replaced by Fred Crerar in October of that year. In addition to free room for him and his family, he was paid $12 a month, a wage that had not increased for at least five years.

It was also in 1929 that the directors formally paid tribute to colleague Tom Orr, whose support of library services in the city dated back to the mechanics institute. In 1930, James Steele was honoured in similar fashion but posthumously. He, too, had been on the board of the mechanics institute, before spending 27 years over two terms with the SPL. He was appointed to the executive of the Ontario Library Association in 1924, and at the time of his death, in 1929, he was president of the OLA. His children, Murray and Katie, later donated a brass plaque to the Stratford library in recognition of his contributions.

As of March 1930, the library's full-time staff comprised Misses Louise Johnston, Jennie Daly, Lois Thompson and Doreen Bishop. As a stand-in when needed, was Miss Winnifred Henderson. When Bishop resigned in September of that year,

Henderson, who had started working in the library while in high school, was appointed to take her place as circulation assistant.

Theirs was a library whose reference department lacked for little, especially in the area of encyclopedia. The centerpiece was the 14th edition of Britannica, a 24-volume set known for its "quicker, easier reading for the hurried businessman." However, Miss Johnston deemed it not as good in some ways as its preceding edition. Written mostly by British contributors, the earlier version was a more scholarly work, thought the chief librarian.

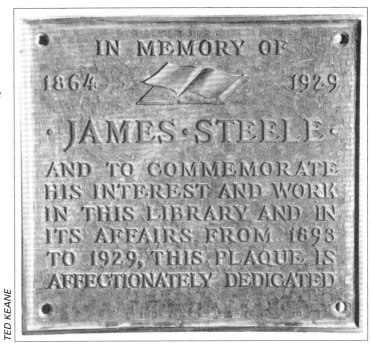

IN MEMORY OF 1864 JAMES·STEELE 1929 AND TO COMMEMORATE HIS INTEREST AND WORK IN THIS LIBRARY AND IN ITS AFFAIRS FROM 1893 TO 1929, THIS PLAQUE IS AFFECTIONATELY DEDICATED

TED KEANE

Another British encyclopedia in the SPL collection was the Harmsworth. There were other general knowledge sets, as well, among them Chamber's, Nelson's and World Book.

And there were specialized works that reflected the interests of the day, such as Everyman's Guide to Radio, the Cyclopedia of Food, Dyke's Automobile and Gasoline Engine Encyclopedia, the A-B-C and X-Y-Z of Bee Culture, the Library of the World's Best Literary Quotations, the Index to Poetry, the Century Encyclopedia of Names, the Cambridge History of English Literature, the Encyclopedia of Social Reform, Fairbairn's Crests of the Leading Families of Great Britain and Ireland, and the Library of Literary Criticism of English and American Authors.

There were similar works that shed more than a little light on music, art, horticulture, architecture, natural history, engineering, hymnology, the Bible, languages, politics, monograms and ciphers.

The history section was anchored by a set

called the History of Ontario and flanked by the Makers of Canada. For those wanting statistics, the selection included the Canada Trade Index, the Canada Year Book, the World Almanac, the Canadian Almanac and the Statesman's Yearbook.

For current events, the library had newspapers, files stuffed with newspaper clippings, and an assortment of magazines. It also had a copy of the Reader's Guide to Periodical Literature, to assist in the navigation of those magazines.

In June 1931, ill health force Miss Johnston to stand down, and Miss Daly was named acting chief librarian until the end of the fiscal year. Two months later, the board hired Misses Jean MacDougall and Kathleen Arnold as assistants.

In October the directors accepted the resignation of Miss Johnston, who, according to Alex Fisher, a board member at the time, had been with the library for "a term of some 40 years." In his history, he wrote: "She had been diligent in the pursuance of her duties and had earned the encomiums of both inspectors and patrons of the library. A lover of books and a qualified schoolteacher with a diploma for library work from McGill University, she entered upon her work with a high appreciation of a library's value to the community."

Along with that high appreciation was a strong Scottish will, which, in her early days as chief librarian came to the fore as she locked horns with the scholarly J. Davis Barnett, an Englishman. While he insisted she place the call number of a book on the top right corner of its catalogue card, she argued she had been trained to put it on the top left corner. He won that showdown, but behind the checkout counter she continued to number the shelf-list cards on the top left corner.

Louise Johnston died on Dec. 27, 1935.

The grand oak counter that until the renovations in 1974-75 was the SPL's checkout desk.

The Jennie Daly years
1931-1953

As of Christmas 1931, the SPL's new chief librarian was Jennie Vanstone Daly, whose obsession with running a no-noise, no-nonsense operation was not soon forgotten by the patrons of her day. But that was de rigueur for libraries then.

She was the youngest of Robert and Eliza (Vanstone) Daly's seven children, all descendants of one of Perth County's pioneer families. "I didn't ask for a position (at the library)," she said in later years. "I was asked to come to the library and told to send an application to the library board. The application was accepted, and J. Davis Barnett (secretary-treasurer of the board) came to my home to tell me that I had been appointed assistant librarian." Her starting salary in 1911 was $4 a week. By 1922 she was up to $700 a year.

In 1932 the Girl Guides of Stratford sought and were given permission to mark the 21st anniversary of their organization in Canada by planting a tree on the library grounds. They acceded to the SPL board's request for a black oak, but the tree did not survive. A more lasting memorial from that year has been the bronze plaque on granite rock that the Stratford Board of Education situated on the library lawn near the corner of St. Andrew and Church streets, to recognize the site of the former Central Public School.

In that year, the Great Depression forced Canada's unemployment rate to 30 per cent. Few were unaffected by the 42-per cent decline of the country's gross national expenditure. In an effort to keep its property tax rate down, the city asked the SPL to forego about $750 of its annual municipal grant, and the library agreed. In 1933 there was no asking; the city simply reduced the grant by 15 per cent.

Better news came from outgoing board chairman Harry Strudley, the president of Imperial Rattan Co. He donated furniture for the library boardroom.

Also, SPL continued to get good grades from government inspectors; in spite of the tough times, it was thriving. The reasons for that, concluded Jim Anderson in his history

ON THIS SITE STOOD THE FIRST SCHOOLHOUSE BUILT IN STRATFORD 1841 ALSO THE CENTRAL SCHOOL ERECTED 1855 — RAZED 1917 PLACED BY THE BOARD OF EDUCATION — 1932 — STRATFORD CENTENARY 1832-1932

DEAN ROBINSON

DEAN ROBINSON

The rock and plaque that since 1932 have marked the site of Stratford's first schoolhouse, a log building that went up in 1836, five years earlier than the inscription suggests.

of the SPL, were fairly straightforward: "By then the Great Depression had descended, with thousands of people out of work and money scarce. The library managed to get by with reduced appropriations for several years, but with the additional burden of serving the needs of the unemployed who filled the building to keep their bodies warm and their minds busy. Circulation was at an all-time high. Concern was expressed over lost and stolen books, which had never amounted to more than 100 a year before this. It was necessary to put reference works out of bounds except by application."

In the face of such odds, the board and its staff were increasing their book purchases, broadening their selection of reference material, expanding their clipping files,

acquiring picture collections and running more activities in the children's department. "There were attempts to find out the particular reading matter that the public wanted, and a system to rotate it under a book committee," said Anderson. To that end, the directors decided each of them would come up with 20 book recommendations a month and make their choices known to the library staff. Further, each board member was to assume responsibility for the merits and morals of the books they recommended. Under the weight of 240 books a year per board member, it was an exercise that fast faded.

The workload was also getting to staff members, and for the first time, they began to complain openly about six-day workweeks that featured 11½-hour days. In the last half-hour, the employees were required to tabulate and record the library's circulation numbers for that day. They also counted and stashed the cash, some of which had been generated by the overdue notices prepared each evening by a member of the staff. There were several locks throughout the building, and at day's end each had to be secured. The last of those was on the front door, and it was turned only after the staff was sure there was no one left in the building.

In March 1935 a delegation from the city's historical society appeared before the SPL board seeking the use of a room in the library for the storage of its exhibits. The directors appointed William Blakeston and James Smith to meet with the society for further discussion of that request.

In November of that year the directors asked Alex Fisher to "prepare an article for the *Beacon Herald* appropriate to the occasion" – the occasion being the 100th anniversary of the birth year of the benefactor of their building, Andrew Carnegie.

It was in 1936 that the library modified its hours of operation. Like Stratford merchants, it chose to close on Wednesday afternoons in June, July and August. And it remained closed on those Wednesday evenings. But that was not a popular move among library patrons, and the directors ultimately went back to six days a week. It wasn't until May 1971 that Sunday afternoons were added to the rotation, but the building stayed closed on Wednesdays.

Initially, the hours of operation for the children's department were the same as those for the rest of the library, but they were eventually reduced so the children's librarian could visit schools and talk to students about the wonders of the Stratford collection. After some years of fluctuation, the hours of operation for the children's department were brought back in line with the rest of the library, and there, for the most part, they have stayed.

It was also in 1936 that the directors replaced the furnace in their library.

In the winter of 1937-38, in conjunction with the Stratford board of education, the SPL hosted a series of exhibits and lectures presented by the Royal Ontario Museum. But attendance was scant, and the library directors decided the series did not warrant their expenditures.

At the library
(author unknown)

This is a lovely place to be.
The books are everywhere,
And I can read them here, or take
Them home and read them there.

It is a kind of secret place
Where I can enter in
And no one tells me where to stop
Or where I should begin.

The books sit waiting on their shelves,
As friendly as can be,
And since I am a borrower
They all belong to me.

On June 6, 1939, the SPL closed early so staff and patrons could take in the whistle-stop visit to Stratford of King George VI and Queen Elizabeth.

In 1940 the library got a grant of $8,581.50 from the city, and from the province a further $209. By then its shelves were holding 29,106 books and its circulation was close to 136,000. About 300 books had been lost, damaged or mutilated in recent years, and, while that news was not comforting to the board members, they were assured such losses were commonplace among public libraries. Compounding the problem, however, was the Second World War, which had made buying books from overseas sources slower and more expensive. It was a situation that was some years away from resolution.

By 1940 the library auditorium had become a popular meeting place for various organizations. As a result of representations made to the SPL board, one of the groups, the Workers Educational Association, was

The McLennan books

While the Stratford Public Library has bought most of its collection through the years, on occasion it has been on the receiving end of books at no cost, though not necessarily without conditions.

Such was the case on April 20, 1940, when the SPL directors were invited to dinner at the residence of Janet McLennan, whose parents had emigrated from Scotland and lived in Blyth and Clinton before settling in Stratford in about 1883.

After dinner, Miss McLennan presented to the library an elaborately bound volume that documented the story of the pioneers of North Easthope Township. Its author was her sister, Mary Louise McLennan, a teacher who had died in 1938 at age 58.

The book was locked in a wooden and glass box, visible through a framed glass lid. And there it was to stay for 20 years, declared the donor. The key to the box, she said, was to remain with the youngest member of the library board. As they accepted the gift, the directors assured her that the book would be "given the proper attention while on display for the next 20 years."

Janet McLennan died on Christmas Eve 1942 and is buried in Toronto.

In its box, her sister's book continued to sit in a corner of the library, available but not accessible. The key to its wooden case was entrusted to lawyer John Anderson, who kept it when he retired from the board in 1943.

In the evening of May 31, 1960, the box was opened with some ceremony. Anderson, long since off the board, was vacationing in Europe, but he had given the key to chairman George Edwards. The latter invited Daisy Lightfoot to unlock the case. She had just retired from the board after serving for close to three decades.

What she found in the box was not one book, but three. In addition to A History of the North Easthope Pioneers from Perthshire, were Children's Artist Friends, and Memories, 1923 to 1930. All were bound in royal blue morocco, and all were somewhat dusty.

After closer examination by the assembled, the books were returned to the box, which was again locked. But, upon request, the three remained available for inspection by library patrons.

In 1974 the books and their case were moved across the street to the Stratford-Perth Archives, where they have remained in a back room.

asked to submit a list of its upcoming lecture topics. The association's secretary, James Skene, a teacher at the nearby collegiate and vocational institute, was quick to assure the library directors that no improper subjects would be discussed at WEA meetings.

Another of the groups meeting regularly in the library was the Stratford Camera Club, which, like the WEA, had been granted use of a room in September 1939.

In a wartime spirit that had infected most communities, the library extended special privileges to soldiers. It also shipped books to northern Ontario and elsewhere.

In May 1940 the board directed some of

SPL exterior 1942

post signs to that effect, the directors left it up to their staff to inform their canine-accompanied patrons.

On occasion, the library would try to recover books from delinquent patrons by making pleas in newspapers. One such occasion, in 1941, resulted in the return of many of its outstanding volumes. On the other hand, a call in the *Beacon Herald* for volunteers to submit reviews of popular books went unanswered.

its attention towards dogs, specifically their banishment from the library. But rather than

By 1942, four members of the library staff were covered under the federal government's newly introduced Unemployment Insurance Act.

At the end of that year the board decided it would spend 75 per cent of its 1943 book-buying budget on adult titles, the rest on works for its juvenile department. It also opted to send discarded books to the Ontario Reformatory in Guelph.

Early in 1943, board members George Edwards, Chris McKeough and Alex Fisher petitioned city council and were successful in getting the SPL annual grant raised to 53.75 cents per capita from 50 cents. The increase was to be directed to the staff salaries.

There was direction of another kind in 1943, specifically heat from the basement to the upper reaches of the library. To comply with a government wartime mandate to reduce energy consumption, the directors placed a fan in their janitor's quarters.

George N. Edwards, a long-time public school inspector, was also a SPL board member for 27 years, 15 of those as chairman.

Ontario Library Association Regional Meeting

Stratford Public Library Children's Room

MAY 3, 1944

MORNING SESSION

Registration on arrival.

10.00. Greetings. Mr. A. W. Fisher, Chairman of the Stratford Public Library Board, will introduce His Worship the Mayor, J. Waldo Monteith.

10.10. Business.

10.40. Address. Pension Schemes. Miss Dorothy Carlisle, Sarnia Public Library.

11.00. Round Table Discussions :
Problems of the small Library, led by Miss Greta Thompson, Seaforth Public Library.
Children's Work. Miss Alethea Johnston, Kitchener Public Library.
County and Regional Libraries. Miss Dorothy Carlisle, Sarnia Public Library.

12.30. Luncheon. Mr. S. B. Herbert, acting Inspector of Public Libraries, will be asked for a brief talk.

AFTERNOON SESSION

2.00. Address. Library Finances. Miss Ruby Wallace, Niagara Falls Public Library.

2.45. Question Box. Miss B. Mabel Dunham, Kitchener Public Library.

3.15. Address. Preserving of Local Records. Miss Elsie M. Murray, University of Western Ontario.

4.00. Afternoon Tea. Delegates to be guests of the Stratford Public Library Board.

6.00. Dinner. Informal.

SPL

OLA meeting notice 1944

On May 3, 1944, Stratford hosted a regional library conference. Mayor J. Waldo Monteith brought greetings from the city, and SPL board chairman Alex Fisher presided over the day's events. The topics of discussion that day included pension plans, problems of small libraries, children's work, county and regional libraries, library finances, and preserving local records. The delegates had lunch at nearby St. Andrew's Presbyterian Church, where they were invited to listen to Samuel B. Herbert, the acting inspector of public libraries.

In 1944 the SPL spent $1,949 on new books, but they were hard to get because of the war. A buying trip to Toronto by Misses Daly and Thompson was cancelled when they learned the books they wanted were not available.

In 1945 the directors were able to increase the salaries of their staff, but only slightly. They said they hoped more money would

Also in 1943, representatives from across Perth met twice with the SPL board to discuss the formation of a county-wide library. Stratford officials favoured such a creation and offered to assist with its organization. To that end, they appeared before county council seeking some financial assistance, but to no avail. The councillors were equally passive when it came to followup requests in 1944 and 1945.

Alex W. Fisher

It was 100 years earlier that the mechanics institute had been established in a log schoolhouse on what was now the SPL's front lawn. To mark the centenary, chairman Alex Fisher, whose day job was at the liquor store on Ontario Street, wrote a history of the library. He had been a director of the SPL since 1929, and for a dozen years headed its board.

This is how he ended his work, 12 legal-size pages of single-spaced lines: "In concluding this sketch of the ups and downs of the Stratford library board and its predecessors, one is prone to claim that this institution, under different names, has made a very substantial contribution to the mental and moral education of both the masses and the classes of Stratford's population.

"In the selection and distribution of books, which is the foremost duty of a library board, it is most difficult at times to determine when, for alleged moral reasons, a book should be banned from library shelves. Board members have constantly asked themselves the question: Where is the line of demarcation between what a librarian should hand out to the public and what a public whose morals have been inculcated to a great extent by a century of library reading, demand? Members of the Stratford library board have endeavoured to use their practical good sense in their selections and hope their choices have been at least reasonable.

"In the past decade we, in common with most other libraries of our size, have been hampered through lack of funds to properly carry on. For 20 years a substantial percentage of our income has gone towards liquidating the cost of an expensive, though much needed, addition to our library building. The war and the years of economic stress preceding it tended to vastly increase prices for books, fuel, salaries and other things essential to the well-being of a library, so that boards have been obliged to curtail book purchases in

be forthcoming in the following year, perhaps because they were about to unburden themselves of the 20-year debenture to which they had been tied since they expanded their library in 1926.

Regardless, the directors came through as hoped in 1946. They appeared before council and managed another increase in their grant from the city, and then gave their employees a raise. Miss Daly's annual salary as chief librarian went to $1,450. Miss Thompson's pay, as head of the juvenile (children's) department, was upped to $1,350 a year. The hikes for Winnifred Henderson and Jean MacDougall brought their annual salaries to $1,100. Margaret Rosamond, as a part-time assistant, was to be paid $250, but she died soon after the new pay scale was set. The average earnings for salaried female employees in Canada in 1946 were $1,305 a year, $25.91 a week, and 66 cents an hour – all less than half of what their salaried male counterparts were averaging.

order to keep within their rather meagre allowances.

"Now, however, our debentures having been retired, our building free of debt and with the wish that the 'powers that be' may see fit to dole out to libraries their just needs, we are hopeful that the years to come may see constant improvement in serving a public which knows what it wants and is determined to get it.

"One wishes also at this time to express keen appreciation of the splendid pioneer work of those who carried on in the earlier history of the mechanics institute, the 'paying library' and the free library as it now stands. Many of those men and women have been mentioned in this sketch, but unfortunately, because of the fire which destroyed valuable records, a considerable number have been overlooked, simply because it seems impossible to learn their names."

Fisher no doubt had some capital expenditures in mind when he wrote of improvements, because the library – leaking roof aside – has never been need-free in that department. In 1948 the directors installed some new lighting and redecorated the children's section. By then they were overseeing an institution estimated to be worth $75,000: land $5,000, building $45,000, furniture $5,000 and books $20,000. Their insurance policy covered books to a value of $15,000. (Ten years later, those tangible assets totalled $116,000: land $5,000, building $70,000, furniture $11,000 and books $30,000).

It was also in 1948 that the SPL became home to the Stratford Film Council, an organization that in time became redundant because of the ever-widening services offered by the library. The council eventually gave its projectors to the SPL. With them came the group's minutes (from 1945 to 1957 and from 1961 to 1968), its records of film rentals and memberships (1956-1968), and its cashbooks (1952-1968).

In 1950, members of the library's board and staff presented a series of addresses in the interest of the SPL on CJCS radio. It was Lois Thompson's assignment to use the airwaves to tell one and all about the children's library, which she did on a Sunday afternoon in February. She was back in the radio on a Sunday in May 1951, talking about "the library and the community."

By then the SPL's circulation numbers totalled more than 104,407.

From 1951 through 1954 the board members rejuvenated their building by repairing and repainting its exterior, by upgrading the heating equipment, by refurnishing the auditorium, and by redecorating the main floor, the reference room and the auditorium. Above the front entrance, they attached a solid brass PUBLIC LIBRARY sign, which they bought from Bernard Cairns Ltd. in Toronto for $185 plus tax.

In 1953 the city's grant to the library was $12,992, of which $30 was used to decorate the interior in celebration of the coronation of Queen Elizabeth II. It was also in that year that the SPL made a donation to the group putting up a tent and starting a Shakespearean festival in lower Queens Park.

In November 1953 the trustees hired John Gaffney Construction Ltd. to repair the library roof and copings, at a cost of $700. Some of the work was to be done immediately, the rest in the spring.

Early in 1954, Joyce Banks joined the library staff. Not long out of Stratford Collegiate and Vocational Institute, she had been working as a cub reporter for the *Stratford Beacon-Herald*. Her beat included the library, and in December 1953, SPL secretary-treasurer Jean Gordon asked her if she might be interested in changing careers. Still a teenager, Miss Banks made the switch and launched a career in library services. The opening in Stratford was a result of

Jennie V. Daly

Jennie Daly's retirement.

As full-time staff, that left Lois Thompson, Winnifred Henderson and Jean MacDougall, to which Joyce Banks was added. "They were all very good women," she says today. "They were really nice people, warm and patient. They were devoted to their jobs, and they were good at them. And they weren't well paid. I got along with all of them, and I learned an awful lot from them. Those were good years. They were good training years for me."

In 1954 the annual salary for library's newest recruit was $1,600. "I had a raise every year until I left," she says, "and I don't think I was making more than $50 a week." For the same year, Miss Thompson was paid $2,800, Miss Henderson $2,350 and Miss MacDougall $2,200. Part-timers were paid 75 cents an hour to start, to a maximum $1 an hour.

Jennie Daly's resignation took effect Dec. 31, 1953, but, in recognition of her exemplary service, the board gave her a three-month paid leave through to March 31, 1954.

One of her lasting contributions was the establishment of a room that housed nothing but Canadiana. She also put together a booklet called The Stratford Public Library Welcomes You, and saw that it was delivered to all newcomers to the city. It explained the SPL's facilities and services.

Miss Daly might have been on paid leave for the first three months of 1954, but Joyce Banks recalls her being around the library. She also remembers being invited to the Daly home, where Jennie was living with her brother Fred and sister Mabel. "I was asked to come for dinner, or for the evening; I can't remember which," she says. "And they (Miss Daly and her siblings) were very kind. They all were so interested in me, the new one (at the library). They were very, very kind. It was a magnificent house with a beautiful dining room with a chandelier in it. In my memory there was a round room, whether it was the dining room or the sitting room, but it was just beautiful. The house was on Brunswick Street (no. 96), where the Bell Telephone parking lot is now. I think of it every time I walk down Brunswick Street. I look at that parking lot, and I think what a shame (that the house was torn down)."

Jennie Daly died on March 19, 1957.

Joyce Banks left the employ of the SPL in 1965 when she enrolled at Wilfrid Laurier University in Waterloo. She later added graduate degrees in the field of library science and spent most of her working days with the rare book collection at the National Library of Canada. "It all started at the Stratford Public Library, with Jean Gordon and learning from Lois Thompson and working with people I respected," she says. "I just went on from there."

The art of the SPL

While never mistaken for an art gallery, the Stratford Public Library has always been a place for art. Among the most visible in its collection these days are three portraits on the north wall of the main floor.

One of those is of Andrew Carnegie, the man who put up most of the money to build the SPL in 1903. His likeness was donated to the library in 1935 by the Carnegie Corporation in New York, on the occasion of the 100th anniversary of his birth year.

The second portrait is of R. Thomas Orr, the man who had requested that money from Carnegie and was instrumental in getting the library built. This painting was donated in 1950 by artist A. Bruce Stapleton, one of Orr's nephews.

The third portrait, also by Stapleton, is of William (Tiger) Dunlop, a military physician, journalist and politician who worked for The Canada Company as it surveyed and settled the Huron Tract. In the fall of 1956 this work was moved from the boardroom to the entrance of the library, from where it has since made its way to a place above the library's main bank of computer stations.

The SPL has long provided those from near and far a space in which to display their creations. In 1947, when the board sought to mount a show by local artists, it enlisted the help of Jean Cameron, a teacher at the Stratford Collegiate and Vocational Institute, to help select the paintings.

Also in 1947, the SPL had a display of photographs by Mary E. Smith.

The Stratford Art Society was an active group in the 1950s, and in July 1958, from its collection of Canadian works, Ann Gregory presented to the library a painting by Carl Schaefer titled the Great Oat Field. In March 1959, Shirley Anderson of the SAS gave an etching titled Past-Future, by Nicholas Hornyansky, to the library.

In the spring of 1963 the SPL found itself in receipt of a small original watercolour titled Shanty John. Dated 1851, it was signed by William Nichol Cresswell (1818-1888), a native of Devonshire,

Bruce Stapleton's painting of R. Thomas Orr

England, who lived and painted near Seaforth in Huron County. He was a charter member of the Ontario Society of Artists (1872) and the Canadian Academy of Arts (1880). Shanty John was described only as a pioneer of Tuckersmith Township.

Reg White remembers the work sitting for some time atop the card catalogue on the main floor of the library. In the early 1970s it was moved to the Perth County Archives. In the 1980s, Shanty John was loaned to the National Gallery of Canada and toured the country as part of an exhibition. For insurance purposes, it was evaluated at that time and estimated to be worth thousands of dollars. It remains out of view at the Stratford-Perth Archives.

In March 1966, the SPL hosted a free week-long exhibit of original lithographs by the American firm Currier and Ives. The show, arranged by Orr Insurance, was presented by the Stratford Art Association and featured original prints from the Travellers Insurance companies.

SPL

Shanty John watercolour

In a break at the showing of films during the Canadian Library Week open house in 1966, the Perth Regiment of the Imperial Order Daughters of the Empire presented a framed picture of Queen Elizabeth to the SPL. Representing the IODE were Elsie Inglis and Gillian Taylor.

In the fall of 1974, the library had a showing of 56 works done by John De Vry, by then deceased. When the show ended, the De Vry family gave one of the paintings to the library.

In February 1977, 22-year-old Stratford artist Milton Newbury donated three of his paintings to the library. They were of the Perth County courthouse, the Festival

theatre and Stratford City Hall. He said the last of those took him 55 hours to complete.

In March 1980 the SPL received a collection of 14 signed Inuit carvings. It was willed to the library by Florence Murray, formerly of Avonton. She had been a teacher and occupational therapist, the latter at a sanatorium in Hamilton, to which many Canadian Inuit were sent in the 1950s and 1960s for the treatment of tuberculosis. There, they were encouraged to carve in soapstone, which was supplied by the hospital. To show their appreciation for the help they received, some of the patients donated carvings to the staff. The pieces given to the SPL depict seals, bears, geese and people.

In November 1980, the Stratford Rockhounders used a model of the Festival Theatre to exhibit in the library a collection of their findings.

For two weeks in September 1982, the SPL displayed a full-sized quilt bearing the logo of the Perth County Junior Farmers. With the help of their mothers and grandmothers, 17 members of the club spent about 200 hours sewing the quilt, which became a raffle prize at the Junior Farmers' 60th anniversary party in Mitchell. Its winner, Ross Daly, agriculture commentator with CFPL-TV in London, thought the quilt should have some exposure in Perth County before he took it home. So, in addition to the SPL, he deemed it was to hang in libraries in Mitchell, St. Marys, Listowel, Milverton, Monkton and Atwood.

After the SPL was enlarged in 1974-75, it had more room for the exhibition of art, specifically in the lounge area that was part of the audio-visual department in the basement. And for the next several years, it regularly used that space to showcase the work of dozens of artists, most of them from Stratford and Perth County. Many of the shows ran for a month, and the library often scheduled receptions to which the public was invited to meet each artist.

The media of those artists included oil paints, watercolours, pen and ink, photography, pottery, beads, tole, fibre, acrylic, woodblocks and sculpture.

Among those whose work was shown at the SPL, several on more than one occasion, were Tait Baynard, Beverly Nye, Carolyn Horley, Olive J. Coghlin, Terry Gibbs, Alf Bell, Nina Soltys, Fred Pitts, Bruce Clark, David Leaney, Susan Murar Crean,

The portrait of Andrew Carnegie, given to the library in 1935

Elizabeth Bailey, Mark Fletcher, Veronica Lamb, Pat Bowes-Rowlandson, Jean Edmunds, Jane Turnbull, Sheila Easun, Marjorie Eggert, Mary Lynn Fiske, Dorit Learned, Nancy Wilson, Nancy Devitt, Kitty Howard, Marion Jackson Tyler, Elizabeth Fraser, Robert John Barrett, Tim Mosher, Michael Wheal, Lida Bause, Elizabeth Jay, Joy Walther, Jeanette German, Al-Noor Somani, Jade Blaney, Norma Bald, Lin Souliere and Ron Lightbourn.

Some of the foregoing may have been part of the Mitchell Art Society that had an exhibit at the SPL in August 1983. The Stratford Potters Guild also had a group display, in March 1982.

The Lois Thompson years 1954-1969

Joyce Banks describes the Stratford Public Library of her day as a "lovely" place. "You went in, and there was a huge, oak desk right there, like a big bar," she says. "The fireplace (near the southwest corner of the main floor) was never used for anything, but it was quite handsome. You couldn't see it unless you went back to the back of the stacks, but it was a nice fireplace, with lovely old tiles on it."

She also recalls book salesmen dropping by to meet with head librarian Lois Thompson. One such representative was Jack McClelland, who by then was executive vice-president of the publishing company founded by his father.

One of her earliest memories of those days, however, is also her most grisly. In the first minutes of Feb. 16, 1954, Reuben Henry Norman was hanged within the walled yard adjoining the Perth County jail, across St. Andrew Street from the SPL. A year earlier, he had shot and killed 17-year-old Jean Marie Satchell on Wellington Street.

After helping to close up between 9 and 9:30 p.m., about three hours before the execution, Miss Banks walked out the front door of the library. "There were people out there already," she recalls, "and I could see somebody in the tree, trying to get a look. It was a terrible, wet, foggy night. Talk about pathetic fallacy. It was a dreadful night on a lot of different levels. It was awful. I shudder to think of it even now. I couldn't believe anyone would want to witness anything like that. I can't remember if I was an abolitionist before that night, but I certainly was after."

In the following month, the library sent a delegation to city council seeking an increase of $1,000 in the municipality's annual grant. No doubt some of the money was earmarked for roof repair and elimination of the buckets needed to catch the snowmelt and rainwater dripping from the ceiling in the reading room.

The city responded by bumping its allotment to 72 cents per capita, which amounted to $13,960.80, but only if the SPL would raise its yearly fee for a library card

SPL staffers Dorothy Robinson (left) and Joyce Banks, December 1960

to 10 cents from five cents. That hike took effect May 1, 1954. The provincial money directed to the SPL that year was $2,511.86.

By then the SPL collection held 34,322 books and circulation was about 113,299. The annual cost of buying books was up to $3,554.55, compared to $1,948.61 in 1944.

It was estimated that those who watched films or film strips which were owned by or on deposit at the SPL numbered more than 45,000.

There were 26 children's story hours at the library in 1954. A dozen public school classes visited the SPL, and the library staff made 14 trips to public schools to distribute books and make presentations at home and school association meetings.

There were 61 meetings in the library in 1954. The groups that regularly rented the auditorium at night included the Workers Educational Association, the Stratford Sea Rangers and the Stratford Art Society. A decade later, the WEA was still meeting in the SPL. It was the last of those, in co-operation with the London Public Library and Art Museum, that organized seven

exhibitions at the Stratford library that year. There were also displays on book design and a growing emphasis on live theatre – in response to the Shakespearean Festival that had taken root in the city.

In September 1955, the library rented some space on its second floor to the separate school board, which needed it for a classroom until the new St. Aloysius school was ready for occupancy.

In September 1957, the city's public board followed suit and established its Grade 6 class from Hamlet school in the SPL. And there it stayed until June 1965, when space problems were alleviated with the opening of King Lear, a senior public school.

In March 1956 the most popular requests in the SPL's fiction collection were Marjory Morningstar by Herman Wouk, The Sixth of June by Lionel Shapiro, and The Golden Journey by Agnes S. Turnbull. Their non-fiction counterparts were Inside Africa by John Gunther, A Man Called Peter by Catherine Marshall, and I'll Cry Tomorrow by Lillian Roth.

In 1957 the Stratford board hired Walter (Butch) Kelterborn to succeed Fred Crerar as the library's custodian. The latter had retired after a term of 28 years.

In December 1960, it was announced that the library, the *Stratford Beacon-Herald* and an unnamed partner were contributing $500 each to kick-start a program that would put on microfilm the back issues of Stratford and other Perth County newspapers. One print was to stay at the library, another with the *Beacon-Herald*, and a third was to go to the University of Western Ontario in London.

In March 1962 the board set its employees' salaries for the next couple of years. At that time they were $4,100 for Lois Thompson, $3,900 for Winnifred Henderson, $3,400 for Jean MacDougall and $2,700 for Miss Banks. Over the next two years, each was to receive another $300 each.

By the time the first microfilm reader was in place at the SPL, in April 1962, about 45,000 pages of Stratford newspapers had been filmed and were ready for public viewing.

In May the board summoned the city's animal control officer in an effort to rid its property of pigeons. Apparently, there were just too many of them hanging around.

Near the end of the year, the trustees asked Oliver Gaffney of the Gaffney construction company to assess their building for insurance purposes. When he came up with a replacement value of $140,000, they bumped their coverage with Orr Insurance from $100,000 to $130,000. They also insured their contents for $95,000 and "valuable papers" for a further $5,000.

It was in 1960 through 1963 that the library was redecorated, and new lighting was installed on the main floor. Plans also called for replacing the lighting in the children's department, as soon as there was money available.

By then the staff was issuing about 200 warnings a week to those with overdue books. As many as 96 went out in one day. Many books were returned within a week or two of the warnings, said Miss Thompson. Most defaulters, she said, were students who took out books for essays and projects. In 1962 the revenue from fines, at two cents a day per book, totalled $1,041.

In March 1964 the guest speaker at the library's annual meeting was William A. Roedde, director of the provincial library service, Department of Education, Toronto. After his explanation of newly formed library co-operatives and the subsequent creation of regional boards, SPL board members voted unanimously to join with Galt, Guelph, Kitchener and Waterloo to form the Midwestern Regional Library Co-operative, taking in Waterloo, Wellington, Perth and Huron counties.

Acting on a suggestion from staff, the SPL board elected to close at 6 p.m. on

DR. DON DAVIS

Lois Thompson

Saturdays, effective May 9, 1964.

Beginning in 1964 and stretching into 1966, the Stratford trustees spent $21,246 for upgrades to their library that included a new Cleaver Brooks 25-horsepower gas-powered boiler for heating, new carpet in the children's department and boardroom, linoleum on the main floor, electric perimeter heating in the basement, fluorescent lighting, aluminum storm windows, and some shelving and furnishings. They also resurfaced the roof, gravelled the parking lot, replaced the fire escape, installed public washrooms, and did some masonry repairs to the front of the building, where they restored some steps.

Dorothy Robinson, who began working at the library in 1959, recalls how those washrooms became a place in which students from nearby Central Secondary School smoked marijuana during their noon hours. "When Mr. McDougall (head

Lois B. Thompson

Lois Beatrice Thompson was born in Mount Forest, the youngest of the five children in the James and Annie Thompson family which moved from Mitchell to 268 Douro St., Stratford in 1920.

On Feb. 8, 1921, she took a job with the Stratford Public Library, where she worked for almost 49 years.

A library school graduate, she had a special interest in children's books and soon took charge of that department for the SPL. She also became chair of the children's section of the Ontario Library Association.

Miss Thompson was regularly a guest speaker at home and school association meetings, at which she talked about the many facets of children's literature.

In March 1954 she was appointed head librarian in Stratford, the job she held until she retired on Dec. 31, 1969.

"I have enjoyed my work at the library," she said at the time. "They have been very happy years. The children's department is the foundation of a library, and I feel I have been fortunate in having this experience and to work my way up through all departments."

On June 29, 1970, Mayor Jim Neilson hosted a dinner at which the city recognized Lois Thompson's considerable contributions to the library and her community. It wasn't the first such outpouring. On Dec. 9, 1967, at a dinner at the Victorian Inn, she was feted for her longtime service. On that occasion, Ald. Peter Case, pinch-hitting for Mayor C. H. (Dutch) Meier, presented the guest of honour with an end table.

The Chairman and Members
of
The Stratford Public Library Board
request the pleasure of your company
at a dinner
on Saturday, December 9th, 1967
at the Victorian Inn, Stratford
to recognize the services of
Miss Lois Thompson
Chief Librarian
R.S.V.P.
SPL
6:00 p.m. for 7:00 p.m.

"I think I was her favourite nephew," says Dr. Don Davis of his unmarried aunt, "maybe because she was my godmother. Anyway, there was a book in the library about a kid driving a train, and I loved it. I would read it over and over again, so she would save it for me. She would come up to our house frequently, and she would usually bring a book or two for me and my brothers. She was always interested in us and what we were doing."

Away from the library, Miss Thompson supervised the primary department of the Sunday School at St. Paul's Anglican Church.

She never drove a car, but she certainly got around, especially in her roles as an elocutionist and thespian, both of which she was well into before joining the staff at the SPL.

As the former, she was featured dozens of times at band concerts, fowl suppers and revues. She drew readings from the likes of A. A. Milne, Pauline Johnson and Edgar Guest and performed in the Opera House in Mitchell, in the Baptist Church at Fullarton, in the United Church at Trowbridge, in Listowel, Monkton, Lakeside, Gorrie and Woodstock. Closer to home, she was a regular at lodges, at the Lakeside bandshell, at the YWCA and at the city churches' varied entertainments, anniversaries and celebrations.

She helped to raise funds for the Protestant Orphans' Home in Richmond Hill, for the Perth County Music Festival and for the Community Welfare Bureau in Stratford.

Over the span of six nights in March 1927 she did readings at an organ recital in Main Street United Church in Mitchell, for the Juliet Home and School Association's "At Home," and at a concert in the Salvation Army citadel in Stratford.

After she had read during a concert at Parkview United Church on March 27, 1928, the *Beacon Herald* reported: "Her numbers received much applause and an encore was given after each presentation. Some of her numbers were of a thoughtful and serious nature and kept the audience in silence, while others were of a comical nature and provided laughter galore for the many people present."

One of her earliest performances in the song and dance arena was as a member of "our beauty chorus of 60

DR. DON DAVIS

Lois Thompson with nephew Don Davis

girlies" when the St. Thomas chapter of the Imperial Order Daughters of the Empire staged The Isle of Love in the Star Theatre in St. Thomas in March 1920.

A few years later she became a cast member with the Knickerbocker Players of St. Paul's Church and played leading roles in productions of Mother, R. F. D. – a play with a moral, Brother Elks, and Am I Intruding? In the "play with a moral," Miss Thompson was "the plucky little stamp clerk."

Lois Thompson died in the Rehabilitation and Extended Care Unit of Stratford General Hospital on June 10, 1979. She was 77.

In the spring of 2003, to help the library celebrate the 100th birthday of its original building, the Perth Regiment chapter of the Imperial Order Daughters of the Empire held an essay contest in memory of Lois Thompson, the SPL's longest-serving employee.

Entrants were invited to write up to 1,000 words on The Library of the Future, My First Visit to a Public Library, or their choice of a library-related topic. For each of the two age categories, 14 to 18 and 13 and under, the IODE awarded $100 for first prize and $25 for honorable mention. The winning submissions were to be published. The judges were Georgina Cameron and Audrey Mageau, retired teachers.

librarian Blake McDougall) was here, we would have to go to the stairwell and smell. We would recognize *that* smell. Then he would call the police to come over right then. They (the police) were appreciative that we would call."

Anne Marie Heckman remembers another washroom-related problem: "We had a peeping Tom in the women's washroom for a while in the 1980s. He had long hair that I think was his, but he looked like a girl. We would just give out the (washroom) key and not question anyone. We weren't keeping track of them (the keys) very well. The women's washroom has two stalls, so he would go into one of them, lock it, and then peek over the top at whoever was in the other one. Brian (McKone) and I ended up confronting him in the washroom."

Book circulation at the SPL reached 138,428 in 1965, an increase of 2,089 in the adult department and 475 in the juvenile department. As well, 1,839 magazines and pamphlets were checked out, which brought total circulation to 140,267.

In June 1966 about 120 delegates from the 42 library boards within the Midwestern Regional Library Co-operative met for a conference at St. John's United Church. They were joined by members of the Niagara and Erie regional libraries, and by a representative of the provincial library service in Toronto.

Guest speakers included Frances Whiteway of the Middlesex County library and Francis R. St. John, a library consultant from New York. The latter had been retained by the Midwestern group, and he hinted at some of the findings he would be presenting in a report that came out a few months later.

At the end of his 13-month study, St. John concluded that "the public library situation in Perth County is sad. Almost half of the population has no service at all, and so many of the libraries that do exist are open only a few hours per week, are under-financed and given minimal service." He said SPL was spending 42.1 cents per capita on books – which was less than what three of the other four major libraries in the Midwestern group was each spending. Only Guelph, at 30 cents per capita, was doling out fewer bucks for books. As well, the other three counties were outspending Perth.

St. John said Ontario libraries were wasting several million dollars a year in duplicate rather than co-operative ordering of books.

There was further slamming in January 1967, when E. Stanley Beacock of Kitchener, director of the Midwestern library co-operative appeared before Perth County council to talk about the benefits of a county library system. In the course of that discussion he criticized the architects who designed the Carnegie libraries, specifically their liberal use of steps. Unwittingly, he declared, they probably discouraged the public's use of Carnegie libraries by incorporating so many front steps. And, that the libraries were so well built, the steps would be a deterrent for years to come. "I sometimes wish they (the Carnegie libraries) were falling down," he said.

In Stratford it was the steps that were falling down, so in June 1967 the board let a $10,900 tender to Guenther Mohrmann Construction Ltd. to rebuild them. The contract also called for refurbishing the front entrance, building public washrooms in the basement, raising a flagpole on the lawn, and putting down a new walkway. The Public Utility Commission was going to illuminate the walkway, from Church Street to St. Andrew Street.

In 1966, some SPL board members toured libraries in neighbouring communities and came home convinced their facility was woefully undersized. So they asked the architectural firm of Kyles Kyles and Garratt to come up with plans and costs for

SPL

It was in December 1967 that the Midwestern Regional Library System was officially formed. Its proponents hoped to buy, catalogue and prepare 20,000 volumes for $100,000, which was expected to save its members about $2.50 a book over previous costs. The initial purchase was 600 books, which were distributed among the system's five main libraries, in Stratford, Kitchener, Waterloo, Guelph and Galt, as well as 20 smaller libraries in the four counties of Waterloo, Wellington, Perth and Huron.

It was also in December 1967 that the city recognized the services of its chief librarian, Lois Thompson, at a dinner at the Victorian Inn.

On Feb. 16, 1968, the *Beacon Herald* called on Stratford and Perth County to set up a county library system. In an editorial, it repeated several of the damning conclusions reached in 1966 by New York library consultant Francis St. John.

Six days later, the paper used the same space to repeat the call, this time citing a survey completed by a trustee of the Burlington Public Library. Frank Rose found that Ontario's public library facilities on a per capita basis were the second worst in Canada, better than only those in Quebec.

"Stratford and Perth County do not help the situation, as per capita expenditures for books in our area lag far behind our neighboring communities," stated the editorial. "Mr. Rose's report estimated that it would cost $20 million to bring public libraries in this province up to standards set in 1956. It would take $65 million to provide for Ontario's library needs over the next 10 years if the 1956 standards were followed. The standards were set in 1956 by the Canadian Library Association in co-operation with the American Library Association, but Ontario's public libraries

an addition to the south side of their building. The architects did just that, and their cost estimate for the addition requested was $290,500. The construction of that addition was set for 1968.

In September 1967, the SPL was visited by 15 Swedish librarians who were making a swing across southern Ontario before spending some time at Expo 67 in Montreal.

It was in that year that the city postponed its plans to put an addition on the south side of the library in 1968, using the plans and cost estimates that had been tabled in 1966. It said the construction would take place in 1970, at a projected cost of $388,000.

To commemorate Canada's centennial year, 1967, the Stratford Junior Chamber of Commerce donated busts of Sir. John A. MacDonald and Etienne Cartier to the SPL.

In the same year, the library received its first shipment of large-print books, purchased through the Midwestern co-operative, and began to look into the delivery of reading material to shut-ins.

simply have not been able to keep up to the standards set jointly with U.S.

"Charles Brisbin, Hamilton's chief librarian, said, 'It's high time we got over our sweaty, apologetic approach in getting decent facilities.' Mr. Brisbin also noted that library facilities in Ontario are basically unchanged since the St. John report was brought down two years ago . . .

"The Ontario Library Association will be holding its annual conference in Hamilton in May at which time an attempt will be made by representatives of Ontario's public and school libraries to establish a uniform system for all library resources in the province. Now is the time for those people in Perth County who are interested in better library service to seek the establishment of a Perth County library.

"Why should Perth continue to lag behind when local taxpayers are already helping to pay for the regional library system from which they cannot really benefit until a county library is set up?"

In November 1968, Mayor John Killer and the rest of the Stratford city council toured the SPL, mostly to get a look at the upgrades that had been completed over the previous half dozen years.

By then the library had about 40,000 books and 90 periodicals. It also had more than 6,000 adult members, and it was estimated that 3,000 children were using the facility. The reference room was busiest when students were out of school – at noon hours and after 4 p.m. The SPL was also offering a 16-mm film service, through which patrons could borrow documentary and travel films at no charge. They could also rent a projector if necessary.

As of January 1969 the main library was still closing at 1 o'clock on Wednesday afternoons. It was open from 10 a.m. to 9 p.m. Monday, Tuesday, Thursday and Friday, and from 10 a.m. to 6 p.m. on Saturday. Operating hours for the children's department were 2:30 p.m. to 6 p.m.

Monday, Tuesday, Thursday and Friday, and 10 a.m. to noon on Saturday. That year, the circulation of its books surpassed 135,000.

It was in 1969 that the city announced its proposed addition to the library was on the back burner until 1971 or 1972.

In October 1969, Nora Martin of Williamsville, N.Y., gave the library more than 100 old coins, mounted in two cases with glass fronts. The coins, valued at $250, were from around the world and included a 1794 British trading token. They had been collected by Nora's father, Maurice Dillon, a machinist with the Grand Trunk Railway, who had moved to Stratford from his native Hamilton.

After leaving the GTR, he was a hotelier in Stratford. He was also a longtime member of the separate school board. He died in 1928. The Dillon family, which included 14 children, lived on Cambria and Huron streets.

The coin collection is now at the Stratford-Perth Archives. Just one of the cases has survived, and some of the coins are now loose in a box.

Lois Thompson's last official day at the library was Dec. 31, 1969. Her term of almost 49 years remains the longest among SPL employees. By the time of her retirement, her annual salary had reached $7,800, which is what Blake McDougall was paid to take her place.

Other full-time staff members and their yearly earnings at the time were Winnifred Henderson ($6,100), Jean [MacDougall] Bain ($5,900) and Billie Kirkby ($4,500). Part-timer Dorothy Robinson was bumped from $1.75 to $1.85 an hour, and two students were getting $1.25 an hour.

Gladys Eickmeier was paid $700 a year as the SPL board's treasurer and Victor Lindsay $350 as its secretary.

Live-in caretaker Walter (Butch) Kelterborn got a $100-a-year raise in December 1969, to $2,200.

School days at the library

In the summer of 1955 it was apparent that the new St. Aloysius school on Avondale Avenue was not going to be ready for the resumption of classes in September. That caused more than mild concern for officials of the separate school board, and they looked to the Stratford Public Library in resolving their dilemma.

For $75 a month they rented space from the SPL and directed Audrey Kennedy, and her Grade 2-3 class of about 24, to a room on the second floor. "I know we went upstairs and through an area where there were a lot of books which were not in use, and then there was a classroom for us," she recalls. "I had a blackboard that was sort of an easel-type thing, but the setup wasn't primitive at all. The setting was wonderful. I wasn't bothered by anybody, and we got along just great. There were also two nuns on staff, just the three of us, and they were at Avon Public with their classes in two rented rooms."

The library was not a strange place to the 18-year-old Miss Kennedy, fresh out of teachers college. She was an avid reader and had been a regular SPL patron during her days growing up in Stratford. "I still love to read," she says, "For me to have my first class in the library was almost like the answer to a dream. Taking the kids into the library was like being lost in paradise."

One of her students that year was John Flood, now a poet, academic, and proprietor and president of Penumbra Press in Manotick, Ont. In June 1987 he wrote to the woman he remembered as Miss Kennedy and said, in part: "I have often attributed my interest in and involvement with books – as a writer, publisher and teacher – to our Grade 3 class at the Stratford Public Library. That was a period of genuine immersion for which I will always be grateful to you. Let me say 'Thank you' for that introduction."

The immersion ended in the spring of 1956, as soon as St. Al's was ready for occupancy. Miss Kennedy left town that summer and for the next four decades or so taught in five centres across the province, mostly in Timmins, and mostly as Mrs. Mageau. Now retired and back in Stratford, she says nothing in her teaching career could compare to those days in the library. "It was an idyllic setup. I would have stayed there forever. I loved it. It's a wonderful memory."

Miss Kennedy was not the only Audrey to teach elementary school in the SPL. Nor were John Flood and his colleagues the building's only full-time students.

In 1957, trustees on the city's public board of education encountered a space problem at Hamlet School, due in large part to the leading edge of the baby boomers. Like their separate school counterparts, the trustees on the public board turned to the SPL. The rental fee was $75 a month plus $1 per school day for caretaker services.

"I don't know who made the decision that it would be Grade 6 that went to the library," says Audrey Gale, "but G. N. Edwards was the school inspector at the time, and he was also connected with the library."

It was also decided that Mrs. Gale would be the teacher at the SPL, in a room equipped with regular school desks and three large blackboards which were initially on wheels. Through the next eight school years, about 300 Hamlet students earned their Grade 6 credits in the library, where they also learned about sharing the only washroom on the second floor. When it was in use, the name of the user was printed in a corner of the blackboard. And not until that name was erased was the washroom deemed to be vacant.

"I certainly did enjoy being there," says Mrs. Gale, "and I think most of the students thought it was a great place, too. I was my

This is the area the SPL board rented to school boards as a temporary classroom, beginning in 1955. The blackboard was eventually added for that reason. The room is near the eastern end of the second floor on the north side of the building. Behind the blackboard was a storage room for magazines, and beyond it a well-furnished boardroom with pile carpet on its floor. The retired wall shelving, at right, was sold by public auction in August 1975. This space is now used for offices and storage.

there. It was a great introduction to the library for the kids. On those afternoons, I was supposed to turn the phone on, so somebody could reach me if they wanted, but lots of times I forgot to turn it on. When we left on those days, I just pulled the door shut and it locked.

"One Wednesday after the kids had gone, I looked around and a man appeared in the library. I was able to get him to leave, but I often look back and think I was awfully lucky that nothing happened. On the following Sunday he came into the narthex of St. Andrew's church. I think the police finally came and got him."

There were no police around on the day Mrs. Gale marched her charges through Queens Park for a tour of the waterworks plant on Romeo Street North. It was a winter excursion, and en route, she slipped through some encrusted snow and dropped into something of a hole. Among the first students to the scene was Jackie Haines, who, according to Audrey, was moved to say, "Well, Mrs. Gale, I don't know whether to pull you out or leave you there." Or words to that effect. A broad smile on his face, Jackie rescued his teacher.

For Mrs. Gale, teaching in the library lasted five school years, and she had as

own boss. Not often did the principal (Hugh Myers) appear at the door.

"We had no playground and no real recess, but we took breaks and played balloon volleyball and things like that. The students would go home for lunch. Twice a week, after the afternoon recess, we'd walk to Hamlet for physical education. When the weather was nice the kids would ride their bikes, and I remember one day, one of the students came running back to tell me that Dennis Petrie had gone over the handlebars of his bike and he was hurt. So I ran down the hill, down by the Legion corner, and sure enough, he had gone over the handlebars, and he was lying on the road. I told the rest of them to go on to Hamlet, and that I would look after Dennis. I don't think he was badly hurt, but I do remember that day.

"On Wednesday afternoons, when the library was closed, we could go into the children's library and spend some time in

many as 46 students in one of those years. "They were five of the best years of my teaching career," she says. "Of course, the roof was often leaking, and we had pails sitting around to catch the water, but it was a wonderful teaching experience. The kids kind of fell into a routine. I expected a certain behaviour from them, and they gave it to me. They had a special feeling about being there, I think. It was one for all and all for one."

One of the all was Marilyn Connor (now Wells), who says, "I thought we were very special to go to school in the library. I liked it. I thought Mrs. Gale was an incredibly good teacher. She was tough, but she was kind. I remember after lunch having to do multiplication tables. I don't think you got out of her class until you knew them. When I became a teacher and she became a colleague, I got to know her much better."

"Nobody seemed terribly offended that we had to go to the library for school," says Brian Hayter, another of Mrs. Gale's students. From where we lived, it took me about five minutes to get to Hamlet school and about seven minutes to get to the library, so it didn't bother me. It was a pretty good year there. We probably became more of a class because we were there by ourselves. I've gotten to know Audrey over the years, and we are pretty good friends now."

The same can be said for Mrs. Gale and Rick Linley, whose paths led each to the library in 1958-59. "That class was kind of a special little unit," he says. "We were on the north side of the building. Our room looked out on the courthouse. As much as we were isolated (from the rest of the school), I never felt that to be a deterrent. I enjoyed Audrey as a teacher. I think everyone respected her.

"I remember her reading The Pegeen and the Pilgrim to us. I've always remembered that book because the story took place in Stratford. And it was Audrey who introduced me to the fact that Halley's

comet was returning in 1986. That stayed with me."

There was another return of sorts in 1986, when Ald. Rick Linley became Stratford's council representative on the library board, and he was once again "mounting those stairs" with some regularity.

When Mrs. Gale left, her place at the library was taken by Mary Murray. One of her students in 1963-64 was Betsy Trethewey (now Kalmusky), who says, "I got my best marks in that class. I thought being in the library was kind of a gas. I had a good time. I was with all my friends, but at that time school was fun.

"I remember it being hot up there, though. We'd have all the windows open. We didn't go outside much. For recess we divided the class in half and played beach-ball volleyball or 20 questions, games like that. We had to be reasonably quiet because the children's library was next door. I remember one day, when we were walking back from Hamlet, there was a fire in an old building, and we stopped and watched it for quite a while."

When King Lear, a senior public school, was opened in September 1965, Hamlet became a kindergarten-to-Grade 6 operation, with enough room that some of its students were no longer assigned to the SPL.

The desks were removed from the library soon after the last class had been dismissed, but the blackboards – eventually slate models that were affixed to walls – remained in use for some. It took three men to hoist the last of those down the stairs when the quarters were renovated in the 1990s. What was once a Grade 6 classroom is now offices.

In later years, the SPL auditorium, formerly the children's department, served as a classroom for students taking extension courses from the University of Waterloo and the University of Western Ontario in London.

Tall stacks, narrow aisles and record-toting, plywood sentinels, 1973

The Blake McDougall years
1970-1971

In February 1969, the SPL's Chris Swanston travelled to Toronto, where he interviewed nine library school students who had expressed an interest in becoming Lois Thompson's assistant – and, they hoped, her successor.

At the end of the day it was Donald Blake McDougall, about 10 days shy of his 31st birthday, who most impressed the Stratford board chair.

In June 1969 McDougall joined the SPL staff as assistant chief librarian. His grandparents had moved west from Hibbert Township in 1911, and he was born in Moose Jaw, Sask. He had worked for the Toronto-Dominion Bank and had been in the Canadian Army. He also had a bachelor of education and a bachelor of library science, the latter from the University of Toronto. He and his wife Norma moved from Regina to Stratford, where they settled into an apartment on William Street.

In January 1970 he was given the top job at the SPL upon the retirement of Miss Thompson. But any hopes he might have had about an expanded facility in the near future were soon dampened, when city council once again postponed the building of an addition to the south side of the library, a project that originally had been pencilled in for 1968. The new target year became 1973.

In May 1970 the University Women's Club of Stratford gave the library $350 to help it start a collection of phonographic recordings. In September of that year the members helped the project along with the donation of 96 records in 19 categories that ranged from classical to jazz to modern to country and western. The new head librarian predicted the SPL would have a further 400 records available for loan by the end of 1973.

June 1, 1970, was the first official day at the SPL for Sue Bonsteel, hired by the board as its reference librarian, a newly created position. She soon learned that most of the questions directed to her by adults would be about local history and the women's liberation movement, but that about 70 per

Blake McDougall in the 1970s

described as educational in nature. The three most popular had to do with drugs, pollution and Canadian Indians. The rental fees were $1 for colour films and 75 cents for black and white.

At that time, the SPL's 10-cent membership card for residents of the city was good for three years. Out-of-towners were required to pay $1.96. Most books could be taken out for two weeks, but those on the best-seller lists and new books were due back after seven days.

To help slow readers, the library brought instructors from London to teach a "rapid reading course." It was in the auditorium, one night a week for 10 weeks. "It's been terrific in terms of response," said McDougall.

It was also in the fall of 1970 that a noon hour book club was started, and it has remained a fixture at the library.

By February 1971, the attendance of older children at the library on Saturday mornings had dropped off. Just 16 or 17 in the grades-3-to-6 bracket were showing up. So McDougall appealed to the public for someone in the community who "might be interested in organizing some type of entertainment for the youngsters" for every third Saturday. He was hoping for something a little less academic and more recreation. "I have found that for older children, it has to be mainly a recreational

BLAKE MCDOUGALL

cent of all questions were from students.

That October, she said, "I think every kid in Stratford was doing an assignment on trees, leaves or flowers, this fall. Without spoon-feeding them too much, we tell them where they can find the information." As well, she said, the library was sending books and other materials to schools, if specific subject matter was requested by a teacher. "We do this because of the inadequate libraries in the schools, particularly the elementary schools."

The library's collection of films had by then grown to 150 in-house, with another 800 available through the Midwestern exchange program. The offerings were

7 DAYS

THIS BOOK MAY BE KEPT FOR

7 DAYS ONLY

BECAUSE OF SPECIAL DEMAND

IT CANNOT BE RENEWED

SPL

program. After sitting in school all week, the kids want mainly to be entertained." He said he was also thinking about adding animals and films to the Saturday morning program. There were no plans, however, to disrupt the long-running Saturday morning story hour, for which about 40 nursery and primary school-aged children were showing up faithfully.

In March 1971 the library offered, on an experimental basis, an audiovisual program that made available to community groups and commercial enterprises a wide range of equipment. The SPL got approval from the Midwestern system to use $2,000 to implement the program.

When Donald Davis was elected mayor for the 1971-72 term, he mentioned a bookmobile and Sunday hours in the part of his inaugural address that dealt with Stratford's library. And when Blake McDougall and his staff surveyed their patrons and other interested parties, they found that both ideas had merit.

McDougall estimated the cost of a city-owned bookmobile and service to be $42,000 for the first year. For the library to be open from 2 p.m. to 5 p.m. each Sunday, the city would be looking at an additional expense of $750 to $1,000 a year, he said. At the same time, he wanted to see an extension of hours in the children's department. He pointed out that Stratford was at the bottom in a study of nine libraries of comparable size when it came to children's library services.

In May 1971, the SPL introduced Sunday hours, after which the staffers who worked those days said they could often smell roasts cooking in the caretaker's apartment in the basement.

In the same month, when Vic Lindsay resigned as a trustee, the head librarian was offered $350 – over and above his $8,500 salary – to add the board's secretarial duties to his responsibilities.

In 1971, the city put off the proposed

addition to the south side of the building once again, this time to 1974 and at an estimated cost of $450,000. The SPL board expressed doubt that the construction would ever take place and began to consider other possibilities.

Blake McDougall's frustration showed through in a document he prepared in calling for the city to forget about the proposed addition in favour of "a substantial mobile book service plus extensive renovations to the existing library building and major improvements in exisiting public services. The mobile book service in itself is not enough." Or, he said, the city could opt for a new public library building.

"At the present time, I feel that the first of the two proposals is most realistic," wrote McDougall. "The adoption of this recommendation would guarantee a strong public library service in the city now and yet still allow for continued progress in the future. The adoption of the first proposal would also only cost a fraction of the amount that would be required for the proposed extension plan. In terms of cost for value, it is my opinion that the utility of the proposed extension plan is questionable.

"This statement, of course, is just my opinion and not that of the library board. The present board has been involved in the operation of this library much longer than I have and may have very good reasons for supporting the extension plan. However, if the library board feels that it wishes to continue to support the extension program, I feel that they should consult an independent consulting service in order to determine the feasibility of adding to the existing library building. The extension of older library buildings in other centres, for example St. Catharines, has often proven to be a very expensive 'mixed blessing.'"

In October 1971, McDougall resigned his position with the SPL and took a job with Edmonton Public Library.

A cost of doing business

Much to the chagrin of staff, library patrons have long marked books they have checked out. While some of those markings are obscene and verge on vandalism, others are a kind of record keeping, a way to remember whether or not they have read those books.

Stratford Public Library has had its share of markers, including the person who has put an unusual symbol at the end of the second paragraph on page 77 in "guy" novels that range from mysteries and espionage to action and adventure.

Others have left initials or numbers in specific places.

Such marking is thought to be more prevalent in series novels such as mysteries, Harlequins and westerns.

More annoying are patrons who underline or circle passages, or mark them with a highlighter.

Jim Anderson touched on a related practice in his 1975 history of the library: "One should see the things people hide in books or use for bookmarks – bacon rinds, love letters, invitations, sand, porno and Aunt Matilda's birthday card."

Then there are the mutilators. Anne Marie Heckman recalls getting back a copy of Martin's Annual Criminal Code that had been nailed shut. "I think the person had anger management issues," she says.

As well, there are those who steal books. Former staffer Ken Clarke, says, "I remember one fellow in the early 1970s who would take books out of the library by the bushel. He was taking more and more and more, and nobody thought to say, 'Maybe we should put a limit on this fellow.' Eventually, we had to send the police around, and we found hundreds, many hundreds of our library books. He was furnishing his (hotel) room with them, and cutting pictures out of them and hanging them on the wall. He had his own branch of the library at his place. Unfortunately, I don't think any of the books were salvageable."

Dorothy Robinson began working at the SPL in 1959, and for many years it was her job to notify delinquent patrons. One of the most memorable of those was a woman who regularly paid the five-cent charge to sign out new releases, which for many years were lined up across the checkout counter. But she had little regard for returning them.

"I'm not kidding around anymore, Mrs. Whitman. You have our book. We have your son."

"One day, Lois (Thompson) said, 'C'mon Dorothy, we're going to get those books.' So, we went to this house, and the son was home. We walked in and just went around and picked up all the new books and brought them all back. The woman never ever said anything. I guess it wasn't the right thing to do, but we did it, and we got away with it."

In her role as book cop, she says she heard every imaginable excuse for not returning books on time, everything from "It's at the cottage" to "It's in my friend's locker at school" to "The dog ate it."

Sometimes dogs did get at borrowed books, she concedes, "but you could always tell when a dog got it."

For many years the library had a free-standing drop box at the front of the building. It was a large, vertical steel box that needed to be opened and emptied regularly. One morning the staff discovered that someone had tossed raw eggs through the deposit slot. On another occasion, someone had tried unsuccessfully to burn the box and its contents.

"I remember getting the books out of the box one time, and all the inside pages of one of the books had been burned," says Sally Hengeveld.

Libraries have long had a system of fines in place to deal with tardy borrowers. Since the mid-1990s, the SPL has also held food-for-fines days, during which patrons facing fines are allowed to donate non-perishable food items in exchange for money owed. In turn, the library gives all that it takes in to a local food bank.

PUBLIC PERFORMANCE RIGHTS
PUBLIC PERFORMANCE

This video has Public Performance Rights. Showing this video outside a home is considered public performance. Materials designated "Public Performance" are for non-theatrical exhibition for non-paying audiences in libraries, schools, churches or other public institutions.
Please note that public performance videos are usually significantly more expensive than those designated for home use only. The additional charge goes to the creator of the work as compensation for public showing. If you are concerned about the replacement cost of this video, a library staff member would be pleased to tell you its price.

PUBLIC PERFORMANCE RIGHTS
HOME USE

This video is for Home Use only. Materials with this designation must be shown only in a private home. It is illegal to show this video in a public place, including libraries and schools, regardless of whether or not admission is charged.

Property of
Stratford Public Library
Stratford, Ont. 271-0220

! Caution !
Do Not Use Book Drop
When Returning.
Damage or Fines Possible

DATE DUE

This item is Due on
or before Date shown.

Library weeks and book days

In 1956, a survey of Canadians revealed that 61 per cent of the population had easy access to public library facilities, but only 15.2 per cent of citizens five years old and older were using them to borrow books. Of those, 28.5 per cent were in the five-to-14-year-old age category.

There was considerable mention of that study in April 1959, when the Canadian Library Association, the Canadian Book Publishers Association, and La Societe des Editeurs – Canadiens des Livres Francais sponsored the first Canadian Library Week, for which the theme was "Wake up and read."

They wanted a "better-read, better-informed Canada," they said. "Limited horizons are dangerous to a free people; so, as we have discovered, is the mindless assumption of superiority and invulnerability."

Libraries across the country were encouraged to publicize their services and attract the masses with open houses and special events.

In Stratford that mandate was met in a variety of ways through the years. There were displays of the most recent and popular books in assorted categories. And the Canadian room in the southeast corner of the main floor was awash in local historical items, ranging from a fire chief's hat to a sizeable hand-carved wooden Indian. These were pre-city archives and museum years, and the library doubled as a repository for such things.

It was in that room that the Stratford Public Library occasionally made available for viewing a number of rare books, which were usually locked away. In that collection were In the Days of the Canada Company, and Humours of '37, by sisters Robina and Kathleen Lizars; Pioneers of Blanshard by William Johnston; and Upper Canada Sketches by Thomas Conant.

For its open houses, the SPL also involved other groups, such as the Stratford Film Council, which in 1960 presented a night of travel films – in colour – including one on the voyage of "the modern Mayflower."

In 1961, members of the University Women's Club of Stratford set up displays, of pottery, Shakespearean Festival costumes, local history, floral arrangements and books on travel.

Costumes and properties from the Festival became a fixture among the library week exhibits, and for many years the man who co-ordinated them was Bob Ihrig.

For CLW in Stratford in April 1962, the Stratford Pastime Gun and Anglers Association put together an array of rifles and shotguns, fishing rods, lines and tackle. Also on exhibit were club trophies and pictures of fish, birds and game animals.

As well, the Stratford YMCA Aquanauts had a display of diving equipment and relics from sunken ships.

For the SPL's sixth annual open house, in April 1964, members of the Stratford Art Society arranged a showing of their scenes of Stratford.

In 1966 there were National Film Board movies, and arts and crafts from a number of Stratford's public schools.

Many of the library weeks featured a coffee hour, and often it was members of the city's Zonta Club who helped with refreshments, which were served in the children's department. They also made available some items for display.

In line with Canada's centennial celebrations, library week in 1967 adopted the theme "The Library and Man and his World." That year, artifacts from the Perth County Historical Foundation featured a set of dishes, and a painting of those dishes done in about 1900. Both were owned by Jean Johnston of Fullarton Township.

For another year, the slogan was "Books are friends, come let us read." The aim of library week, said the promoters was to "remind Canadians of the meaning of reading to free men in a free society."

"The man who does not read is not better off than the man who cannot read," they said.

The last Canadian Library Week was in 1967.

The first National Book Festival week was held in 1978 and ran annually through 1993, when the federal government pulled its funding.

Also in 1978, Canadian Children's Book Week was started, and it has been held each year since. Because of title sponsorship from the TD Bank Financial Group, it is now called TD Canadian Children's Book Week.

The first Ontario Public Library Week was in September 1985, and at the SPL it was celebrated with a storytelling workshop for librarians, teachers and parents. As well, Margaret Beckman was in town to talk about the history of Carnegie libraries in Ontario.

In October 2002 the theme for OPLW was "It's not by the book anymore," and the SPL offered free computer lessons to help patrons make the best use of the library's lastest technology.

As well, it again invited delinquent borrowers to take advantage of its food-for-fines program, through which they could donate a non-perishable food item for each $2 owed in fines, to a maximum $20. Each year, the resulting hundreds of pounds of food have been given to a local charity.

Initiated by the Ministry of Culture and Recreation, Ontario Public Library Week is now administered by a marketing task force whose members represent scores of library organizations from across the province.

It was in 1995 that the United Nations Educational, Scientific, and Cultural Organization declared April 23 to be World Book Day. In the same year, a group of book enthusiasts, inspired by Ottawa author Lawrence Martin, gathered at The Writers' Trust of Canada and decided to dedicate that day to the promotion of the nation's writers. They proclaimed Canada Book Day.

The Friends of the Stratford Public Library have helped the SPL celebrate Canada Book Day, which in 2003 becomes Canada Book Week and runs from April 21 through April 27.

The Noon Hour Book Club

Over the years, there have been assorted incarnations of literary groups associated with the Stratford Public Library. They have taken names such as Bookscene, Reading for Pleasure, Bookbeat, and The Good Book Group.

But none has enjoyed the popularity and longevity of The Noon Hour Book Club, which has been running since the fall of 1970, for most of those years on Thursdays. Its genesis, according to Cathy Clarke, was in the William Street apartment of Grace Reynolds soon after the latter had moved to Stratford. "There had been a book club where she came from," says Cathy. "So she approached Sue (SPL librarian Sue Bonsteel), and they started it." After two or three meetings, the handful of charter members moved to a small room in the library, and the numbers grew.

Originally, members volunteered at the beginning of each session, spring and fall, to read a book and review it when the group gathered.

"We tried to keep the focus on the books and encouraged the people who came out to review books," says former SPL staffer Lorraine Greenberg. "Not everyone wanted to do the reviews, but when they did, I always felt that they were on a very high level. People tried very hard. Occasionally, there would be a guest speaker come in and talk about something that was of interest to the group. Soon the members themselves were generating the speakers and the topics. They were a tightly knit group, which was an advantage and a disadvantage, but they really enjoyed it."

This is a club for which there are no memberships cards or dues. There is no roll call, no record of attendance, no executive, no minutes. There is, however, a cover charge of $1 per meeting. Those who show

up, and there are a few who have been doing so since the beginning, are still invited to bring their lunch. The organizers and the library provide coffee.

Like all clubs, formal or otherwise, the noon hour group experienced change. "In the '80s and into the '90s the original members were getting older, and they just didn't want the responsibility anymore," says SPL director Jane Kirkpatrick. "So the program and the speakers became more staff driven. Then it was pretty much all guest speakers coming in and it got away a little bit from the focus on the books. After Gail Poole (staff member) left, we were really struggling with how to do it, but now, again, it's driven by the members. They're

From left, Helen Kirkpatrick, Kay Weston and Marg Pike at a Noon Hour Book Club gathering in 1990.

not doing the reviews so much, but they're bringing the speakers in, and they're trying to bring the focus back to the books."

"We do have people who talk about books," says Marg Pike, "and this spring we are going to have someone review a book. But our speakers talk about various things." She has been a member of the group since about 1975, and for many years has been

---

among the shrinking circle of organizers, whose numbers also include Mary McCaffrey and Cathy Clarke. Longtime members of that circle, Sue Bonsteel, Madeline Ferguson and Helen Barker, had to step down for personal reasons.

Various library personnel have helped to co-ordinate the club's activities through the years. At present it is Anne Marie Heckman.

The format now calls for 10 Thursdays in the fall and 10 in the spring, all in the second-floor auditorium. The fall session ends in early December with a potluck lunch. The spring program winds up in May with someone from the Stratford Festival talking about the upcoming season. Most recently that has been Pat Quigley, but the Festival has also been represented by Sheila Ferguson, Michal Schonberg, Philippa Lloyd, Paddy Crean, Richard Dennison, Alberta Nokes, Elliott Hayes and Jeff Marontate.

When Rogers had a cable TV office and studio in the city, it regularly taped the Thursday presentations and played them during the following weeks on its local community channel.

On Nov. 10, 1980, the club celebrated its 10th anniversary with songs by guitar-playing SPL staffer Carol Robinson and refreshments.

In February 1986 the members donated a gavel to the SPL board in memory of Lorne Brothers, who had died in 1985. He had been a longtime supporter of the library in many ways.

Those who, through the years, have reviewed books at the club's get-togethers include Thelma Pelley, Dorothy Tupper, Isabel Black, Hildeburg Scheu, Elizabeth Sanders, John Sinclair, Tom Wilcox, Lorraine Greenberg, Carol Robinson, Louise McColl, Jane Kirkpatrick, Cathy Clarke, John Quirt,

Marg Pike, Ted Priest, Hannah Miskin, Judy Robinson, Enid Hamilton, Joan Little, Grace Reynolds, Christina Wilson, Leona Green, Jo Aldwinckle, Helen Kirkpatrick, Nella Benson, John Benson, Anne Marie Heckman, Edna Young, Earl Galbraith, Elaine Wood, Elda Codogan, Frank Leslie, Kay Weston, Len Plotnik, Sue Bonsteel, Katherine Seredynska, Catherine Monahan, Myrtle Walkom, John Patterson, Reg White, and the duo of Ann Gregory and Madeline Ferguson.

Among the guest speakers have been Jim Anderson on Stratford's sesquicentennial,

Staffer Gail Poole hosts a session of the Noon Hour Book Club in 1990. At left are guests Elliott Hayes (wearing glasses) and Rick Whelan.

Bob Miller on swans, Karl Schuessler on the value of laughter, Susan Close on nutrition, Mary Jane Schuessler on researching and writing local history, W. H. Thomas on the poerty of Wilfred Owen, Marg Pike on winter gardening, Rose Barrett on Information Stratford, Heather Pryde on women and drugs, Gordon Hale on aging, Frances Greene on the Stratford General Hospital, Muriel Freeman on quilting as history, John Silverstein on Gallery Stratford, Nella Benson on search and research, Lucky Lott on his life as a hell driver, Gail Poole and Kate Jacob on storytelling, John Quirt on science fiction, William Munnelly on wine, Jim Henry on options for seniors, Reg White on royal family trees, Helen Barker on key books in her life, Scott Wishart on photography, Nancy Milne on indoor gardens and house plants, Barb Leavitt on community connections, Dama Bell on mystery writers, Craig Burtch on genealogy, Mary Hoy-Schmidt on short stories and poetry, Sulea Schlosser on selling books, Dean Robinson on Stratford's railway history, Maureen Davis on the Stratford Field Naturalists, Jane Kirkpatrick on the Stratford Public Library, Daniel Moores on Tai Chi, Lesley Beckett on Hans Christian Andersen, Brian Emery on George Frederick Handel, Nancy Hislop on herbs, Brenda Silver on archeology in Jordan, Ruth Dill on dried flowers, Rob Freeman on Gallery Stratford, Earl Galbraith on toastmasters, John Hayes on children's books, Jack Hamilton on the history of the Stratford Fall Fair, Faye Knott on environmental sustainability, Gerard Brender à Brandis on book-making, Lynne McDonald on the Victorian Order of Nurses, Rheo Thompson on making candy, Nancy Kramer on Brocksden School, Becky Rogers on stained glass, Paul Rhodes on massage, Jane Eligh-Feryn and Eric Eberhardt on the Meadow Rue garden, Carolynn Bart-Riedstra on Irish immigration to Perth County, Barbara Foster on medication safety for seniors, Lutzen Riedstra on the Canada Company, Dave Essex on the Avon Trail, Astrid Roch-Russell on creative dance drama, Rev. James Dickey on T. S. Elliot, Vicki Krotz on planning a wardrobe, Ian Munro on Robbie Burns, Carolyn Badun on planning meals, Katherine Seredynska on Easter traditions in the Ukraine, Diane Goettler on diet and cancer, William Needles on John Updike, Lorene Douglas on open doors, Marian Doucette on "philosophizin," Barb Munro on cancer survivors, Alexander Grygier on Japanese language and calligraphy, Sally Hengeveld on Christmas books for children, Stephen Chandler on children's aid, Geraldine Barnard on stenciling, Karen Webb on Body

Basics, Geoff Hancock on Reveal Ontario, Les Wilker on Carolinian species, Eric Coates on the Blyth Festival, Suzanne Strahan on the Perth County Youth Chamber Choir, Stephen Russell on acting, Barbra Williams on read-aloud classics, Gail Fricker on writing and directing, Betty Larkworthy on painting the house, Bruce

Trigger on the portrayal of native Canadians in Canadian literature, Dave Bradshaw on the Brown mystery, Vicki Ryder on birding, Frank Jenner on Scotland, Susan Chapman-Bossence on from the inside out, Ann Cooper on Canada's correctional service, William Needles on the work of Dan Needles, Allan Watts on container gardening, Natalie MacPherson on missionary work in Guatemala, Bob Boyce on rockhounding, Peter Brierley on

Shakespeare's sonnets, Robert Windrum on Gallery Stratford, Paul Reese on Stratford police home protection, Karen Scott Booth on pottery, Leslie McGrath on the Osborne Collection of Early Children's Books at the Toronto Public Library, Rick Whelan on writing plays, Ray Rutherford and Robert Clayton on Victoria and Grey's new data centre, Stan Beisel on family history, Jennifer Lawrie on Lucy Maud Montgomery, John and Nancy Patterson on Guatemala, and Robyn Godrey, John Brogan and Jason Paquet on fencing and stage combat. The foregoing does not include all of the many writers who have spoken at the Thursday gathering during visits to Stratford and the library.

In the early 1980s the SPL tried to fill the Tuesday noon hour with a bring-your-lunch program that featured films and video presentations. It brought in speakers to talk about financial planning, nutrition, time management, the power of listening, sexual harassment, burnout and speaking effectively.

But no such endeavour has enjoyed the success and staying power of The Noon Hour Book Club.

PLOWing for literacy

One of the SPL's most ambitious projects as it kicks off a second century in the house that Carnegie built, is a literacy project designed to promote reading for young children and offer resources for their parents.

There is plenty of opportunity for that within the library, but the aim of this program is to reach those unfamiliar with the SPL and those living in areas where library services are not easy to access.

Funds for the program have come from a variety of sources, including the sale of the library's literary celebrity posters, the 2002 Stratford Book Festival, and a reading of A Christmas Carol at Knox Presbyterian Church. Support has been pledged from other sources, and the SPL intends to apply for a government grant. The biggest capital expense for the program will be the purchase of a van, which needs to be equipped to accommodate staff, books and assorted other materials.

The outreach project has been labelled Public Library on Wheels, the same name used when the SPL got into the mobile book business in the early 1970s. At that time, its driving force was Blake McDougall, newly arrived head librarian. When he pitched the idea in February 1971, he estimated the first-year costs to be $42,000. But it would be after McDougall left Stratford that the SPL took to the road.

In 1973, the library got an Opportunities for Youth grant, and three students, Brian McKone, Lorraine McGovern and Marlene Forrest, spent that summer travelling the roads of Perth County with a book-filled trailer. Actually, it was McKone who applied for the grant. "At first, township councils said they didn't need rural service, that they had enough books out there," he said. "But we've proved them wrong. North Easthope and South Easthope have no library service at all. They almost wouldn't let us go into Shakespeare, but our best response has been there.

"In some places we had a hard time getting permission to park the trailer. People didn't trust us – didn't trust the public library? They thought maybe we were bringing dirty books for their children to read. We haven't had any complaints though."

Most of the interest that summer was shown by those up to 12 years of age, and

The SPL's mobile branch, summer 1975

those over 30. The trio circulated about 3,800 books and issued 525 library cards.

In 1975, on the strength of a $4,000 grant and a tractor trailer furnished by Steed Standard Transport, students Geraldine Cuerden and Wayne Billo made weekly rounds to Shakespeare, St. Pauls, Fullarton, Sebringville and Rostock. Response was especially positive in Shakespeare and Rostock. In addition to books, the bookmobile offered a story hour, cartoons and a puppet show. By June 23, Cuerden and Billo had issued 300 cards to the Stratford Public Library.

The summer of '75 was the last for SPL's

bookmobile, but not the end of mobile books on the byways of Perth County. In 1976 the library boards in the townships of North Easthope, South Easthope, Ellice and Downie came up with a collective $2,500 to convert a yellow school bus into a motorized dispensary of knowledge and entertainment. They equipped the bus with shelving and other fittings from the SPL's efforts of previous summers and hired University of Waterloo student Jim Commerford of Stratford to be their driver-librarian.

He and his eight-month-old pug pup, Spike, spent about six hours a week in each of Shakespeare, Sebringville, Gadshill, St. Pauls and Rostock. Like his predecessors in summers past, he sold memberships in addition to lending books supplied by the SPL. Response was highest in Shakespeare, lowest in Sebringville.

In 1978, Central Secondary School student Gloria Schumacher was hired with an Experience grant to work on the township-funded book bus.

In 1980, Lawrence Diamond, the owner of Diamond Coach Lines, supplied the bus and taught 19-year-old Ruth Richards how to drive it. She and Mary Lynn Cook, 18, hired with an Experience '80 government grant, papered the ceiling with posters and took to the roads. In place of the bus's normal seats there were shelves, stuffed with books and other assorted library materials.

The regular stops that summer included Dublin, Cromarty, Shakespeare, Sebringville, Rostock and North Easthope Public School, as well as Anne Hathaway Park and Bedford Public School in Stratford.

Chief among the borrowers were children and their mothers. The highest response was in Dublin, the lowest in Shakespeare.

PLOW was back on the road in 1981, with Tina van Heyningen and Jacqueline Herold as the mobile librarians.

But its new life was a short one.

Mobile librarians Ruth Richards (left) and Mary Lynn Cook, 1980

The Sue Bonsteel years 1971-1983

By the time she joined the Stratford Public Library in 1970, Sue Bonsteel's background included some time as a private secretary at Stelco in Hamilton, a stint with the Student Christian Movement in Toronto, a university degree and two years in New York City as youth secretary for the World Council of Churches – all before she married a United Church minister, who eventually became a probation officer and took a job in Stratford.

A native of the Simcoe area, she was named to replace Blake McDougall as chief librarian late in 1971. Her salary was $8,500, and her job description included the secretarial duties of the board. At the same time, trustee Gladys Eickmeier was being paid $700 a year as the board's treasurer.

In January 1972 the board hired Larry Chu as its new reference librarian and assistant to the chief librarian.

In August of that year, when Jean (MacDougall) Bain retired from the SPL staff after 41 years, she was presented with a figurine by the board and her colleagues.

Also in 1972, the city agreed to repair the library roof, at an estimated cost of $4,500. The board had been requesting the improvement for two years.

As of Jan. 3, 1973, the SPL's loan period for books was increased to three weeks from two weeks to coincide with the policy of most Canadian libraries. No longer, however, would the library accept requests for renewals over the telephone – though that stand was eventually reversed.

By August 1973 the library's collection numbered 50,000 books, whose circulation totalled 140,000 annually. The collection also held 500 phonographic records and 1,200 films. The SPL's 8,500 cardholders included 200 from outside the city.

A steel strike in October 1973 caused the delay of new steel shelves for the main floor. In an effort to free up more space, the old but large and impressive oak checkout counter was slated to go out with the fine old shelving, also oak. Most of it was sold to the St. Marys Public Library, where the counter, reconfigured somewhat, continued

Bow-tied staffer Ken Clarke works the checkout desk, Oct. 23, 1973. Paperbacks were introduced at SPL in about 1968.

The view from behind the impressive oak counter, 1973. For many years there was a line of new fiction releases in the centre of the counter. Any of those books could be checked out for a week at a cost of five cents. The desk beneath the pigeon holes was used by the staff who tracked overdue books and collected and recorded fines.

The northeast corner of the main floor, from which doorways led to the reference room, 1973. Most of the furniture was built in Stratford factories.

The reference room, in the northeast corner of the main floor, 1973. The door to the room is in the top right corner.

The view to the left as one walked in the front entrance of the SPL in 1973. In the room through the open door was a corner filled with audio-visual equipment.

Looking southwest towards the north end of the bank (or range) of non-fiction stacks, 1973. The shelving was built when most books were the same size. Newer, larger volumes had to be stored horizontally. The maple floor was covered with plywood and cream-coloured linoleum.

SPL

Stratford teacher Bruce Stewart sits in the northwest corner on the main floor of the library, 1973. Behind the bookshelf was a stairway (not original to the building) to a basement storeroom that contained microfilm and retired Canadiana. In early days the north part of the main floor featured four large oak tables, each with two, green-shaded lamps mounted in their centres.

SPL

The room in the southeast corner of the main floor, October 1973. For years it was known as the Canadiana room. By 1973 it had become part office, part workroom, part lunchroom – complete with teapot and kettle. Staffer Jim Anderson said, "When you didn't know what to do with something, you took it to this office. And left it there. Time takes care of everything."

The staff workroom, to the left of the main entrance, October 1973. The daily take, usually just a few dollars, was in an envelope, which was in a locked box, in a locked drawer in one of the desks. In an adjoining drawer were the keys required to liberate the money.

Looking west from the northeast corner of the main floor, October 1973

to serve until 1988. Much of the shelving remained in use until 1990. Three sections of the shelves thought to have come from Stratford are still performing their intended duty on the second floor of the St. Marys facility.

It was also in 1973 that the Ontario Association of Library Technicians was formed.

Three days before Christmas that year, the library closed, so carpeting and new shelving could be installed on the main floor. That meant lugging about 20,000 books from that area to the second floor. There was no elevator in the building then. Chief librarian Sue Bonsteel lightened the load somewhat by giving away outdated books and magazines, some of them to apartment buildings for seniors and to Spruce Lodge. The library's grant from the province doubled to $32,000 in 1973, and half of it was earmarked for the upgrades.

There was a plea for volunteers to help move the books to and from the second floor. The hundreds who showed up might have included the person who phoned the library to ask how much each volunteer was to be paid.

It was about the third week of January 1974 before the SPL reopened, with hours that now included Wednesday afternoons and evenings.

It was that summer that somebody stole two flags within a month from the pole on the front lawn of the library. It was city firefighters who were called to replace the flags when they went missing or became tattered. Gerry Petrie and Larry Dale were photographed by the *Beacon Herald* when they drew that assignment in May 1986.

In August 1974, the architectural firm of Kyles, Kyles and Garratt was told its initial plans for the library's long-awaited expansion presented a southerly addition that was too grand and too modern relative to the main building.

So the firm came back with revised drawings, which city council approved 7-4 in the first reading of the necessary bylaw. By now the construction cost was pegged at $585,000. Speaking before the vote, Mayor Keith Culliton said, "I think the public library is a Stratford landmark. I think the time is at hand when the Ontario and federal governments are offering a grant to cut 30 to 35 per cent of the overall costs. By dilly-dallying around it is going to slip out of our reach. I think we would be doing the citizens of Stratford and Perth County a real disservice (by not approving the project)."

His position was supported by aldermen Gar Landers, Len Wilson, Fred Pearce, Bob Smith, Dave Rae Jr. and Jim Morris, though the latter said he would have preferred spending the money on a new building.

Dave Bradshaw and Colleen Misener were most vocal among the dissenters. He said he could not abide the city borrowing any more money that year, for the library addition or for the bus garage that the Public Utilities Commission was seeking. She said, "I'm still not convinced it blends in with the remaining building." Bas Schooley said he didn't approve of the new plans, and Dave Hunt said he couldn't support the cost. The city's debt at the time was in excess of $5.6 million.

The plans were sent to the Ontario Municipal Board for approval.

Not long after the vote of council, the matter of parking arose at a committee of adjustment meeting. Specifically, the library was not going to have enough. The addition was going to wipe out some of the lot shared by the SPL and St. Andrew's church, and the church was concerned. By mid-September, however, St. Andrew's had agreed to give the library free use of some of its land, and that satisfied the adjustment committee's on-site regulations.

Also in September, council voted for the second time on the addition, but this time Ald. Morris moved to the other side, fearing the plans would not be approved in time to

A view of the checkout counter from the desk of the reference librarian, December 1974. At right, chief librarian Sue Bonsteel uses the photocopier. At left, two patrons use the card files. Just beyond them is the library's front door.

Looking at the northeast corner of the main floor, December 1974. By then the room to the left of the row of car files had been converted from the reference room to the office of the chief librarian, Sue Bonsteel. The desk in front of the filing cabinets was used by the reference librarian, beneath the portrait gaze of R. Thomas Orr.

On occasion the library's front lawn has been its stage, August 1974

get the government money, and the city would be on the hook for another $175,000. Council voted 6-5 to stay the course. The city then sought and received a four-week extension on the grant approval deadline.

The federal winter works program to which it was applying specified that construction be done between Nov. 15, 1974, and May 31, 1975. Tenders were called on Oct. 3, 1974, and three weeks later the nod went to Pounder Bros., a Stratford company, for $41,344 less than the estimated $585,000.

While there was some fear that officials might be mucking up a fine-looking building with a "haphazard addition," there were also letters to the editor slamming those same officials for their "frivolous

The fire escape that ran down the west (rear) wall, 1974

Banker's view of the SPL from the roof of the Victoria and Grey building, summer 1974. By then the triple-globe lights on either side of the main entrance had fallen into disrepair. Those on the left had simply fallen.

spending" on the library and PUC bus garage.

Muriel Blackmore of Delamere Avenue took her complaint to the OMB. That necessitated a hearing, which began in City Hall at 11 a.m. on Dec. 16 and ran for six hours. There were 15 witnesses called, some of their testimony occasionally interrupted by some of the 50 or so onlookers.

Blackmore and Jake Triller spoke against the project because of its cost, as did Ald. Bradshaw. Jean Gordon also testified against it. Library head Sue Bonsteel and architect Brian Garratt argued for the other side.

At the end of the day, the OMB gave the city the authority to debenture $410,000 to pay for the addition. Fifty-five per cent of the projected cost was to renovate the existing building. Within a few hours of the

OMB decision, the councillors approved the project with a 6-4 vote. For: Rae Jr., Landers, Pearce, Wilson, Morris and Smith. Against: Bradshaw, Misener, Schooley and Hunt.

Ray Pounder of Pounder Bros. said he was optimistic about completing the work by May 31, 1975. "We'll come pretty close to that deadline. We'll do everything possible to make it by then." After a month on the job, he had revised the target date to June 30, 1975, and the city set about getting a work-period extension so it could remain qualified for grant assistance.

On the day after the hearing, library staff began packing books. There had been talk of setting up a temporary operation in a number of locations, including the vacated Scholar's Choice building near the corner of Erie and St. Patrick streets and the former Metropolitan department store building on Downie Street, both owned by the city. But the site of choice was the vacated A&P grocery store at 145 Erie St., a building now housing several businesses, among them Buns Master Bakery and Deli, and Feed All Pet Supply.

A Pounder Bros. crew works on the addition, spring 1975

Reinforcing and refurbishing the main floor or the original building, spring 1975

Winnifred Henderson did not make the move. Rather, she retired as children's librarian, replaced in that role by Jane Crozier, who had joined the SPL staff late in 1974. There were presentations to Miss Henderson from the board and her colleagues, but no open house in her honour because of the upheaval caused by the evacuation of the building.

On Jan. 6, 1975, the library reopened on Erie Street after being closed for two weeks.

It was in that month that the hours for the children's department were aligned with those of the main library: 9:30 - 9 during the week, 9:30 - 5 on Saturday and 2 - 5 on Sunday.

In June the federal government rejected the city's application to have the winter works grants program extended beyond May 31. City treasurer Ray McDonald said he was working with Kyles, Kyles and Garratt to speed up the construction process.

On July 14 the move back to the expanded and renovated library began, but it was complicated because shelves expected in April still had not arrived. To be shipped from Montreal to Stratford, they went instead to Edmonston, N.B. From there, they went to Ottawa. They made it to Stratford in mid-August.

On Aug. 25, 1975, the library was again open for business on St. Andrew Street, though some of its new furniture had not arrived. As well, about 3,000 books from the bookmobile, which had been shut down for the year, still had to be accommodated in the main collections.

"The first couple of days, I couldn't step out of my office without taking someone on a tour," said chief librarian Sue Bonsteel. "The surroundings are much nicer, and it is more pleasant to spend time here. The new lounge area is full all the time, especially at night. We haven't had any criticism at all."

The makeover had signalled the end of anyone living in the library, at least knowingly. The janitor's basement apartment became part of the new children's department, which

was moved from the top floor. "The little kids are just delighted," said their librarian, Jane Crozier. "When we were on the second floor, it was kind of dark. Now it's nice and bright. We have proper lighting, interesting geometric designs on the walls, proper kid-size shelving and scaled-down tables and chairs. The shelves look half empty now, but that only means we have room to expand and build up our resources."

In fact, the new children's area was 100 per cent larger than the old. Its features included three large stuffed animals – a camel, elephant and pony – all made and donated by residents of the Nithburg Retirement Home in New Hamburg, and designed to double as chairs.

Also in the basement was the expanded audiovisual department, where, it was said, "There's something for everyone down here." Among the exclusions, no doubt, were titles then gracing city screens, namely Once is not Enough, based on a novel by Jacqueline Susann, at the downtown Vogue Theatre; and twinbills at the Stratford Drive-in, at Downie Street and Lorne Avenue. The Devil's Rain was paired with The Butterfly Affair, and, on Sunday night

SPL

The west end of the auditorium, on the north side of the second floor, 1973. The enclosure was originally a retreat for staff members who were not feeling well. It eventually became a repository for miscellanea and took on the appearance of a junk room. When the children's department, on the south side of this floor, was moved to the basement in 1975, this area became offices and storage rooms.

only, Teenage Hitchhikers with Teenage Tramp.

The microfilm readers were in the basement, too, as were a screening room, sound booths for records and tapes, and a small film and meeting room.

With the children's department moved, the south half of the third floor became an auditorium that could seat 150. Attached were a projection room and kitchen.

The building was made more accessible for handicapped patrons with a wheelchair ramp and a washroom on the main floor for those patrons.

Television news anchor Lloyd Robertson, a Stratford native, was the special guest when the library was officially re-opened before about 300 people on

SPL

News anchor Lloyd Robertson takes a turn at the microphone during the official opening of the library addition, Sept. 7, 1975.

Other of the dignitaries on that sunny afternoon included Stratford Mayor Betty McMillan, Perth MPP Hugh Edighoffer, Perth-Wilmot MP Bill Jarvis and the director of the Midwestern Regional Library System, Clinton Lawson. They spoke from a podium set up on the steps leading to the library's front door.

Lorne Brothers and Sean O'Reilly cut the ceremonial ribbon. The former was a past board member, the latter a 4$^{1}/_{2}$-year-old member of the library's preschool programs.

Musical entertainment was provided by the Stratford Boychoir and the Royal Canadian Legion Band.

SPL

STRATFORD PUBLIC
LIBRARY

*RE-OPENING
CEREMONIES*

SUNDAY SEPTEMBER 7, 1975

CHAIRMAN: George Smith
Chairman, Stratford
Public Library Board.

Sunday, Sept. 7, 1975. He said his childhood memories of the library included the stuffed squirrels in the children's department and the smell of the janitor making his lunch in the basement. Sue Bonsteel said it was Paul McKone's idea to invite Robertson, who, 11 months later, left the CBC for a top news job at CTV.

As the speeches ended, the assemblage was invited inside for refreshments and to view special exhibits in the enlarged and refurbished library. There was a videotape presentation of She Stoops to Conquer by the Stratford Festival, a display of photography from the National Film Board, and a slide show called A Walk Along the Avon by Charles Trethewey.

That was International Women's Year, and beginning in October, the library hosted a seven-part weekly series with speakers and panel discussions. For most of those nights, 12 to 15 people showed up, but there were just two reporters on hand on Nov. 12, when Mayor Betty McMillan and Ald. Colleen Misener were scheduled to discuss women in politics. "I'm very disappointed that people aren't interested in running for politics," said the mayor. "I'd like to see some women interested." Ald. Misener blamed the washout on the "general apathetic view most people have for politicians, male or female."

In December 1975 the SPL was talking about charging members from most townships outside Stratford $15 a family per year. At that time, 711 families from outside the city were using the facilities.

INTRODUCING

Stratford Public Library

Serving Stratford and District since 1842

19 ST. ANDREW ST.
STRATFORD, ONT.
N5A 1A2

TELEPHONE 271-0220

A Member Of The
Midwestern Regional Library System

DISPLAYS
A series of displays take place during the year. If your organization wishes to mount a display in the library, we would be delighted to arrange for it. Please phone the librarian.

PROGRAMS
The children's department has pre-registered preschool story hours weekly. There are also Saturday programs during most of the year, featuring films, crafts, puppet shows and special guests.
A series of Feature Films is regularly planned by the AV Department.
The Thursday Book Lunch Club meets weekly except during vacation periods. Bring your own lunch.
Other programs will be announced. Watch our bulletin boards, the local newspapers, and listen to the radio and channel 12 cable TV for up-to-date news of the library—the place where Things Happen!

SPECIAL FACILITIES
There is a ramp at the back door so that wheel chair patrons may come to the main floor. They can also come into the lower floor through the side door. Washroom facilities are available on both floors. Please phone before you set out for the library, so that we can help you.
Public washrooms are located on the lower floor. Please ask for the key at the main desk.

SHUT IN SERVICE
For patrons who are unable to come to the library due to age or illness, we have a list of volunteers who are willing to pick up and deliver books. Please phone for information. We also have book deposits in two senior citizen apartment complexes and are planning more.
Please phone for information on our Talking Book program. We have a large number of books on cassette that may be borrowed for a lengthy period, and also a couple of cassette players.

LIBRARY CARDS
For city residents, library cards cost 10¢ and are renewable every third year. New applicants must show suitable identification and proof of residence.
Patrons who live beyond the city limits will have their cards renewed yearly at a cost of 10¢, providing their municipality has a financial arrangement with the library. If there is no such arrangement, the cost is $15.00 per family per year.

CIRCULATION
Books are circulated for a three week period, renewable only if they are brought back to the desk. We reserve the right to limit the number of books on one subject at any time. Some magazines circulate except for the latest issue.
Overdues are 5¢ per day per item in the adult section, and 2¢ per day for children. Maximum fine for a child is $1.00.
Patrons are responsible for lost, damaged or mutilated library materials.

LIBRARY HOURS
Monday - Thursday   9:30 a.m. - 9:00 p.m.
Friday, Saturday   9:30 a.m. - 5:00 p.m.
Sunday   2:00 p.m. - 5:00 p.m.
with limited services.
Closed Sundays during the summer.
We observe all statutory holidays.
Any changes in hours will be well advertised and posted.

AUDIO VISUAL DEPARTMENT
The AV department is on the lower floor in the new wing. Go down to the children's department and turn left.

Film Service
You may select 16 mm. films from our catalog of 2,000 titles, in person or by telephone. We also have access to over 5,000 titles from the National Film Board. Persons wishing to use projectors must know how to handle the equipment. The AV staff will be pleased to show borrowers how to operate the projectors so that they can be used to their best advantage for a smoothly run show. Films and equipment must be booked well in advance. Check the AV department for rates.
We also have a good selection of Standard 8 and Super 8 films for home showing.

AV Equipment
We have 8 mm. and 16 mm. projectors, a home movie camera, a reel-to-reel tape recorder, overhead projectors, slide and filmstrip projectors, cassette players, and a public address system that is completely portable. This equipment is all available for rent, and should be booked in advance.

Records
We have six listening jacks complete with easy chairs, and more are on the way. Take the record of your choice to the film librarian, check out the headset using your library card, and the record will be played for you. Records may also be rented at 25¢ per week using your library card.

Microfilm
We have the BEACON HERALD and its predecessors on microfilm back to 1855, along with history and a printer. We also have available the census rolls of Perth County for the years 1851, 1861 and 1871, through the courtesy of the Perth County Archives. Please phone ahead to reserve a reader.

Four pages of a six-panel flyer outlining the library's services and programs, 1975

Only Fullarton, Downie, Logan and Ellice townships had paid their share of the library's expenses, which worked out to $17 a person, excluding the costs of the just-completed facelift and expansion.

By January 1976, the SPL's circulation was up 10 per cent over January 1975. The library's budget was also up – to $212,315, from $172,549 the previous year. While provincial grants, county library fees and memberships were going to cover some of those costs, the tab for city taxpayers was going from $119,892 to $157,815.

The big items were a $20,000 increase for salaries and $23,000 for the purchase of books. While Mayor McMillan called it a "real bare-bones budget," Ald. Dave Bradshaw looked at the $24,000 the library paid part-time workers in the previous years and suggested it reduce its hours of operation from 9:30 a.m. to 9 p.m., to noon to 8 p.m, and lay off its part-time staff. He later praised the budget and took aim at union salaries, which he claimed were responsible for increasing the budgets of city departments. "Why should I come in here and fight with you people (library personnel) over a few bloody books?" he asked rhetorically. "I'm not going to do it this year."

Meanwhile, the enlarged and refurbished library was proving to be a hit. It was booked for a wine appreciation course, beginning in January 1976, and in the following month the University of Waterloo offered a free philosophy course over four nights, starting with a lecture on love. The Noon Hour Book Club each Thursday was outgrowing the lounge in the audiovisual department, and the Sunday afternoon travelogues were more popular than ever in the new auditorium.

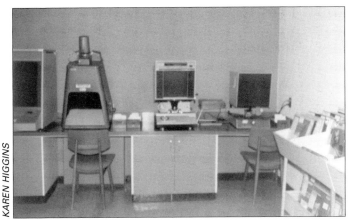

KAREN HIGGINS

The microfilm readers used by students in the late 1970s and early '80s to index historical information for the Stratford-Perth Archives.

The feature film program resumed on Thursday nights, and there were plans for another series featuring actors who had appeared on the Stratford stage. On tap, as well, was a lecture series about plays in the upcoming season at the Festival. It was to be taped and shown to summer visitors.

In April 1976 the SPL added 300 volumes to its foreign-language collection. The library also had a catalogue from which its patrons could order from about 4,000 foreign-language books at the central library in Toronto.

In May, university students Geraldine Cuerden and Janet Robertson, both of whom had been student employees at the SPL, were hired back for 14 weeks with an Experience '76 grant. Their job this time was to index stories in the Stratford *Beacon Herald* by going through copies of the newspaper on microfilm. They were hoping to index the issues from 1855 through 1900 "this summer." That job went on for several summers. In 1978, Joan Smythe and Elizabeth Lotz were hired with an Experience '78 grant.

In July 1976, the library's audiovisual director, Brian McKone, and its children's librarian, Jane Crozier, held a week-long film-making course that attracted 10 participants aged 11 to 15. The course was the outgrowth of a one-day session on film animation offered in the previous winter.

By then McKone had accumulated several cast-off radios, which he put on display in the audiovisual department. Then he made a plea for more, as well as for music boxes, gramophones, clocks and a piano to complement his antique player piano. It was in August 1976 that the library

The addition to the south side of the library, soon after it was completed in 1975. The external improvements included walkways, landscaping and replacement of the tri-globe lights bracketing the front door with single-globe lights.

exhibited the collection of 22 clocks owned by Paul McKone (Brian's brother) and Ron Thompson, both bound that fall for Carleton University.

That was the summer that Anne Marie Heckman added menus from Stratford restaurants to the library's reference collection, though she made it clear she and fellow staffers would not be making recommendations to inquiring patrons. Eleven eateries in the city responded to her invitation to put their menus on display.

The hiring of Heckman (reference department), Jennie Montgomery and Theresa Talsma (reference and inter-library loan) brought the library's number of full-time staff to 10. It also included Sue Bonsteel (head librarian), Jane Crozier (children's librarian), Billie Kirkby (circulation), Dorothy Robinson (circulation), Florence Henry (children's circulation), Brian McKone (audiovisual) and Russ Marlow (caretaker).

They were joined by 13 part-timers, namely Jim Anderson, Jean Bain, Kenny

MINUTES OF STAFF MEETING OCTOBER 15, 1976

1. Telephone. Will everybody please keep track of all requests on the part of the public to use the telephone. Keep two lists - one for general requests, one for taxis. Do this until further notice.
2. Volunteers: Suggest we can use volunteers for
   a) clipping newspapers
   b) labelling paperbacks (alphabetically by author only)
   c) checking new expensive books before they are put back on shelf, for damage.
3. Tours. Please be sure to check the bookings for all tours. All hands to check every morning. Be sure to write in all tours.
4. Limits on lending. No more than 3 books on one subject in adult, 2 on one subject in children's. Be strict about this.
5. Cards left in books. There was discussion about this. Should we charge to get their card back? Investigate getting plastic covers to help with this problem. (Sue)
6. Chair lift. Investigate a chair lift for the back stairs (Board)
7. Stamp to be ordered for top of date due slips: "This card must not be removed." Put a book mark in each group of books taken out by one person, with the remark "Please use this for a marker, not the date slip".
8. Label to be ordered - bright color - to put on new and older expensive books:"Upon return this book will be examined for marks or damage. The borrower will be responsible for replacement if necessary".
9. Book drop unsatisfactory. Investigate installation in front door, or wall of building. (Board)
10. Sink in AV area. Good idea. (Board).
11. Break times. Anyone who comes on at 1 p.m. should take a break at 2:45, no later. From 3 p.m. to 4 p.m. one person must be at the desk and one person on reference at all times.
12. Staff room. The sink is being left in a mess again. A sign will be posted. Gordon will be notified to check in the evening.
13. Back door. Needs a covering, and a windbreak for the winter. (Board).
14. One-way Sign in front driveway is on wrong side. Sue to get it changed, also get driveway marked.
15. Vandalism has been noted in book drop and at front of building.
16. United Way. When this comes around, please consider it carefully. Last year the total contribution from city employees was $300 from 300 persons. Disgraceful. Suggest one hour's pay every two weeks, or something like that.

Highlights of the library staff meeting on Oct. 15, 1976

Brien, Jeane Ferguson, John Groothuizen, Guy McKone, Grace Reynolds, Catherine Robertson, Cathy Rothwell, Fred Rynor, Gloria Schumacher, Gord Vandervliet and Eleanor Waldie.

From September to December 1976, the library had a six-night series of old movies on alternate Thursdays, beginning with Bob Hope and Bing Crosby in The Road to Zanzibar and wrapping up with the same leads in The Road to Utopia. Tickets were $1 for single-night admission, $4 for the series.

Also that fall, the University of Waterloo offered a credit course in philosophy at the SPL. And the library presented an evening lecture series of its own, varied in nature and without scholastic credit.

In November 1976 the SPL received the first of its new videotape equipment, which enabled it to make prerecorded videotapes available to patrons.

By then one of the novel features of the revamped library was a bathtub, which the chief librarian rounded up from a city junk dealer. The tub was filled with books the SPL was discarding, and patrons were invited to help themselves.

Through the first full year of its reincarnation, the library hosted about 550 programs, including films, travelogues, book-club meetings and a variety of events for children. Chief librarian Sue Bonsteel estimated the cost of those programs to be in excess of $1,100, or "way over the programming budget." But, she said, "People want these programs, so by golly we're giving them. Everyone on the staff participates, and we've had a lot of favourable feedback. People are saying this is the place where things are really happening. I've got a lot more ideas, but money is always a problem."

On the night of Sunday, Jan. 9, 1977, or early on Monday the 10th, a valve in the heating system on the third floor failed, and, for hours, water made its way to the main floor and basement. Much of it was soaked up by about 1,000 books, dozens of ceiling tiles and hundreds of square feet of carpeting. Library staff and 10 volunteer high school students spent most of Monday arranging the damaged books so they could dry in front of fans. Carpet restoration experts from Kitchener squeezed what water they could from the flooring.

The audiovisual department escaped damage, and only 20 or so children's books were among the 350 that could not be salvaged. By Thursday the library had reopened for its scheduled film night and for a University of Waterloo sociology lecture, but the story hour for that day was cancelled. It took a couple of more days with high heat and six dehumidifiers before the rest of the library was available to the public.

The damage estimate was less than $3,000, most of it for repairs to the heating system, for repainting affected areas, and for replacing 30 to 40 ceiling tiles

It was also in January 1977 that the SPL board decided to charge residents of

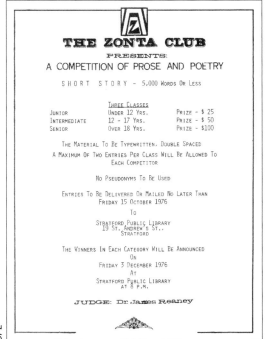

THE ZONTA CLUB
PRESENTS:
A COMPETITION OF PROSE AND POETRY

SHORT STORY - 5,000 WORDS OR LESS

THREE CLASSES

JUNIOR	UNDER 12 YRS.	PRIZE - $ 25
INTERMEDIATE	12 - 17 YRS.	PRIZE - $ 50
SENIOR	OVER 18 YRS.	PRIZE - $100

THE MATERIAL TO BE TYPEWRITTEN, DOUBLE SPACED

A MAXIMUM OF TWO ENTRIES PER CLASS WILL BE ALLOWED TO EACH COMPETITOR

NO PSEUDONYMS TO BE USED

ENTRIES TO BE DELIVERED OR MAILED NO LATER THAN
FRIDAY 15 OCTOBER 1976
TO
STRATFORD PUBLIC LIBRARY
19 ST. ANDREW'S ST.,
STRATFORD

THE WINNERS IN EACH CATEGORY WILL BE ANNOUNCED
ON
FRIDAY 3 DECEMBER 1976
AT
STRATFORD PUBLIC LIBRARY
AT 8 P.M.

JUDGE: Dr. James Reaney

Mitchell, St. Marys and Blanshard Township $15 a year for using its facilities because the library boards in those areas chose not to support the SPL. Most municipalities without libraries received federal government grants, from which they could pay neighbouring municipalities for library services. By then the idea of a county-wide library system was being floated again, an idea that Bonsteel said "could solve everyone's problems."

In April 1977 the SPL unveiled its opener in a series of displays relating to sports, designed to encourage people to read. Baseball was the first to be featured, and each exhibit, which included books, photographs, equipment, pennants, trophies and videotapes, was up for two weeks. Scuba diving and skiing were two of the other sports in the series.

It was also in April 1977 that the SPL attracted more than its share of media attention, when there was found to be no Nancy Drew or Hardy Boys books on its shelves. Those books were cheaply bound and deteriorated quickly, explained children's librarian Jane Crozier, so many of them were not replaced and others were sold back to publishing houses. Two of the letters to the editor calling for the return of the Hardy Boys books came from Mike Graham and Mark Ferguson. The latter was the junior winner in the Zonta Club's first literary contest in the previous December.

"A lot of school libraries here have

the Nancy Drew and Hardy Boys series," said Crozier. "Why would I duplicate what is already available to children? I only have so many of the taxpayer' dollars, so I have to choose carefully. In no way am I saying that kids shouldn't read them."

Crozier's boss, Sue Bonsteel, said she wasn't aware the books had been withdrawn. "Each department is pretty well independent and operates under board policy guidelines."

Board chair Sharon Malvern said, "Jane is trained in that field, and if that's her decision, then I'll certainly support it."

The furor was enough to interest Global TV, which sent a crew to check out the shelves and interview the principals.

The dust eventually settled, but Jane Kirkpatrick, who replaced Bonsteel in 1983, chuckles when she reflects on the fallout. "It was a case of the books being old and tatty and being withdrawn because of bad condition. But everyone got it into their head that there was censorship going on, and for years we were on the Book and Periodical Council censorship list for the

An airier entrance and more patron-friendly checkout counter after the renovations of 1974-75.

SPL

censoring of Nancy Drew. It took me about three years to get us off the list."

"When I accepted the job in Stratford," says current children's librarian Sally Hengeveld, "they told me in Toronto, 'Oh, you're going to that place where they banned the Nancy Drew books.'"

While censorship and book-banning are words not embraced by most librarians, the same can not be said of all library patrons. "Most of the challenges (today) are for children's books," says Kirkpatrick. "We get a lot of challenges with fairy tales."

Hengeveld says anything with the word devil in it is certain to stir unrest with some members of the public, mostly parents concerned about the content of children's and teen books.

"If a library is doing its job properly, we should be offending somebody all the time," says another SPL staffer, Anne Marie Heckman. "Everyone should find something offensive in the collection."

There was nothing offensive in May 1977 when Mayor Keith Culliton helped to officially open the Stratford and District Information Centre, whose quarters in the northeast corner of the main floor were provided to the city by the library rent free. Beth Garland was the centre's first co-ordinator.

Government agencies, community groups and organizations of all kinds were encouraged to make their literature, contacts and calendars available through the centre.

"It was at a time when the province wanted to make itself more accessible to the local citizenry," says Lorraine Greenberg, who worked first as a co-ordinator for the centre and then joined the library staff as program co-ordinator. "Sue (Bonsteel) was

In 1979 the SPL's entry was awarded first prize in the Festival City Days parade. Mother Goose (Sue Bonsteel) and some youngsters eager to listen to her tell nursery rhymes were joined on the float by Little Bo Peep (Gloria Schumacher) and her sheep, Old Mother Hubbard (Marilyn Cunningham) and her dog, Little Miss Muffett (Ann Gagnon) on her tuffet and Little Boy Blue (Kyle McKone).

the driving force behind the community information centre in Stratford. It was a wonderful service in the community."

Wendy Wilkinson was another of the co-ordinators.

When government funding dried up, most of the centres were closed in the 1980s.

In October 1977, the SPL presented inscribed pens to 52 people who had been particularly helpful to the library on a volunteer basis. For their contributions to the Sunday travelogues, pens went to Paul Carey, Irma Connor, John Conroy, Donald Davis, Betty Jean Davis, Barry Eckstein,

John Emery, James Ferguson, Dave Gibbard, Elsie Gibbard, Mac Gilmore, Vera Golightly, Frances Greene, Jean Isbister, Henry Kalbfleisch, Marion Kalbfleisch, Gordon Kechnie, Helen Kechnie, Sylvia Leser, John Miller, Anne Moore, Ian Munro, Ted Priest, John Quirt, Evelyn Quirt, Wes Shrubsall, Cliff Taylor, Charles Walkom, Myrtle Walkom, Tom Wilcox, Erlyn Wilker, Robin Wilhelm, Len Wilson and Elaine Wood.

Maureen Blaney, Vi Cheney, Joan Dickson, Sheila Grose, Ruth Lawson, Miriam Scott, Gordon Scott, Jill Skinner and Cheryl Tucker were recognized for their work with mothers' programs.

Others honoured were Raffi Armenian, Chuck Beatty, John Hayes, Perry Hill, Urjo Kareda, Harald Scholz, John Skinner and Jeff Van den Hurk. Florinda Johnson was singled out as a special volunteer.

There was talk of making such awards an annual event, but it never happened.

The SPL has rarely been without some form of information vehicle in the city's print media. In 1980, Anne Marie Heckman wrote a column called "'round the library," which appeared in the short-lived *Stratford Weekly News*. For a while, the library also sustained a column in the *Beacon Herald* called "Books and People." It included information about books at the library and some background information about the people who wrote them.

Soon after her arrival, Jane Kirkpatrick had a weekly column in the *Beacon Herald* called "Ask Marion the Librarian." Patrons would submit written questions, and she would answer then in the newspaper.

Most recently, the print vehicle has been "Library Lines," also in the *Beacon Herald*. Like most of its predecessors, it has been written by various SPL staffers, though for the past few years that task has fallen to Sharon Malvern, a retired educator, former library board chair, and past president of the SPL foundation.

In February 1978, the SPL was awarded a $70,000 Wintario grant for the installation of an elevator to assist elderly and handicapped patrons. In the following month, city council adhered to its policy and accepted the lowest of six tenders, $59,598 from Guenther Mohrmann Construction Ltd. That was against the wishes of the SPL board, which had recommended the bid of $59,741 from Pounder Bros. because of that company's familiarity with the library building.

Designed by Kyles, Kyles and Garratt, the project was started immediately, and on Sept. 24, 1978 – coinciding with the 75th anniversary of the original library building – the elevator was officially opened. It was one of the first public buildings in Stratford to be accessible to the handicapped.

Guest speaker for the opening was Bruce McCaffrey, MPP and parliamentary assistant to the minister of culture and recreation. Past board member Lorne Brothers was back to cut another ribbon, and he was among the first to use the new service, joined by representatives from the Stratford and Area Handicapped Club (Bernice Thomas), Equalaction for the Physically Handicapped, the Eileen Langley Training Centre, L'Arche and the Festival City Kiwanis Club (Harry King).

Among the other dignitaries were Perth MP Bill Jarvis, Mayor Keith Culliton, and library board chair John Devlin. After the official ceremonies, members of The Noon Hour Book Club served refreshments in the second-floor auditorium. As well, there were films in various departments, displays from the Perth County Archives and a birthday cake in the shape of a book. Music for the day was provided by the Kiwanis Youth Band.

To further mark the 75th anniversary of the building, the library staff offered free library cards to anyone born in 1903.

In April 1978 the library was asking patrons to drop off their used (as in unlucky) Wintario tickets, which could be redeemed in the purchase of new Canadian books and magazines. With those tickets, the SPL received a credit of $412 toward an invoice totalling $2,000.

In December 1978 the library had a display of teddy bears, whose purpose was to wish everyone a "beary Christmas."

In 1979 the SPL started a free literacy program to assist those unable to read. Provincial statistics indicated there were about 600 functionally illiterate adults in Perth County. A 1981 survey of the county presented a more depressing picture: 10,750 functional illiterates (5,224 women, 4,526 men). Of those, eight per cent were completely illiterate.

A display of photographs in the audio-visual department in the summer of 1980. The room also featured a jukebox and antique radios collected by the McKone brothers.

Volunteers used the Laubach method to teach the program at the library. One of the charter volunteers, Dorothy Tupper, said teaching people how to read was "the most rewarding thing I've done in my life." In three years, the SPL had about 25 people successfully complete the program. On April 30, 1991, Bob Laubach of Laubach Literacy International was at the library to talk about world literacy.

On May 12, 1980, the staff proclaimed Sue Bonsteel queen for a day to mark her 10th anniversary at the library.

In June of that year, 21-year-old Chetan Bahri, one of those staff members, took three weeks to create a 78-word puzzle on actors who had played Shakespearean parts at the Stratford Festival. She offered a SPL metal bookmark to the first seven people to solve the puzzle, which was so popular she followed up with others.

In July 1980, the SPL began sending books to the jail, just across St. Andrew Street, on a six-month trial basis. It was part of the library's outreach program. "I remember taking books to and from the jail," says former staffer Lorraine Greenberg.

"We were not allowed to give them (inmates) Helter Skelter, Go Boy and Papillon. I think they (library officials) sent me because I was older. I think they thought if it was someone older and matronly there would be no trouble. There would be no trouble if it wasn't somebody young and sweet."

It was in 1980 that the SPL bumped the fee for its membership card to 25 cents from a dime.

In the spring of 1981, 1982, 1983 and 1984 the library hosted a weekly series on the works of Shakespeare with Jack and Susan Gray from the University of Waterloo. It also showed Shakespearean films through the summer months, sometimes twice daily.

On July 29, 1981, the library opened at 5 a.m. so one and all could watch live television coverage of the royal wedding of Charles and Diana. The SPL brought a giant television set into the audiovisual department and, for the dozen or so early risers, there was also coffee, muffins and Danish pastries.

"Billie (staffer Billie Kirkby) brought her (teddy) bears, and they were in the front row," recalls Anne Marie Heckman. "When

Staffer Billie Kirkby and her bears Edward and Mr. Grimthorpe, at the SPL's royal wedding get-together, July 29, 1981.

we saw that dress, we knew it (the marriage) wasn't going to last," says Lorraine Greenberg with a chuckle. "It was too 'fairy princess.'"

In addition to city residents, the library's showing attracted tourists from Philadelphia, New York, Chicago, Quebec, Howell, Mich., and other parts of Ontario.

From January to April 1982, the library had a "classic cinema" series, for which it charged $7, or $1.50 single admission. It was while that series was running that the SPL endured another spring flood in the basement.

In March 1982, the library announced a get-tough policy to reduce delinquency among its borrowers. More than 2,500 books, representing a loss of about $18,000, were not returned to the SPL in 1981, so a decision was made to take offenders to small claims court if they did not respond to a phone call and followup invoice.

Increased postal costs had made it more costly to use repeated mailings to retrieve overdue books, said chief librarian Sue

Soggy ceiling tiles lie broken on an office floor after the library roof leaked yet again, spring 1982.

Bonsteel. "This may sound hard-nosed and unfriendly, but we believe these books belong to the citizens of Stratford, and that anybody who does not return them is guilty of stealing."

Beginning at 10 a.m. on Saturday, April 17, 1982, there was another big-screen showing at the library, this one featuring Prince Charles's mother, Queen Elizabeth. The occasion was her proclamation of the Canadian Charter of Rights and Freedoms.

On April 25 of that year, the library invited all writers, published and unpublished, to a reception to meet each other and discuss their work.

In August 1982 the SPL held a nonsense poetry contest in honour of the 150th anniversary of the birth of Lewis Carroll. The rules called for limericks, acrostics, jingles, tongue twisters, and "other plain bad verse." Those deemed the best at supplying same were Sarah Brennan, Peter Smith, Lorne Richards, Heather Lightfoot and Lorrie Matthews.

On Oct. 31, 1982, a Sunday, the library hosted a free afternoon "ghostly gathering" for families of all ages. Participants were invited to dress as their favourite literary character, and there were prizes for the best costumes.

In the following month, the SPL bolted into the computer age with receipt of a Telidon unit, furnished and installed by the federal government. Looking a lot like a small-screen television with a keypad and an accompanying box about the size of briefcase, the acquisition was a data bank that head librarian Sue Bonsteeel described as the tip of the information iceberg. "It (Telidon) started in December 1980 and became available to the public in April 1981," she said. "There are units in libraries, in banks, in hotels and in shopping plazas. With 50,000 pages of information, it is the largest (data) bank in the world. It started out to tell the public what services were available through the government. Now

there are all sorts of subjects.

"Telidon will be used in business to supply electronic mail, the printing of manuals, travel bookings and staff training. In education it will be used as a teaching

STRATFORD PUBLIC LIBRARY

19 St. Andrew Street
Stratford, Ontario N5A 1A2
Telephone 271-0220

Please present your library card
when borrowing materials.

Identification is required when
obtaining a library card.

New Card 25¢ Replacement Card $1.00

Library cards available to
county residents.

Visitors' cards available with a deposit.

The library reserves the right to limit
the number of items that may
be borrowed.

The library reserves the right
to not renew materials.

Damaged or lost materials must
be replaced.

Overdue Charges

Adult Department—5¢ per day per item

Boys and Girls Department
—2¢ per day per item

AV Department — Records
—5¢ per day per item

PLEASE DO NOT REMOVE
DUE DATE SLIP FROM THE BOOK
OR RECORD POCKET

Library Hours

Mon. to Thur. . 9:30 a.m. - 9:00 p.m.

Friday, Saturday 9:30 a.m. - 5:00 p.m.

Sunday . . . . . . 2:00 p.m. - 5:00 p.m.

Closed Sunday during June, July and
August

June 1982

SPL

Some of the rules and regulations, June 1982

aid, as a research tool, as a registration and course program, and for home study where you will get instant contact with the teacher. In the home, Telidon may give us electronic newspapers, covering weather, sports scores and news features. We will be able to call up pictures of products from catalogues, check prices, order and have the item delivered. This can be done now in Toronto with one distributor. We may have a community bulletin board with instant information such as is available now through the information centre."

On May 31, 1983, a once-postponed retirement ended Sue Bonsteel's years as chief librarian at the SPL. In an unprecedented move in 1982, Stratford city council had amended its retirement bylaw to allow her an extra year on the job, a year in which she was to train a replacement.

"I've had the best job in the world for the past 12 years," she told one and all at the time of her leaving. The library board and staff made her last official day a memorable one. From noon until 5 p.m. there was an open house at the library for those wanting to wish Sue a warm farewell. Then the SPL was closed for the day so her colleagues could attend a dinner in her honour at the Stratford Country Club.

"I wasn't completely looking forward to it (retirement), at least initially," said the well-liked librarian, known for her warm smile and penchant for wearing comfortable shoes. "Of course, that's the problem with retirement – all of a sudden you have no excuse for not living, for not doing all the things you always said you wanted to do. All of a sudden you have to take responsibility for your own life. So, it has taken me a few months to get over that hurdle."

By then a widow, she said her plans for retirement included more involvement in the many associations and goodwill organizations to which she belonged, chairing the city's 1983 United Way campaign, and a stint with Canadian Executive Services Overseas. "I don't really want to fade off into the sunset," she added.

Longtime friends Marg Pike (left) and Cathy Clarke flank Sue Bonsteel during her retirement reception at the SPL, May 31, 1983.

MARG PIKE

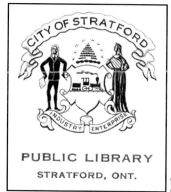

CITY OF STRATFORD

INDUSTRY ENTERPRISE

PUBLIC LIBRARY
STRATFORD, ONT.

SPL

The Ed Neigh history collection

In the 1970s, Stratford secondary school teacher Ed Neigh Sr. began to capture on videotape the recollections of residents who had a hand in shaping the city's parks system, its sports programs, and its industrial and cultural base. He wanted to preserve their oral impressions of what life had been like before the automobile and television, and during the world wars, the Depression and the early days of the Stratford Festival.

To do that he enlisted the help of the local cable TV outlet, which had the necessary equipment and also welcomed the programming. And he gave the edited tapes to the Stratford Public Library for distribution by loan.

One of his first subjects was Tom Dolan, a longtime newspaperman with a passion for researching, recording and relating the history of his home town. A year after the interview, T. J. Dolan died. And in 1981, Ed Neigh died.

In March 1981, four members of the Noon Hour Book Club at the SPL got a federal grant for seniors to fund what they called Programs Unlimited. They sought to buy padded chairs for the club's meeting room, design and cultivate a garden in front of the library, and expand the Neigh collection of taped historical interviews.

Government officials never warmed to the padded chairs idea, but they did like the other two proposals. Upon approval of the grant, SPL personnel helped the seniors use some of the money to buy a video camera, a video cassette recorder and an editing deck. They later added a large-screen projector and two television sets with money from a New Horizons grant.

In May 1983 the library board officially named the tapes the E. G. Neigh Memorial Local History Collection. By then, city native Frank Leslie, in his 80s, had become a driving force in expanding the collection. Lugging and setting up the camera and other necessary equipment, he did about 35 interviews, many in the subjects' homes.

One of his most cherished was with Amelia Hall, the first woman to walk onto the stage of the Stratford Festival (as Lady Anne in Richard III). She said she was writing her memoirs and didn't want to give away her story in interviews. But she agreed to talk to Frank on condition the tape not be used beyond the scope of the Neigh collection.

Not far behind him in enthusiasm for the project was Erlyn Wilker, who had a special touch when it came to keeping that equipment in good order. Others in the group took to editing the tapes, assisted by Brian and Guy McKone of the SPL.

The tapes are now housed in the Stratford-Perth Archives.

Erlyn Wilker and the equipment used to record local history.

If I had a million dollars (for the library)

What would you do if you had a million dollars to spend on the public library?

That's what SPL officials asked city schoolchildren as they expanded their facilities with an addition in 1975. The invitation was in the form of an essay contest, open to those in grades 5 through 8, and the prizes were books.

The winning entry came from the pen of Marion Lindsay, a Grade 6 student at Avon school and a resident of 62 John St. N. This is what she wrote.

What would you do if you had a million dollars to spend? Maybe you would buy a good horse or a car; maybe the family's house of dreams. Or perhaps you would do what I would do, which is to rebuild the library.

There would be three floors. I have an idea! Why don't I give you a grand tour? Let us go first to the adult section. On the left there are eight librarians ready to assist you. When you step into the library you get the red carpet treatment although it is shag blue, wall to wall. When the librarian comes you tell him what you are looking for and he will get the book for you.

Now I will take you to the relaxing section. Go to the door with 'Tapes' written on it. Here we are. Have a seat. As you notice this is purple shag carpet with purple plush curtains. In front of you are the names of the various categories of music — classical, pop, folk, dance, country and western, and so on. You punch out the name of your selection and the composer on this machine which looks like an electronic typewriter, and when the sign lights up you may hear your tape through the earphones attached to the chair in which you are sitting. This is all very relaxing but there is more to this library than that.

We will go to the hall which takes us to the record library. In here you see the shelves filled with records. At the front there are a few chairs to use while you look at the covers to decide whether or not you want to hear the records, and if you do there are two record players on which to play them. We should move along or else we shall not be able to see the whole building before it closes.

The next room is for films of every kind, from Mary Pickford's silent ones such as Little Lord Fauntleroy to cartoons on cats and history. These films may be borrowed to take home. On some days the films are shown here. Now we are back where we started. Oh, before we go upstairs, I will show you the place where you can read outdoors on benches under the trees, with flowers and birds to look at all the year round. You will feel just as though you are in the Bahamas except for the water. This fabulous place is located in the inner courtyard between the four red walls of the building. It has a plastic dome-shaped bubble over it to keep out the rain and snow, and to keep the air warm for the birds and flowers. Shall we go upstairs now? If you choose to go by elevator you may but I shall go by the silver slithery escalator.

Let us visit the children's library. In there is a section on Enid Blyton with all of the series, plus all the great books of today and the favourites of yesterday. This room has dark green short carpet, dark green curtains and light green, painted walls. In the far corner before the door there is a cage with gerbils and an aquarium with small fish from every corner of the earth.

The room next to this is used by the children's theatre group and you are allowed to watch their rehearsals or even join in sometimes. The regional ballet class also uses this room on the weekends. Now, here we are at the music education room which is filled with music books and all kinds of musical instruments that are taught to students from kindergarten to grade eight. Next to it is the studio where art meetings are held and you learn to draw. Your legs are probably aching but we should go on to the third floor. This section is for nothing but animal observation. It is a miniature zoo filled with small, but unusual, animals together with pamphlets on observation of them. This is where meetings of the naturalist club are to be held.

May I now invite you for a coffee? You are surprised but we even have a coffee shop just off the courtyard where we can rest and enjoy our lovely library. Can you think of a better way to spend a million dollars?

"I couldn't believe I was getting paid for that job."

Sue Bonsteel worked at the SPL from June 1970 through May 1983, mostly as head librarian. These are some of her memories, written in 1975 and 2002.

For about a year I worked at Fanfare Books for Ellen Stafford and got acquainted with Miss Thompson – Lois Thompson – the chief librarian at Stratford Public Library. She used to come into the bookstore at the end of the month to spend what was left of her monthly book budget.

In those days the budget was a monthly thing, with the board exercising authority over money, since most of it came from the province. The board had a treasurer who paid all the bills.

Miss Thompson was a very dignified, warm and friendly person, and I could quite believe that she had spent much of her life as a children's librarian. At the library, there is a fine picture of her standing in front of a crowd of about 50 kids, holding them spellbound.

My husband Dick and I had decided that since our children were coming to the end of high school, we would need money for their going to university. A classmate of Dick, who was chief librarian of the

Chief librarian Sue Bonsteel and staffer Jim Anderson wait on a patron at the oak checkout counter, Oct. 23, 1973.

Metropolitan Toronto Library, suggested I might be interested in a library career, and talked of the new School of Library and Information Science – SLIS – which had just opened at the University of Western Ontario in London. I accumulated all my credits, including some from Columbia in New York, and was accepted as a student at UWO, starting June 1, 1969.

I graduated on May 31, 1970, and was immediately hired, at the instigation of Miss Thompson, by the Stratford board as reference librarian, to start June 1, 1970. Miss Thompson was retiring, and the new chief librarian was Blake McDougall, who was bringing new ideas and a fresh approach to the library.

Stratford had never had a reference librarian, and I had a ball. I weeded out the vertical files (which is to say I threw out old newspaper and magazine clippings), and relished such questions as: "How do I get to Formentera?" (an island in the Mediterranean), "Why has Ontario not got an ombudsman?" "How do you make a still?" "Do you get rid of bees with cyanide, and how much?" "Can my landlord kick me out?" and "What is in a trout stream besides trout and water?"

Most of Michigan seemed to be populated with descendents of Stratford pioneers, and they all wanted to know who they were, where they lived, and what they did. At that time there was no Stratford-Perth Archives, so they came to me. It was a wonderful job, and I probably had as big a store of useless information in my mind as my husband had. I couldn't believe I was getting paid for that job.

I reorganized the checkout system at the library and got rid of the date stamp on every book and every library card. Most libraries had a Kodak system for checkout, but I didn't like it because it didn't seem to save any time, involved reading miles of tape every day, and was expensive. It turned out that the system we devised led directly into the automatic system we have today.

Blake McDougall was the first to see that the library had to be renovated. We women were quite in agreement because we had lost many nylon hose as we manoeuvred around the old oak shelving with its splinters and musty smell.

Blake made such a fuss about, among other things, our salaries, including his own. When he was told by a council member not to be greedy, Blake promptly resigned. The councillor backed off, and Blake reconsidered when he got at least some of what he had been asking for. Salaries in those days were very low. Elderly women had no benefits. I believe there had to be a special bylaw enacted to give Miss Thompson a pension when she retired.

With an increase in the annual government grant, work was quickly started on renovations to the library. The caretaker had lived in the basement for years, underneath about 10 tons of books. The children's library was upstairs, to which small children had to be carried, and certainly few babies showed up for anything. Incidentally, the library was built on perhaps the only hill in Stratford, contrary to the rules laid out by the Carnegie foundation when it provided the grant for construction in 1902. There were several steps outside the front door, as well as more up to the adult section inside the door.

We sold our old shelves to St. Marys Public Library for use in its storage rooms, and eagerly awaited new movable shelving from Montreal. It was a long time coming – I believe it went from Montreal to Fredericton, then back to Montreal, thence to London and back again. I like to think we intercepted it on the way through Stratford for the second time. When it arrived, we were given half a day to unload the truck.

When we were about to clear the main

floor, we put out a call over CJCS radio for help in moving books upstairs. At first, small boys showed up and ate all our doughnuts; then some teenagers arrived and the work went apace. One willing volunteer was Festival actor Tony Van Bridge, who lived across the street. He would arrive in the morning, get this pipe going nicely, and carry books with genial good humour for two or three hours.

The sight upstairs in the auditorium was of a huge sea of books standing on their edges, spine up, with a pile of books here and there to step on.

Staffer Billie Kirkby takes a time out after the main floor had been cleared in preparation for new carpeting and shelving, December 1973.

On the main floor, new carpet went down, and the new shelving was installed, along with a new checkout counter. It was a joy to work there again.

At that point, we still had the card catalogue which took up most of the room immediately to the right of the main entrance to the library.

After Blake McDougall had accepted a position as head of adult services at Edmonton Public Library, I was appointed chief librarian. That was in February 1971, and I well remember walking into the library on the first morning after

Chief librarian Sue Bonsteel lugs books to their new main-floor shelving, January 1974.

my appointment. There was Jean Bain and Billie Kirkby, and upstairs Winnifred Henderson, the children's librarian. All had been there for years. I felt like a green newcomer whaling in. Finally, Jean came over, put her arms around me and hugged me, and they all said how pleased they were that I had the job. I have never forgotten the great sense of relief and gratitude to them for their friendship.

We always had an ambiguous relationship with the county and townships. They applied for and were given a yearly grant on a per capita basis for library services to those living outside the city – the same grant that we received. However, at the end of every year I would have to list all the people outside the city that used the library by township, along with the number of times they had used our services. In the pre-computer age, this kind of record keeping entailed a fair amount of time. We would submit the lists to the townships concerned, then wait to see what they would do about reimbursement. One township clerk used to call each of the users on the list to see if, in fact, they had used the library. We generally got that list back with various names deleted because some people had used the library only once, and the clerk felt we shouldn't get paid for just one service.

In about 1974 we applied for and secured a grant to set up PLOW – Public Library on Wheels. We rented a trailer the first year, and went out to areas where there was no public library – Sebringville, Shakespeare and Gadshill among them – and set up shop once a week for the summer season. The service was well used, and the students who ran it had a good time. Brian McKone did most of the driving each morning and late afternoon. One year we had a big trailer from Steed Standard Transport. The first morning we went out, I broke a bottle of champagne over the trailer hitch. Actually, I had trouble breaking the bottle and realized only later that we shouldn't have drunk the champagne first, before refilling the bottle with water. The program lasted three or four seasons and created quite a bit of goodwill on behalf of the library.

We always thought of the library as a public servant, and when the opportunity came in 1974 to extend our services, we jumped at the chance. Information centres were all the rage, and we were the first public library in our region to set up an official information centre. After working hard to set up and collect all sorts of information, both governmental and local, it was a real thrill one morning to have a phone call from a prominent lawyer in town who said he had a client who wanted to give some money to 100 Huntley Street. He wanted to know who or what on earth was 100 Huntley Street. Somebody who

happened to be in the centre at that moment filled him in. He was suitably impressed and passed the word on to his colleagues. Others working in the information centre over the years included Lorraine Greenberg and Cathy Cuerden. Cathy was there when there was some library construction going on, and she gave us valuable advice regarding how to make the building more accessible for disabled people.

After a few years, the Stratford Information Centre moved out, to the lower floor of the city hall annex at 38 Albert St. The centre began several services when it was operating. The Stratford *Beacon Herald* began listing community calendars a couple of times a week. And the visitors centre attempted to make listings so that major events in the city would not overlap. That, of course, is an impossible thing to do, but it was the information centre that created the public awareness of the need for such services, and it is a sign of its relevancy and success that other agencies have taken up the task of trying to keep Stratford in some sort of order.

For some time we discussed expanding the library, and we finally decided that enlarging the main library would be preferable to a branch, since the library is in the centre of town. The front portion had been added in 1926, and people complained it had spoiled the beautiful old Carnegie building.

This time the board hired Brian Garratt's architectural firm, and his partner, Larry Parsons, took on the responsibility of planning another extension. We had done dozens of surveys of library use, including counts of people coming into the library, what they did while in the library, and of course, how much material they checked out. I had also personally checked the parking situation. We had to make arrangements with the people of St. Andrew's Presbyterian Church to share part of their parking facilities, and I even paced off the distance from the free parking behind the courthouse, for possible use in the evenings. It turned out that that there are fewer steps to that lot than there are between trains and buses in the Yonge-Eglinton subway station in Toronto. However, Stratford people like their parking two feet from the door, so there was plenty of discussion on the subject.

In December 1974 there was an Ontario Municipal Board hearing at City Hall. The council chamber hadn't had such a crowd since Howie Morenz was given the freedom of the city back in the '20s. The crowd did not have much to look at. Inside the magic circle were ranged, on one side, the librarian, some members of the library board, lawyer Perry Hill and the city treasurer, and on the other side one woman whose argument had won a delay in the OMB's approval of plans for the library addition.

The hearing, which started at 11 a.m., was well named; absolutely everybody had a hearing. It was not until 4:30 that the verdict was handed down – approval to go ahead with the issuing of debentures to cover the cost of renovating our ancient Carnegie, probably the oldest still in use as a library in Canada, and to put an addition on her side. Of course, it could all have been done by telephone, or a perusal of the city's balance sheet. As an exercise in public relations it was questionable, particularly since it caused a delay of one month in the winter works

program.

However, the third reading of the bylaw was handled with only the usual amount of flak that evening at city council, and then the library board was given permission to rent the unused premises which were vacated by the A&P when it left Erie Street for the new Stratford mall a couple of years earlier. That was Monday. I draw a veil over the remainder of that week. We moved out of the old building, lock, stock and barrel during Friday, Saturday and Monday. On Tuesday we closed shop and staggered home for Christmas.

On Jan. 6, 1975, we opened for business in one of the first supermarket libraries in this part of Ontario. We had acres of floor space and drafty walls. The only steps in the building were the 24 steep ones down to the washrooms. The children's library was in BREADS, with "Jane Crozier" covering the original Jane Parker sign. Jean Plaidy was under FROZEN FISH and Ian Fleming in COOKED MEATS. The classified shelves covered the holes in the floor where the coolers had been. I announced to all that pornography would go in DEEP FREEZE. The staff room was in the vegetable section;

The former A&P grocery store at 145 Erie St., temporary quarters for the SPL in 1974-75.

TED KEENE

The SPL's children's department in the former A&P store – under the words CAKES, COFFEE, EGGS and CHEESE. Working the desk are ???? and Jane Crozier, spring 1975. To better serve the building's new tenants, another staffer, Paul McKone, changed the surname in the food section's Jane Parker sign to Crozier.

The checkout counter on the checkered floor, spring 1975. Staffers, from left: Florence Henry, Jim Anderson and Jane Crozier. The portrait atop the bookshelves is that of Andrew Carnegie.

Plenty of space, lots of windows and few steps, spring 1975

A makeshift projector room in the old frozen fish section, spring 1975

paperbacks were under POULTRY; newspapers and records at the checkout. The copy machine was also at the checkout, using the electrical outlet that once operated the grocery store's doughnut-maker.

The public loved the setup, especially those swinging doors, and we did too, despite the fact that we had to wear long underwear all winter, and the washrooms were deep underground.

People wondered why we didn't stay here. We wondered a bit ourselves. The parking lot – that was the great thing. Opening through a whole block from one street to the next, it was a handy drive-through unless the staff cars were parked strategically in the way. It was used by people who worked at the factory next door, by people who worked or shopped downtown, by people who lived on Wellington Street, and by people who had not heard the latest price quoted on newsprint. The local environment club used

In the spring of 1975 the library gave students from the Perth County board of education's continuing education art program at Stratford Central Secondary School some of its new-found space for a display of their work. Those setting up that display in this photo are unidentified.

the lot for newspaper and glass collection over a period of several months, and the idea had persisted. Several tons had to be carted to the dump when we arrived, and one day I saw a member of the board drop off a couple of bundles and hastily drive away.

Meanwhile, work was going ahead on our old building, where we discovered that nothing but a network of two-by-fours held the tons of books on the main floor from descending on the heads of the inhabitants of the basement apartment.

Beginning in July, we took about a month to move back to St. Andrew Street and work through about a thousand efficiency lists. When we reopened in August 1975, Stratford discovered what a library should really be like and how it can serve the community. Our patrons especially enjoyed the eight-foot avocado plant in the reading area, courtesy of the Stratford Horticultural Society. The reading area was in the alcove behind the main desk, and it featured a huge old bathtub in which we tossed material such as magazines and worn books for the public to pick up. My office was beyond the reading area; it later became part of the reference department.

Miss Henderson had retired by then. It's too bad that for 40 years she had to climb those stairs two or three times a day to get to work. Now the children's department was in the basement, after several new supports had been added to hold the weight of the main floor. The audio-visual department had its own location to the left of the children's department, next to the side door off the parking lot.

The AV department had become one of the best in the region, thanks mainly to the efforts of Brian McKone, his brother Guy McKone, and for a short while their brother Paul McKone. We were the first library to have videos for rent, and later on, compact disks (CDs). For years we had been the source of National Film Board films and had several projectors which were widely used. As technology changed, so did the AV department, and now most of the videos are catalogued and put on the shelves with books.

The old auditorium had been on the second floor, to the right of the children's library, and had been

Chief librarian Sue Bonsteel in her new but temporary office in the former A&P store, spring 1975.

used as a meeting room, a venue for university classes that were offered each winter by the University of Western Ontario and the University of Waterloo, and as a temporary schoolroom. The new auditorium was carpeted (with carpet recycled from the main floor – that's how we kept the construction costs down to the budgeted amount), and it had a projection booth at the back.

With our spanking new auditorium, we felt that we could make a real contribution to the life of the community, and the auditorium was generally busy. We had begun Sunday afternoon slide shows by local residents some years earlier, and continued them for several years,

actually until my retirement. Many local travellers shared their expertise and their experiences to packed houses.

We also began a program called Mondays at Eight, to bring a variety of experiences to the public. Nuala Goldberg brought in such people as Raffi Armenian and several members of the K-W symphony orchestra, Walter Learning of the CBC, and Elwy Yost of TV Ontario to do programming for us –

Head librarian Sue Bonsteel moderates an early session of The Noon Hour Book Club, in the audio-visual department of the library, 1978.

all excellent and all for free. We also had programs such as Ralph Pike talking about car maintenance.

The Noon Hour Book Club had begun in 1973, when Grace Reynolds suggested we have something for book lovers. We had our first meetings in the evening at the old YWCA on Waterloo Street, and then changed to Thursdays at noon in the auditorium. We began in the AV department, but outgrew it, and the club is still holding a series of programs twice a year.

In the summer, I felt that we could offer an audience for young musicians who were studying at university, but who were home for the summer, and for several years we had Thursdays at Noon with many young people who have since gone on to make names for themselves in the world of music.

The children's department took off, program-wise, when the new auditorium was available, and a wide variety of entertainment and education for children was offered over the years. Each librarian brought ideas and skills to the department, and it has become one of the best departments for children in the region.

We also had literacy programs in the 1970s and '80s and provided many adults, as well as children, with one-on-one instruction.

In the spring of 1978, I got word that there was provincial money for elevators in public libraries, so I immediately applied and got a grant. The elevators did not cost the city anything, but the councillors objected strenuously to signing a contract that would make the city responsible for the maintenance of the elevator. Over the summer of 1978 we had weeks of construction, with a great deal of heavy banging because the workers discovered several boulders underneath the building. They had to be broken up and removed, almost by hand.

However, in September 1978 the first

In September 1982 the Stratford and District Horticultural Society recognized those who tended the floral gardens that accent the front of the library.

elevator in a public building in Stratford was officially opened. The ceremony included the band from Central Secondary School and several speakers. A whole procession of people in wheelchairs sat on the driveway during the ceremony and then went up to the auditorium, one by one, to an area that had always been a mystery to them.

It was also a celebration of the 75th anniversary of the construction of the library, and Jim Anderson, who was then on the library staff, made most of the arrangements. He wrote a history of the library (typed by myself) and had it published.

The flower beds on the front lawn were designed by Joan Dickson, planted by the members of the Stratford Horticultural Society, and maintained for several years by volunteers who secured the likes of rakes, shovels and trowels with a government grant. For many years, Marg Pike watered the flowers in those beds. For about the last 15 years, she has been taking care of the inside plants.

Sue Bonsteel

The Sunday travelogues

Films and slide shows became part of the fare, albeit sporadically, at the Stratford Public Library soon after they became available and affordable.

When the Stratford Film Council made its home in the SPL in 1948, such programs became less sporadic.

From the beginning, presentations that involved travel were an easy sell. Patrons were eager to soak up the sights and sounds of lands near and far.

On a Sunday afternoon in January 1972, the library joined Stan Blowes Travel Service and Hymans' Travel Ltd. in sponsoring two half-hour film features, both in colour: Portugal, and Iberian Delights – Wings to Spain.

By March 1975 the SPL had in place a program called Sunday Afternoons with Stratford Globe-Trotters. That month the trotters were Ted Priest, Irma Connor, Egerton Ryerson and Ron Dearing, and the stories they told shone forth from carousels of coloured slides.

"Those travelogues were so popular," says former staffer Dorothy Robinson. "They were all done by local people. I would stand by the window and watch people rushing down the street to the library, to get in to see the travelogue. Many times, I had to sit on the floor. One time, Erlyn Wilker used three screens. It was fabulous. Everything just fell into place. There's one couple that still says, 'Dorothy, we really miss those travelogues.'"

In the fall of 1988 the travelogues moved from the library to Gallery Stratford, and interest waned. "I think a lot of the people that had been doing them stopped travelling," says Lorraine Greenberg, another former staff member. "We had such a loyal group of presenters. Along with their slides, they would give this wonderful talk, which made it all so interesting. But

they were getting on in years and stopped travelling."

As well, says SPL administrator Jane Kirkpatrick, "People started to do video, and the videos didn't show very well."

The Stratford Camera Club was a popular presenter at the library, but so were the dozens of couples and individuals who brought the rest of the world just a little closer to Stratford on chilly Sunday afternoons.

Among their numbers were Henry and Marion Kalbfleisch, Africa; Bob and Marj Ballantyne, Australia; Royden Brien, Haiti;

```
            STRATFORD PUBLIC LIBRARY

              FALL PROGRAMS

TRAVELOGUES    Sunday, 2:30 p.m.   FREE
          Contact Dorothy Robinson.

     Oct. 5    Yugoslavia
     Oct. 19   Arizona
     Oct. 26   California
     Nov. 2    Oregon
     Nov. 9    Cuba
     Nov. 16   Scotland
     Nov. 23   England and Switzerland.

These travelogues are all by Stratford
citizens. The series will be continued
in the spring.

"ASCENT OF MAN".  Contact Brian McKone.
     This famous film series which deals
with evolutionary, cultural and
intellectual steps in the history of
mankind, is being shown Monday nights
at 8 p.m.:                        FREE
     Sept. 22 - Grain in the Stone
     Sept. 29 - Hidden Structure
     Oct.  6 - Music of the Spheres
     Oct. 20 - Starry Messenger
     Oct. 27 - Majestic Clockwork
     Nov.  3 - Drive for Power
     Nov. 10 - Ladder of Creation
     Nov. 17 - World Within World
     Nov. 24 - Knowledge or Certainty
     Dec.  1 - Generation Upon
                    Generation
     Dec.  8 - The Long Childhood.

LECTURES ON CANADIAN LITERATURE   FREE
                Contact Eleanor Waldie.
     In October a series of lectures on
Canadian Literature by professors from
the University of Waterloo will be held.
Call for subjects and specific dates.

12
```

Page 12 of the flyer outlining SPL's fall programs in 1975.

Bea Riley, Great Britain; Jo Ann Hayes, Italy; John and Eunice McArthur, Switzerland and Paris; Des and Lorna Booker, western Europe; Otto Van Heyningen, Holland; Ian Munro, Hong Kong; Robert Boyce, Chile and Peru; Glen Schlotzhauer, Costa Rica; Ted Priest, Europe; Chris Borgal, Uganda; Harold and Margaret Erb, British Guiana; Bob Neely, Morocco; John Conroy, Nicaragua; Arden and Lois Feltz, living in Florida; Rhea East, New Zealand; Wes and Irene Shrubsall, Portugal; Rob Gordon, trekking in the Himalayas; Jim Neilson, the USSR; Elaine Wood, Bulgaria and Turkey; Lester Wilker, the Holy Land; Jim Scott, Saudia Arabia; Jane Kirkpatrick, Malta; Bruce and Lois Scott, Haiti; Margaret Whyte, Fiji and New Zealand; Lillian Shepherd, the Keukenhof Gardens in Holland; Mary Lou Kingham, Kenya; Irma Connor, Yugoslavia; Denise and John King, down under; Michael Griffin, Israel; Alfred Ropp, Arizona and California; Len and Dennis Young, Normandy; Rev. James Ferguson, Austria and Vienna; John Hall, camping in Canada; Margaret Price, Germany; Jim Ferguson and Ivy Chung, China, Hong Kong and Macau; Ron and Rosemary Richards, Newfoundland's great northern peninsula; Cecil Mickleson, Russia; Mike Mitchell, sailing the Mediterranean; Elizabeth McKay, Nigeria; Jean Isbister, Switzerland; John Chalmers, Alaska; Rita Vanden Heuvel, Ethiopia; Gwen Carlton, Europe; Nancy Milne, the Arctic; Charles Ryde, cycling in England and Holland; Jack Hamilton, India; Judy Morley, Albania; George and Alice Herbert, Greece; Sue Bonsteel, Brazil; Marg Boemer, Arizona; Frank and May Dodds, Hawaii; Robert Wittig, Papua New Guinea; Allan Bossence, Mexico and Las Vegas; Jo-Anne Willment, Nepal; Charlie Gates, PEI and the East Coast; and Jo Aldwinkle, Colombia. Many were guests more than once, talking about other of their destinations.

Poets, writers and playwrights

In November 1943, 17-year-old James Reaney used puppets to tell the story of Cinderella to a gathering of youngsters in the children's department at the Stratford Public Library.

The native of South Easthope Township was no stranger to the wonders of the SPL, where he could find a wealth of novels, plays and poetry. And he has remained no stranger.

On Dec. 3, 1976, by then a renowned author, poet and playwright, he was back in the library to announce the winners of the Stratford Zonta Club's first prose and poetry contest. Those winners, in the prose section, were Mark Ferguson, junior; Marguerite La Haye, intermediate; and Harry Ellis, senior. The top poets were Lisa Boyce, junior; Paula Hurst, intermediate;

and Alan Shore, Judy Robinson and John Reed, all senior.

On the same night, another Stratford writer, Susan Amy Gearing, was awarded top honours in the annual Dorothy Shoemaker literary contest at the Kitchener Public Library. The guest speaker at that event was Canadian poet Earle Birney.

On the eve of St. Patrick's Day 1982, more than 100 people crowded into the SPL auditorium for a reading by Birney, then writer-in-residence at the University of Western Ontario in London. He read from his work for about an hour and then fielded questions. The evening ended with a reception during which the audience could meet the celebrated guest.

While the SPL has always been filled with books, it has on numerous occasions been filled by the people who have written many of those books. Indeed, its list of guest wordsmiths includes a page or two from CanLit's who's who.

Some, Reaney among them, have been invited to help celebrate national or provincial book weeks, some to promote recent works, some to encourage local writers. Others have been in town to present awards. In November 1983, Irving Layton and Nella Benson were at Stratford City Hall as judges when the Shoemaker winners were named for that year. That afternoon, Layton was at the SPL for a reading of his poetry.

Jane Urquhart and Colleen Thibaudeau (James Reaney's wife) were in Stratford for the same reason in May 1987 when the Shoemakers were announced at the Kiwanis Community Centre.

Still others made their way to the SPL while serving as writers in residence at nearby universities: David McFadden (the University of Western Ontario in London) and Susan Musgrave (the University of Waterloo).

In 1989 the library had its own writer in residence, Welwyn Wilton Katz of London. For that year, the Ministry of Culture and Recreation paid her $30,000, for which she was required to spend 17 hours a week at the SPL, on Thursdays, Fridays and Saturdays. Besides the writing consultations she offered to patrons, she also visited schools and presented free workshops. By that time in her career, the former high school math teacher, had written five fictional books, mostly fantasies for teens and young adults, and had been nominated for a Governor General's Award (which she won for The Third Magic).

Many of the writers to visit the SPL were

scheduled for the Noon Hour Book Club on Thursdays. "Cynthia Good, who is now a bigwig at Penguin (president and publisher of the publishing group) was the agent for a lot of those people," says former SPL staffer Christina Wilson. "And I remember there was never a problem getting people to come. It must have been because it was Stratford. I think a lot of times they had

STRATFORD BEACON-HERALD

Canadian poet Earle Birney (right) with Sue Bonsteel, head librarian, and John Devlin, head of the English department at Central Secondary School, March 1982.

friends here, so they wanted to come. And they'd come for free to the book club. For a while we had a bit of funding, but we were able to draw people in without it."

In addition to those mentioned above, the people "drawn" have included Jim Essex, Erika Ritter, Eric McCormack, Betty Jane Wylie, Edna Staebler, Joan Barfoot, Laurali Rose (Bunny) Wright, Ted Wood, Allan Stratton, Anne Chislett, Michael Cook, Rick Whelan, Charles Mountford, Amber Underwood, Sheila Ferguson, Raymond Skye, Joan Clark, Geoff Hancock, Virgil Burnett, Brendan Howley, Greg Nelson, Paul Ledoux, Janis Rapoport, Beverly Fink Cline, John Mellor, Mary Brothers, Joan Macleod, Barbara Novak, Sheila Martindale,

John Curry, Michael Dean, Gerry Shikatani, Richard Truhlar, Margaret Hollingsworth, Daniel David Moses, Ric Wellwood, Cathy Matyas, Gay Allison, John Benson, Ken Nutt, Elizabeth Woods, Andrea Spalding, Jean McKay, Beverly Cooper, Henry Beissel, Penn Kemp, Len Peterson, Carol Shields, Arthur Black, Dean Robinson, Joanna Glass, Robert More, Rex Deverell, William Needles, Marianne Brandis, Nancy-Lou Patterson, Victoria Branden, Barb Reid, Lynda Weston, Barbara Smucker, Peter Cumming, Nino Ricci, Thomas L. Friedman, Bob Shrier, Maurice Good, Stafford Johnston, Jean Johnston, Lynne Gordon, Hrant Alianak, Rita Kohn, Marie-Lynn Hammond, Catherine Hires, Vancy Kaspar, Peter Baltensperger, Ayanna Black, Peggy Sample, Janice Wiseman, Paul Thompson, Dale Hamilton, Cora Taylor, Ludmila Zeman, Rod Staples. Mary Pettit, Patricia Ann Nelles, Bruce Hunter, April Bulmer, Roger Bell, Carol Bolt and Miggs Wynne Morris.

In May 1995, author Marianne Paul was in Kitchener to announce the winners in the Dorothy Shoemaker Literary contest, and that year those from Stratford and area included Alan Barenberg, tied for first in the intermediate poetry division; Alison Innes, third in intermediate poetry; Bonnie Thompson, first in junior prose; Margita Gailitis, first in senior prose; and William B. Clark, second in senior prose.

Selling the outdated and worn out

Even libraries, mostly because of space restrictions, have limits when it comes to housing books.

In August 1981 those limits at Stratford Public resulted in a sale of thousands of volumes, all 10 years old or older, outdated, worn out or unread. As well, the SPL got rid of some phonographic records for many of the same reasons.

The sale was advertised as the first annual, but there wasn't one again until National Book Festival week in May 1984. That year, most of the offerings were priced from 10 cents to 50 cents, and all money raised was directed to the SPL's new-book fund.

In April 1985 the library held what it called its second annual book sale, and followed with a "special" sale in September of that year.

There was one sale in 1986 (May), two in 1987 (February and October), and two in 1988 (March and September, the latter part of Ontario Public Library Week).

In October 1989 the SPL joined forces with the YMCA and had a book sale at the Y.

In October 1990, 1991 and 1992, the library returned to its original format, with sales in its building.

In 1993 it staged a two-week sale, from June 26 through July 9, but on the first day it also sold obsolete furniture and equipment, which included 24 student desks, coffee tables, a film strip projector, a drafting table, chairs and drapes. For that day and the duration, there was also the regular fare of books, records, compact disks and magazines.

In 1994 and 1995 it was back to a one-day event in October, with as many as 4,000 books on offer.

Since 1996 the annual book sale has been the responsibility of the Friends of the Festival, which officially formed in June of that year. Their first effort was a two-day affair that netted $3,836.

The format was back to one a year in 1997 (with proceeds of $3,119), 1998 ($3,378), 1999 ($3,323) and 2000 ($3,139).

In 2001 the library staff helped the Friends considerably, and the sale ran from Sept. 8 through 14, with new selections set out each day as long as they lasted. Their effort realized $4,436.

In September 2002 it was back to one day, but off site. The Friends used the former Griffith Saddlery and Leather Ltd. building at 240 Norfolk St., where the hours were 8 a.m. to 4 p.m., and the take home was $3,600.

Staffers Karen Higgins (left) and Chander Bahri preparing for a book sale in the early 1980s.

For more than two decades the SPL has been culling its collection through public sales, and that practice is likely to continue for some time. But now, the library is also accepting "gently used" books, videos and CDs (but not old periodicals, school textbooks or encyclopedia more than five years old). If patrons have something to offer, they are invited to make an appointment for the last Friday of the month, which has been declared donation day.

Music at the library

Music has played a role in much of the life of the Stratford Public Library. The SPL has always housed books on music, and through the years has added phonographic recordings, videos and compact disks.

Long a staple in the children's and youth services departments, music has also been a part of the library's special events, whether the celebration of an official opening or the observance of a season.

On the first Saturday in December 1976, Canadian opera star Jan Rubes and Anne Linden of Toronto entertained parents and children at the library with a concert that included Christmas songs in German and Dutch.

In December 1981, the New Hamburg Bell Ringers, led by Jerry Zeigler, put on an afternoon Christmas concert in the second-floor auditorium. In the following December, the 16-member Renaissance Singers of East Lansing, Mich., gave a free noon-hour concert at the library. Wearing period costumes, they presented a program of late 16th- and early 17th-century music, including English madrigals.

The Stratford Kiwanis Youth Band performed at the SPL in January 1982. In

Stratford Public Library presents

Music for a Summer's Day

Thursdays at noon

JUNE 18	ALAN ROTHWELL – BARITONE	AUGUST 6	ZEPHYR WOODWIND QUINTET
	SARAH DRAKE – VIOLIN		JASMINE VOCAL TRIO
	ROBIN MCKENZIE – PIANO	AUGUST 13	TOM KAY – FLUTE
JUNE 25	CAROL ROBINSON – VOCAL & GUITAR	AUGUST 20	CAROL BAILEY – PIANO
JULY 2	AUSTIN STRING QUARTET		
JULY 9	KAREN GOREN & FRIENDS	AUGUST 27	CATHERINE ROBERTSON – PIANO
JULY 16	CEDRIC COLEMAN WOODWIND ENSEMBLE	SEPTEMBER 4	LESLIE FLYNN – PIANO
JULY 23	SUSAN TRETHEWAY BRASS QUINTET		
JULY 30	JULIA PENISTAN – OBOE		

Stratford Public Library
19 St. Andrew Street,
Stratford, Ontario
(519) 271-0220

Free admission

12:00PM
IN THE AUDITORIUM
BRING A LUNCH
COFFEE AVAILABLE

SPL

January 1985 the Gallery Singers of Stratford, featuring Marilyn Schuster and Michael Rouse, were there to sing "mostly songs of love for Valentine's Day." In the following month, director Raymond Daniels and the Stratford Concert Choir presented a preview of Handel's Samson.

The frequency of musical entertainment at the library was hardly regular until 1978, when, from then through much of the 1980s, the SPL offered Music for a Summer Day. Most of the days were Thursdays in July and August, and the noon-hour concerts were free. Patrons were invited to bring their lunch, and the SPL supplied the coffee, also free.

Through the years, most of the performers were from the Stratford, London and Kitchener-Waterloo area, some from the Stratford Festival. They sang and played instruments that ranged from piano to violin, French horn, trumpet, viola, flute, oboe, trombone and cello. There were soloists, duets, trios, quartets and quintets.

And there were appreciative audiences. "We'd always exceed the fire marshal's regulations for the number of people in the room (auditorium)," says former library staffer Christina Wilson. "That was our big worry."

Those who, through the years, filled that hour with music included Michel White, Kathy Armstrong, Kevin MacMillan, Terry Goodden, Margaret Elligson, Kenneth Hall, Tom Kay, Dan Riley, Pat Mullen, Brian Emery, Carol (Bailey) Smith, Sylvia Henry, Elizabeth Fraser, Marianne Wiedman, Christine Wiedman, Sarah Drake, Robin McKenzie, Nancy Gildner, Allan Rothwell, Daniel A. Hansen, Randi Schonning,

Elizabeth Morris, Dodi Layton, Stephen Green, Anne Whittaker-Cumming, Wade Whittaker-Cumming, Angus Sinclair, Thomas Drake, David Drake, Charles Trethewey, Michael Wood, Alan Ridgway, Susan Trethewey, Susan Barber, Richard Jatiouk, Rick Avery, Judy Greenhill, Marilyn Schuster, Michael Rouse, Paula Babb, Robert Gloor, Beryl Hultin, Len Bradfield, Warren Leighton, Lutzen Riedstra, Claudette Wagner, Gail Selkirk, Melba Bingeman, Noreen Waibel, Gary Kidd, Randi Patterson, Colleen Johnson, Andrea Barstad, Ken Varley, Jack Hayter, Wally Gladding, Bill Reid, Jean Hodgins, Jan Pearce, Chuck Deighton, Laura Burton, Ian Harper, Elizabeth Brickenden, Elizabeth Adams, Linda Knechtel, Sandra Donatelle, Leslie Flynn, Yvette Valad, Kim Silver, Julia Penistan, Leslie Belland, Alison Kastner, Michael La Leune, Geoff Thompson, Angela Rudden, Bill Ripley, Janet Robertson, Catherine Robertson, Rhyll Peel, Earl McCluskie, Paul Aston, Candy Forest, Andrew Bensler, Karen Goren, Chadwick Bensler, Ronald Greidanus, A. James Ford, Holly Shepherd, Derek Conrod, Don Sweete, Caroline Burchill, Donna Chiasson, Sandra Mogenson, Jerry Johnson, Bruce McGillivray, David Murray, Dominik Franken, Peter Shackleton, Peter Carter and

SPL

Sisters Catherine Robertson (left) and Janet [Robertson] Woolfrey entertain with some music for a summer day at library, August 1982.

Mark Rowsom.

Some of the foregoing performed alone, others as part of the following: the London Symphony String Quartette, the Eclectic Brass, En Passant, the Bozar Trio, the Stratford Concert Choir, the Austin String Quartet, the Northwestern Secondary School Senior Band, the Bierdo Brothers and Sister Sheila, the Venturi Winds, the Tretheway Brass Quartet, the Knox Chamber Ensemble, the Cedric Coleman Woodwind Ensemble, the Stratford Ensemble Woodwind Quintet, the Zephyr Woodwind Quintet, the Jasmine Vocal Trio, the Woodwind Sextet, Eleveight, the Ken Varley Jazz Quartet, the Festival Fanfare Brass and Friends, and the Stratford Ensemble.

The Jane Kirkpatrick years
1983-

To replace Sue Bonsteel, the board hired Jane Kirkpatrick, a 33-year-old native of Kingston. She had an English degree from the University of Guelph and, like her predecessor, a master's degree in library and information science from the University of Western Ontario in London.

Most recently she had been head of the Merivale branch library in Nepean, but had also worked at four branches of the Toronto public library, namely Gerrard-Ashdale, City Hall, Yorkville and Palmerston. She was assistant branch head at Yorkville and branch head at Palmerston.

She spent some time in the SPL during the last couple of weeks of May 1983, and assumed full duties on June 1.

A one-time resident of Sebringville, Kirkpatrick said she was keen on the Stratford position because "I'm a big theatre buff. I used to come to Stratford two or three times every season. My first impressions were great. This area is totally appealing. People will stop and give you the time of day, and if you are looking lost,

they will offer help. And the staff here is wonderful. They're warm and welcoming. Most people think being a librarian is boring, but it's actually very exciting. There is so much variety, and I meet so many new people."

She also said she expected to make some changes at the library, but not before she studied its services and gathered information about the community. "Then I can set goals and objectives for short- and long-term plans."

In moving to Stratford, Kirkpatrick was accompanied by her 30 or so teddy bears, all of whom were delighted to meet SPL staffers Billie Kirkby and Nuala Goldberg and their collections of bruins. The Stratford and area bears had been holding an annual picnic at the Brocksden School Museum, northeast of the city, since 1978.

Billie Kirkby, Ms. Kirkpatrick soon learned, was the Stratford library's best-known animal lover. In her house, she had all manner of creatures as pets, including a monkey.

> "When I worked at the library I always felt that I was part of the world. Everything was there: the books, the magazines, the newspapers, everything. When I left the library, that's what I missed the most, besides the people that I worked with. And I used to say that to people, 'I'm not part of the world anymore.' You really are part of the world when you work in a library. It was the best job I ever had. It sounds sort of romantic, and I don't mean it to sound that way, but it's true. Everything is in a library. It's a busy place."
>
> Lorraine Greenberg
> staff 1979-1988

One of the first tasks faced by the new head librarian was getting the money needed to automate the SPL, for which 100,000 items had to be bar-coded. Most of that was done during the week of Aug. 29 to Sept. 5, 1988, when the library was closed to the public. The Dynix system installed by the SPL went into operation in the following month, during Ontario Public Library Week.

It was in the fall of 1983 that the SPL had three exhibits from the Royal Ontario Museum in Toronto: Fluorescent Minerals, September; Pipes of the Iroquois, October; and Lock, Stock and Barrel, Ontario Gunsmiths and Firearms 1850-1880, November.

In 1984, in recognition of Heritage Day, the third Monday in February, the library featured a film and artifacts related to Stratford and area.

In April that year, Shaun Burns, director of the Big Brothers Association in the city, gave a free talk in the auditorium about "streetproofing your children."

In the 1980s, one of the groups meeting regularly at the library comprised employees of social service agencies from in and around the city. They got together monthly over lunch to discuss common problems, to listen to speakers and to network. One of those representatives was Steve Chandler of the Children's Aid Society. He says the group was loosely knit, and that attendance fluctuated between half

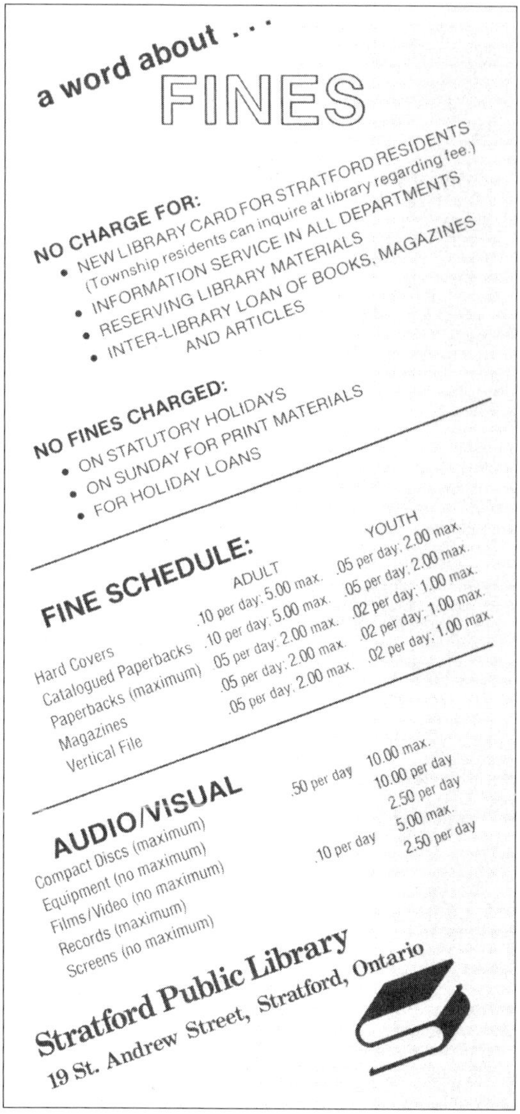

a word about . . .
FINES
NO CHARGE FOR:
• NEW LIBRARY CARD FOR STRATFORD RESIDENTS
(Township residents can inquire at library regarding fee.)
• INFORMATION SERVICE IN ALL DEPARTMENTS
• RESERVING LIBRARY MATERIALS
• INTER-LIBRARY LOAN OF BOOKS, MAGAZINES AND ARTICLES
NO FINES CHARGED:
• ON STATUTORY HOLIDAYS
• ON SUNDAY FOR PRINT MATERIALS
• FOR HOLIDAY LOANS
FINE SCHEDULE:
ADULT
YOUTH
Hard Covers
.10 per day: 5.00 max.
.05 per day: 2.00 max.
Catalogued Paperbacks
.10 per day: 5.00 max.
.05 per day: 2.00 max.
Paperbacks (maximum)
.05 per day: 2.00 max.
.02 per day: 1.00 max.
Magazines
.05 per day: 2.00 max.
.02 per day: 1.00 max.
Vertical File
.05 per day: 2.00 max.
.02 per day: 1.00 max.
AUDIO/VISUAL
Compact Discs (maximum)
.50 per day
10.00 max.
Equipment (no maximum)
10.00 per day
Films/Video (no maximum)
2.50 per day
Records (maximum)
.10 per day
5.00 max.
Screens (no maximum)
2.50 per day
Stratford Public Library
19 St. Andrew Street, Stratford, Ontario

SPL

A word about fines . . . 1984

a dozen and 20. He also recalls many of the lunches as being bring-your-own, brown-bag affairs. Corrections, housing, and family counselling were some of the other groups represented at the get-togethers.

Before she left the library, Sue Bonsteel had started to do an inventory. It was completed by her successor, who found losses to be running between 10 and 15 per cent of the collection each year. In April 1984, Jane Kirkpatrick successfully appealed to city council for the funds to install a $20,000 security system in the SPL. Most convincing in the case she presented was the fact that the library had lost $54,000 worth of books to delinquent borrowers over the previous eight years. The aldermen wasted little time in authorizing the expenditure. They also gave the library $70,000 towards the cost of a computer system that was expected to run to $200,000. Among its many tasks, the computer would be used to detect missing books and other materials and to prepare the overdue notices which to then had been done laboriously by hand.

In addition, the library's operating budget that year was bumped to $488,709 from $450,979.

With a security system on order, the SPL took further steps to deter the theft that had been inflating its costs. It increased its fines for overdue books, recordings, films and videos: 10 cents a day to a maximum of $5 for adult hardcovers; five cents a day to a maximum of $2 for adult paperbacks and children's hardcovers; two cents a day to a maximum of $1 for children's paperbacks; 10 cents a day for records; $2.50 a day for films and videos; and $10 a day for audiovisual equipment. As of Sept. 1, those not picking up reserved films and equipment were to be charged for the full amount. There would be no charge for cancellations with at least 24 hours notice.

The SPL also signed a contract with the Stratford Credit Bureau, whose job was to

track down borrowers who did not settle their accounts with the library after receiving two phone calls and a written invoice.

The new security system was not long in being tested. Staffer Anne Marie Heckman recalls the embarrassment of those patrons who tried to leave the library with a book or two stuffed in their pants. The more creative took to dropping their selections through the windows of the 1975 addition, which forced the board to spring for screens to better secure the building.

In his book, published in 1975, Jim Anderson talked first-hand about the fines and the fined at the SPL: "In today's permissive society, fine-card reminders are all too often resented as an annoying byproduct of efficiency. Residents of the city may not know it, but thousands and thousands of dollars' worth of many of the best books from this library, paid for with tax money, will probably never be returned. Hand in hand with this is the sickening mutilation of books, particularly by student essay writers who remove pages, cut out pictures and underline passages in ink. Patrons clearly do not wish to be checked up on this matter, either. It makes one wonder whether selfishness is on the increase."

It could have been worse, said Jane Kirkpatrick. "For me, coming from a large urban centre where we had lots of problems with young people, we've not had problems here. Some minor things now and again. They get a little rambunctious when they're involved in a project. I think we're very busy because of the school (Central) being there, because it's so easy for them (students) to come here. There certainly was a difference in the late '80s when they went into the self-directed learning projects. They became quite intense, so that changed the nature of some of the reference work, but in terms of discipline problems, they haven't been bad."

In the summer of 1984, the SPL used a federal student employment grant to hire Robert Groothuizen and Bea Renton, whose task was to determine how Stratford and area residents were using the library, what they thought of its services, and how they wanted those services expanded or changed. Of particular interest to the library officials was their patrons' take on

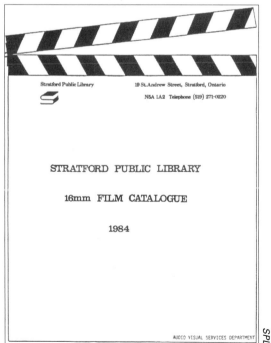

computers for use by the public.

By 1984 the titles in the library's 16-mm film collection filled a 48-page catalogue. The categories included children's, Christmas, conservation and wildlife, fine arts, general entertainment, health and safety, humour, Indians, labour and industry, religion, social comment, and sports. The individual offerings ran from A is for Architecture to Zookeepers, from Black Ice to Witch's Night Out.

It was in 1984 that the provincial government revised the Public Libraries Act, and the changes had a profound effect on library business in Ontario. When the 14 provincial library regions were reduced to eight, the Midwestern system, of which Stratford was a member, was joined with the Georgian Bay group to form the Saugeen Regional Library Service.

Further, the government put the Library Services Centre, which had been started by the Midwestern system in 1967, under the direction of an independently appointed board, to which Jane Kirkpatrick was named a charter director.

In 1990, more government streamlining resulted in the province being divided into north and south library services. Much of what had been the Saugeen area became one of eight divisions in the Southern Ontario Library Service. Each is overseen by a trustee council that meets three times a year.

The Library Services Centre, though it has changed locations, continues to operate out of Kitchener. The SPL buys about 85 per cent of its books, as well as compact discs and videos from the LSC.

On Jan. 26, 1985, the SPL sold some used furnishings, which included chairs, tables, paperback racks, display cases and a microfiche reader. Most of the items were from its audiovisual lounge. There was another such sale on Feb. 6, 1988.

In 1985 the SPL was advertising itself as the first library in Canada to rent out laser

associates. She was charged with administering a $115,000 budget and realizing a $60,000 profit. The head of the SPL's audiovisual department, Brian McKone, was enlisted to oversee the microphones, projectors, video cassette recorders, films and related equipment for the event's almost 50 sessions and related events. And Christina Wilson, the head of adult services in Stratford, worked with the Canadian Library Association president in presenting an overview of the co-operative work program at the School of Library and Information Science at the University of Western Ontario in London. All three were back at the 1987 convention in similar roles.

Early in 1987, the head of youth services, Warren (Socks) James, recruited some SPL patrons and created a training film based on Daniel Pinkwater's novel The Moosepire. The book features a character named Blue Moose and contains a lengthy description of the Moose doing research in the Yellowtooth Public Library.

"The text seems to present a blueprint on how to conduct research utilizing the resources of an average public library," wrote Socks, in seeking Pinkwater's

A/V director Brian McKone didn't always dress like this.

disks and the compact disk players with which to use them. The library spent about $1,000 on three players and 84 disks that ranged from orchestral music to Dire Straits' Brothers in Arms and Wynton Marsalis's Hot House Flowers.

At the same time, the checkout area in the audiovisual department was enlarged, to ease a congestion problem that had long annoyed patrons and staff.

With its student employment grants in the summer of 1986, the SPL hired Margaret Hackney to work on problems in the card catalogue, Ed Pass to develop and administer computer workshops in the youth services department, and Manjeet Sehra to prepare books for automation procedures.

In November 1986, three full-time staffers played active roles at the Ontario Library Association's 84th annual conference, in Toronto. The director of Stratford's library, Jane Kirkpatrick, also an OLA councillor, was treasurer of the four-day gathering of about 1,000 librarians, trustees and

permission to adapt The Moosepire. "It also draws attention to some of the additional services (such as story hours) offered by us and many other libraries."

The author OK'd the project, and the SPL

The front of a six-panel brochure in 1987, featuring a sketch by library employee Norma Bissonnette. By this time the SPL was closed on Sundays from Victoria Day to Labour Day.

wound up with a humorous introduction to its many and varied offerings.

In March 1987, staffers Anne Marie Heckman and Sally Hengeveld were given permission by the SPL board to share the job of youth services department head. "Job sharing represents a significant development in the Stratford Public Library's personnel policy and one that we deem to be reflective of contemporary social trends," said Joan Smith, chair of the board's personnel committee. Heckman was returning to the SPL after a two-year absence, and Hengeveld was coming back from a maternity leave.

In the following month, the library moved its closing time on Fridays from 9 p.m. back to 6 p.m.

In May 1987 the SPL and the outreach program of the Ministry of Citizenship and Culture combined to present a free lecture, called In Search of Your Roots, by Canadian genealogist Angus Baxter. Admission was free.

In June, staffers began converting the more than 120,000 entries in the SPL's card catalogue to a $281,000 Dynix computer system. Christina Wilson was the automation project manager, and the library got a $70,000 grant from the provincial

SPL

government to help with the database. The target date for checking out a book on the new system was August 1988, and by the end of that year, said Jane Kirkpatrick, it was hoped that automation would be saving the library time and money.

In October 1987 the SPL hosted a free, one-night program for inventors and innovators. It was presented by the Innovation Centre of the University of Waterloo.

It was in the late 1980s that the library set down a revised set of objectives, namely: to serve as an information provider; to be a literacy advocate; to provide material dealing with popular culture; and to support self-directed education.

In 1990 the SPL used half of a $100,000 donation from the family of Floyd S. Chalmers to establish a public theatre resource centre in the main-floor room that formerly housed the reference department and later the community information centre. An editor, publisher and patron of the arts,

Chalmers had been instrumental in the development of the Stratford Festival.

The collection that bears his name in the library contains books, videos, newspaper and magazine clippings, microfilm, periodicals, and biographies relating to the Festival, William Shakespeare, stagecraft

STRATFORD PUBLIC LIBRARY
19 St. Andrew Street
Stratford, Ontario N5A 1A2
(519) 271-0220

YOUR CARD IS YOUR RESPONSIBILITY AND THE KEY TO:

—*unlocking wondrous places!*

—*be whoever you want!*

—*travel anywhere!*

—*learn about anything!*

—*solve mysteries*
  or build robots!

THE WORLD IS IN THE PALM OF YOUR HAND . . .
WITH YOUR LIBRARY CARD

BUT . . . REMEMBER: YOUR CARD, AND ANY MATERIAL BORROWED USING IT, IS YOUR RESPONSIBILITY.

Please remember that the next time family or friends want to "borrow" it.

SPL

A reminder, designed by Mary Lynn Cook in about 1988

and theatre in general. The materials are non-circulating. "It was a highlight of my career to do the research, choose the books, and set this room up," says SPL director Jane Kirkpatrick.

The room, decorated with posters, masks, hats and other artifacts on loan from the Stratford Festival, was opened in June 1990 and soon was attracting about 70 tourists a week. It also became popular among secondary school drama students.

Investment income from the other half of the Chalmers donation is used by the library to annually update the collection. In addition to what is housed in that room, the SPL has on its main floor an extensive theatre collection, from which books and other materials may be borrowed.

In 1990 there were almost 190,000 searches on the library's computerized catalogue. In fact, there were often lineups

Annual report 1990

STRATFORD PUBLIC LIBRARY

CHALMERS PUBLIC THEATRE RESOURCE COLLECTION

SPL

Chalmers Public Theatre Resource Collection card

of patrons waiting to use the terminals – three in adult services, two in children's and one in the teen centre. More terminals were planned for 1993.

In June 1991 the SPL began offering a fax service, which meant that, for a fee, patrons could send or receive faxes any time during regular library hours.

On the last day of July 1991, the staff took their lunch to the Shakespearean Gardens for the ninth annual library picnic, an event initiated by Jane Kirkpatrick, who provided drinks and a special dessert. On this occasion, they extended best wishes to Cathy Matyas, who was leaving the SPL.

It was in 1991 that Burt Reid and Joan Smith were recognized by the Ministry of Citizenship for their years of service on the SPL board. They were honoured at a ceremony in London.

> "I remember the day a guy cursed and swore at me because I asked for ID (identification). He was yelling real loud and cursing and swearing and calling me a Communist."
>
> Marion Gibb
> 1978-1992

In June 1995 there was similar recognition for three more friends of the SPL. Irene Dutchak and Margie McCarthy were lauded for their contribution as board members, and Marg Pike for her 10 years as the library's volunteer horticulturalist – caretaker of the indoor plants and the small outdoor garden.

It was in the early 1990s that the SPL became the new home for the Perth Foundation for the Enrichment of Education's career centre, which was moved from the second floor of the Gordon Block. For a number of years the foundation gave the library some money to keep the centre's resources current, but the funding eventually dried up. So the library is now adding the material which is still relevant to its main catalogue.

From April to November in 1993 the Chalmers room housed the first Canadian installation of Pageants of Delight, an exhibition of the theatrical influences on Shakespeare. Presented by Records of Early English Drama, University of Toronto, it included display panels, a brochure and a 25-minute video. The exhibition had recently returned to Canada after almost a year in London, England.

It was in 1993 that library planners, along with the media and the business world, began to devote some attention to the Internet, a burgeoning innovation that was sweeping the world. It was in the previous year that the phrase "surfing the Internet"

had been coined.

As of July 1, 1993, patrons were able to use SPL computers to reserve items for themselves. If reserved items within the library were not picked up, the fine was 50 cents. If reserved items that were brought to Stratford through the inter-library loan system were not picked up, the fine was $2.

On Oct. 6, 1993, the SPL brought in Marvin Post and Michael Keller to conduct a free book clinic. Members of the public were asked to bring their treasured books to the experts for appraisal and advice on restoration.

On Feb. 17, 1994, during Healthy Sexuality Week, the same public was invited to hear nurse Irene Wheeler present "How to talk with your children about sexuality."

From June 20 to July 18, 1994, the SPL closed its main floor, so that floor could be recarpeted. For that period, the bestsellers, the magazines and the reference desk were moved to the lower floor, where they comprised a temporary adult section. The children's and teen departments continued to operate as usual on the lower floor. The upgrade was delayed while repairs were made to the concrete floor.

During the main floor's down time, the SPL added two CD-ROM (compact disk with read-only memory) terminals to its reference department. For use with the terminals, it had seven disks loaded with assorted information, from summaries of magazine articles to global books in print, to all Canadian newspapers in 1993. Plans called for adding another five stations and a link to INFO, the provincial information network. To make room for the new equipment, the microfilm and microfilm reader were relocated across the street at the Stratford-Perth Archives.

When the shelving and books were reassembled on the new carpet, the aisles were widened to 42 inches.

By assuming the role of movers, members of the library staff saved the city an estimated $35,000 in the main floor renovation project, which came in about $9,000 under budget. That gave rise to thoughts about the lower floor, where the appeal of its aged orange carpet had long waned. It was decided, then, the $9,000 be directed to replacing orange with hazelnut. To that end, the youth services department was closed from Sept. 6 to Sept. 20, though materials related to September school projects were made available on the main floor. In addition to the carpet makeover, the walls on the lower floor were repaired and repainted.

At the same time, the library's front steps were lifted to facilitate the repair of crumbling foundations, and workmen installed automatic door openers. That part of the overhaul made the St. Andrew Street door the provisional main entrance.

In October 1994 the SPL announced it had joined parties in London, St. Thomas and five neighbouring counties in a co-operative computer network called Hometown. Its purpose was "to develop and provide universal and affordable access to a comprehensive communication and information service." The group looked to become the first community network in Canada to extend access to a large rural community, and in so doing equalize the opportunities for rural and urban users of the information highway.

The area involved encompassed the counties of Huron, Oxford, Middlesex, Elgin and Perth, and the server was based in London. (The HOME in Hometown is taken from the first letter of four of those counties.)

As well as provide access to the Internet, Hometown was to hook into other free nets and community-driven databases.

Organizers expected the annual fees to be about $25 for individuals and $40 for families. They also planned to be up and running by June 1995. Co-ordinating the SPL's involvement in Hometown was its technical co-ordinator Becky Rogers.

The Ontario Federation of Agriculture donated $10,000 to the project, and there

The SPL crew gets last-minute instructions before wading into the library's major interior makeover, June 1994. From left: Carol Smith, Barbra Williams, Gail Poole, Astrid Roch-Russell, Lorraine Gordon, Perry Wilson, Guy McKone (on chair), Nancy Poppe, Kathy Grant and Cathy Perreault.

was promise of a $492,180 grant from the Ministry of Economic Development and Trade. There was also to be funding from the Ministry of Citizenship and Culture through its library strategic development fund. Other support came from the University of Western Ontario and Bell Canada. All funding requests were put on hold when the provincial government called an election in May 1995.

A six-month testing period began in February 1995, and officials predicted the operation would be self-sustaining after five years, when revenues were expected to reach $700,000. The SPL held a number of information sessions in an effort to interest clients.

But in October 1995, Mike Harris and his newly elected Progressive Conservative government cancelled the $492,180 grant. By then, Hometown had 535 registered users and was growing by five users a day. Because of the Tories' change of plans, the network's membership fee for a single user was hiked to $60 a year. "We tried to make it work," says Jane Kirkpatrick. "Some of the partners were able to get HRDC funding to keep them going. We all believed in the concept so much and really wanted it to work." But that wasn't enough to give Hometown the financial footing it needed. Nor did it help that Elgin County pulled out of the partnership.

After running from Sept. 1 to Dec. 15, 1995, Hometown was shut down when the agreement with its service provider was terminated. It then signed on with another provider and eventually came back on line.

By July 1996 the network had more than 1,000 members and more than 40 phone lines for improved service. In the same month, the SPL started its Community Access Program site with the assistance of a $16,500 grant from Industry Canada, and additional funding to hire three students to implement training and web design services. Participation in Hometown was a

key factor in the SPL getting CAP funding, says Kirkpatrick, but the CAP initiative was not the reason Hometown didn't make it. "Hometown failed because it couldn't sustain itself, and that was because we didn't have a solid financial base once the government withdrew its initial grant," she says. The end for Hometown came in January 1997.

As of July 1996, however, the SPL was offering free Internet access and free introductory workshops for people to learn how to navigate on the information highway. The three students it hired were Philip Bonner, Eric Falconer and Brad Smith, And, because of CAP funding, the library was able to keep them on through the summer of 1997. In 1998 and 1999, Bonner and Falconer, by then attending university, were retained by the SPL to maintain its Web site.

Most of the computer and Internet seminars offered by the library, beginning in 1996, were two hours in length, and for

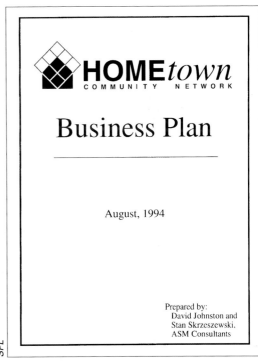

SPL

> "The Internet means we can help people a lot more, but it also means they expect more, too."
>
> Sally Hengeveld
> staff 1980-

most there was a $15-per-person fee – for a user manual created by Smith.

To help finance those training sessions, the SPL tapped into Industry Canada's Community Access Program, from which it continues to receive funding. For a while, Kirkpatrick served on a national advisory committee for CAP, which necessitated her travelling to Ottawa and Vancouver.

Meanwhile, library staff continued to instruct patrons on the use of its Internet terminals. There were no instructional fees attached to those sessions, but there was a $3-per-hour cost for connection time.

From 1997 through 1999 the library had no systems person on staff. Rather, it had a company out of London, CIMS, maintain its network. It was the company that had helped in the attempt to save Hometown.

In 1995 the SPL inflicted budget cuts of its own. It closed seven additional Sundays from May 7 through Oct. 8, and as of Sept. 11, didn't open until 1 p.m. on Mondays. As well, it didn't renew the contracts of two part-time employees. "The thing that really bothers me the most is that there hasn't been a budget increase in three years," said SPL board chair Harry Nesbitt, in announcing the cost-cutting measures. "The way things look at the present, it could be worse in the future." Nesbitt was also the city council representative on the board.

At the time, the library had 29 full- and part-time employees, who were serving about 700 patrons daily. Its budget was just over $1 million, the same as in 1994. The city cut a proposed $11,000 increase, which was slated to cover some maintenance costs, and also held back that year's $25,000 installment for the SPL computer system.

On Aug. 1, 1995, just six people showed up during a three-hour period to air their complaints about the provincial government – its ministries, agencies, boards and commissions. On hand to hear those complaints was Mike Sauer, a district officer out of the London office of the Ontario Ombudsman.

In October 1995, vandals fired three shots from a pellet gun through windows at the SPL, causing an estimated $2,000 in damages.

In the summer of 1996, the Tory government was looking at allowing libraries to charge user fees to make up for money that would not be forthcoming through transfer payments. It was a notion that played to mixed reviews among the electorate.

User fees and cost cutting were certainly on the mayor's mind when he addressed a breakfast meeting of the Stratford and District Chamber of Commerce on Sept. 17, 1996. Dave Hunt suggested the city might be wise to talk with boards of education about opening their libraries to the public, and reduce or eliminate the service it provides with the Stratford Public Library.

About a week later, in an interview, he said, "Maybe we should be cutting costs of the library, and one way might be to work with school boards and get rid of the library." That quote appeared in a *Beacon Herald* story under the headline "Mayor suggests closing the library, letting public use school facilities."

In a followup story, about 12 days later, Hunt called the headline misleading and said, "I certainly never said we should just close the library. I would never suggest that."

By then, however, the pot was stirred, and a wave of support for the SPL flooded forth in letter after letter to the editor of the

"Public libraries are not just these quasi governmental bodies. We're one of the few areas where people really are free to ask questions. It's the thing that keeps us unique. Libraries truly are, I think, democratic institutions. They are the things that keep democracies really democracies – the fact that anyone can come in here and find out the answer to anything, freely, without anyone looking askance at them, making them feel guilty.

Libraries have had a poor image because people are concerned that people are looking over their shoulders wondering what they're reading. I think in the past it's been one of the images of libraries that we have battled with, to keep it free, to make people feel comfortable coming in and borrowing whatever. The collection and the ideas here are not just a mirror to the community. We are more a window on the world. And that's reflected in the collection but also in the policies and procedures, the access to things beyond the walls here."

Christina Wilson
staff 1985-1988

newspaper. More than one writer indicated a willingness to pay user fees if that's what it would take to maintain the downtown library.

Reg White and Heather Pryde, president and vice-president, respectively, of the Friends of the Stratford Public Library, invited the mayor to "meet with us and to tour the library to better inform himself of library services and the great demands our community places upon them." There was a similar invitation in another of the letters, from Pat Stanley, chair of the library board. She also pointed out that, in addition to catering to about 700 patrons a day, the SPL staffers were fielding between 1,500 and 2,000 queries a week while working the reference desk.

On Oct. 15, about a month after Hunt had touched off the firestorm, his colleagues at City Hall did what they could to douse it. At a meeting at which the mayor was absent, the councillors unanimously endorsed a motion that affirmed its recognition of the importance of the library as a centre of culture, education, information and fellowship.

In the following month, the SPL had another fire on its hands, notably a blaze in its men's washroom. City firefighters, who cleared the building at about 8 p.m., said someone had ignited a paper towel dispenser. Damage, mostly from smoke, was estimated at about $800.

By then, patrons needed to ask for a key if they wished to access the library washrooms. It seems on this occasion, a key was taken without permission.

In October 1998, Human Resources Development Canada established an employment resource centre on the lower level of the SPL. In a small office, it set up two computer workstations loaded with software for preparing resumes and writing job applications. It also furnished materials and programs to help users determine aptitude, brush up on interviewing techniques, and search for employment. There were no fees for using the centre.

For many years, the SPL has provided talking book exchanges for Canadian National Institute for the Blind clients living in Perth County. In March 1999 it was the launch site for the Southwest District Spinoza program, designed to put 17-inch talking bears in the lives of three-to-eight-year-olds who are blind or visually impaired. Each bear has a built-in four-track

love of learning, and, because of corporate sponsorship, are available at no cost. Four blind children were given bears when the Spinoza program was introduced in Stratford.

Later in 1999, the library became a meeting place for a newly formed writers' group, initiated by David Pratt, who had recently moved to Stratford. The members still gather at the SPL, where they present and critique their work.

It was on Aug. 6, 1999, that library staffer Guy McKone died of a heart attack at age 42. In his honour, his colleagues placed a wrought iron bench in the gardens in front of the SPL.

audio cassette player, which is used for reciting talking tape books. The cuddly bruins were designed to promote a lifelong

DEAN ROBINSON

The Guy McKone bench, 2003

Snow-crows of the library

SPL colleague Paula Janveau
wrote the following in memory
of Guy McKone,
who died in August 1999.

The hall of knowledge stands,
Lonely and wise,
As the workers of wisdom exit
Sadness emanating
While one whistles his humour,
A clown who washes the floor with clouds.
Among night branches,
The snow-crows caw,
The furry paws of the dog-tree
Providing a home
For all of them
While the black sky
Shields them
In its warm, dark cloak.
Mesmerized by the snow-crows,
Guy's informational know-how
Shines through
Like a divine ray
From the classical film light
Of the theatre moon.

From April through August 2000, the SPL was bordered by scaffolding, as crews from a Mississauga company extensively restored its exterior brick and masonry work, and repaired and replaced windows. There was some inconvenience, especially with reduced parking, but the building remained open.

It was in 2000 that the SPL board put the finishing touches on a new strategic plan. In preparing the plan, the trustees reviewed the three service roles adopted by the previous board, namely "to provide general information and leisure collections to meet the need for information and answers on topics related to work, school and personal life; to meet basic and information literacy needs; and to provide opportunities through collections and services to meet lifelong learning needs and to meet post secondary education needs through distance learning."

They also incorporated the results of focus-group meetings that were held in the fall of 2000. In the end, most of the fingers pointed to a lack of space, a problem that had been plaguing SPL staff and board for some time.

On March 8, 2001, the SPL was evacuated after roofing contractors, trying to melt snow with a torch, accidentally burned a heating filter and sent smoke through the library's air vents. After the situation was under control, city firefighters set a large fan in front of the main entrance and blew fresh air into the building.

In April 2001 the SPL hired Krista Sutherland as its information technology training librarian. Her job is to help patrons use information technology in various ways – to look for books and other library material and check its availability, to learn to use the Internet, and to set up e-mail accounts. Gone were the drawer-laden wooden cabinets to the right of the main entrance, where patrons had long been able to access catalogue information on small white cards. They were replaced by On-line Public Access Catalogues (OPACs). To help everyone through the transition stage, the library planned two-hour workshops from November 2001 through March 2002.

As of May 2001, the SPL was depositing large-print books at 10 sites in the city, including Woodland Towers and People Care. Wayne Schmidt and Patti Chapman from the Eileen Langley Centre were helping to transport the books.

That summer, 16-year-old Dominque Lepage-Cote from Ste. Foy, Que., worked at the library as part of a work exchange program for students. Saying he wanted to learn English and have fun, he put in seven-day weeks, at $6.85 an hour, shelving books, helping with the kids reading program and

SPL

doing yardwork.

In October 2001 the SPL officially launched an interactive computer network in its children's department.

In the following month, in the library board's annual report to the city, chair Dr. Susan Tamblyn told the councillors the SPL was in dire need of more space. She also outlined four options, namely: do nothing, make significant renovations to the interior of the current building, create a satellite location or locations, or move to a new facility.

By then the SPL's operating budget had reached $1,213,561, of which $1,005,543 came from the city and $51,402 from the province. Provincial and federal government projects grants totalled another $29,315.

The library's capital budget that year was $96,295. Most of that money, $71,559, was in reserves, while the rest came from the city. All of it was spent on children's Internet facilities and completion of the outside brick restoration project.

By far, the SPL's biggest expense in 2001 was for staffing – $797,948 to pay 14 full-time employees, nine part time and three on contract for Sunday work. Books, periodicals, compact disks and videos cost the SPL $128,034 in 2001. Other expenditures included $97,433 for utilities, maintenance and insurance; $74,118 for computer services; $31,525 for telecommunications; $20,018 for general administration costs and services; and $14,184 for electronic reference subscriptions and CD-ROMs.

From its operation in 2001, the library was able to direct $50,300 to capital reserves. By then its collection included 100,000 general circulation books, 6,000 reference books, almost 4,000 videos, 2,000 CDs and 172 periodical subscriptions.

It was also in November 2001 that the city hosted the inaugural Stratford Book Festival, from which proceeds were directed

A public thank you, June 2002

to the library's literacy project. The SPL presented some of the weekend events. The second SBF, in November 2002, resulted in a further $6,760 for the project.

In April 2002 the library added an open-mike contest to its celebration of national poetry month. Nine entrants were given a chance to read their poetry, and the audience determined the top three to be Beth Beech, Jen Frankel and Mary Hoy Schmidt. The winners later read their work on CJCS radio, which co-sponsored the event.

In the fall of 2002, the culinary section of the SPL collection was enhanced with the receipt of a selection of books from the Stratford Chefs School. "We had them at the school, but it's so much better if people have access to them," said SCS program administrator Elisabeth Lorimer. "Everybody can enjoy them," she said. "Cooking is very much the in thing. More people are interested, not as a way to put

POSITION AVAILABLE

The Stratford Public Library requires one part-time page. This position involves shelving materials, shelf-reading and related duties.

QUALIFICATIONS: Ability to work effectively with public of all ages. Ability to exercise independent judgment and initiative.

TERMS: Approximately 15 hours per week. Must be available for daytime and Saturday hours. Occasional evening hours may be required.

COMPENSATION: $8.49 TO $9.99 per hour plus vacation pay.

Please submit a written application by September 3rd to:

Theresa Talsma, Page Supervisor
Stratford Public Library
19 St. Andrew Street
Stratford, Ontario
N5A 1A2

The Library thanks everyone for their interest; only those selected for an interview will be contacted. No phone calls, please.

SPL

Advertising for a page, August 2002

food on the table but for the sheer pleasure. We all have to eat, so we might as well make it fun."

Described by the SPL as a semi-permanent collection, the books are catalogued and can be signed out by the public on a two-day limited loan basis. As well, the school's students will have greater access to them because of the library's generous hours of operation.

Nov. 15, 2002, was the deadline for the centennial committee's contest for designing a quilted hanging. The winner was Don Dolton, an artist who recently moved to Stratford. For his design entry, he received $100. Runner-up Jennifer Cohrane of Ethel got $50.

In November 2002, board chair Dr. Susan Tamblyn and executive director Jane Kirkpatrick told city council the SPL needs two to three times more usable space, and all of that space should be on one floor.

Further, they said, a consultant's report due out early in 2003, will indicate that patrons want the library to remain in the city core, a finding not unlike those in previous surveys.

Dr. Tamblyn told the councillors that the present building has about 10,000 square feet of net usable public space, but the current need is for 17,000 square feet. She

THE GOOD BOOK GROUP

September 24, 2002
After You'd Gone
Maggie O'Farrell

October 22, 2002
Isobel Gunn
Audrey Thomas

November 26, 2002
Mercy Among the Children
David Adams Richards

January 28, 2003
The Storyteller: Memory, Secrets, Magic and Lies
Anna Porter

February 25, 2003
The Ivory Swing
Janette Turner Hospital

March 25, 2003
Dreams of my Russian Summers
Andrei Makine

April 22, 2003
The Suspect
L.R. Wright

May 27, 2003
Unless
Carol Shields

June 2002

SPL

said that need will jump to between 22,000 and 30,000 square feet over the next quarter century.

The SPL now has about 20,000 cardholders in the city, and its services are used by an average of 600 patrons per day.

Space limitations have resulted in reduced reading areas, off-site storage and division of the young adult collection into two sections. The space problems are becoming "more and more pressing every year," said Dr. Tamblyn.

Kirkpatrick said possible solutions include a branch library, and that the consultant's report is certain to address that option.

As 2002 wound down, the SPL and its many friends turned their attention to 2003 and a year-long celebration of the 100th birthday of their original library building. In response to an invitation from the SPL's centennial committee, members of the Stratford Horticultural Society spent about 1,400 person hours gathering materials and decorating the front entrance of the library for the Christmas season. Their goal was to replicate a style that would have been

Stratford Public Library
Christmas 2002
Staff Songbook

What Book Is This?
(to the tune of 'What Child Is This?')

What book is this
that crammed itself
on the shelf so tightly

Which patrons greet
with many a curse
while the trace list keeps growing

This, this is the problem
while librarians buy and pages shelve
Space, space is the problem, the future of the library!

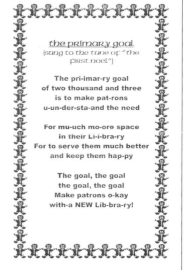

the primary goal
(sung to the tune of "the first noel")

The pri-imar-ry goal
of two thousand and three
is to make pat-rons
u-un-der-sta-and the need

For mu-uch mo-ore space
in their Li-i-bra-ry
For to serve them much better
and keep them hap-py

The goal, the goal
the goal, the goal
Make patrons o-kay
with-a NEW Lib-bra-ry!

That the SPL has outgrown its present space did not escape the lyricists involved in producing the library staff's 2002 Christmas songbook.

popular in 1903. To that end, they used grapevine, dogwood, evergreen, sumac and dried hydrangea to create wreaths, urns, panels and pillars. It was an effort of some significance for the SHS, too, in that it is 125 years old in 2003.

Using a bequest from the estate of longtime colleague Violet Russell, the SHS members also redesigned the floral beds on the library lawn and planned some interior displays at the SPL in June and September 2003.

In January 2003 the library launched SPL@sh!, a newsletter designed to "cause a stir and propel information about the library into your space." Its editor is veteran staffer Anne Marie Heckman.

Some of the Stratford Horticultural Society's floral decorations inside the SPL, December 2002

On Sunday, Feb. 2, 2003, about 50 people gathered in the SPL auditorium for the launch of the Stratford Camera Club's 40th anniversary photographic exhibit, which

Stratford Horticultural Society members Nick Waras (left) and Bruce Wilkinson help to decorate the front of the library for Christmas 2002.

The main entrance, Christmas 2002

was to be refreshed monthly in that space through Sept. 30, 2003.

The club's relationship with the library goes back to 1939. In September of that year, the SPL gave the club the use of a meeting room. Members of the present organization aren't sure how long that first group operated, but the records of their club date back to 1963. Thus, the 40th birthday celebrations.

STRATFORD PUBLIC LIBRARY
19 St. Andrew Street, Stratford ON N5A 1A2

- Phone   519-271-0220
- Website   www.stratford.library.on.ca
- Email   spl@pcin.on.ca

HOURS OF OPERATION

Monday	1:00 p.m. - 9:00 p.m.
Tuesday	9:30 a.m. - 9:00 p.m.
Wednesday	9:30 a.m. - 9:00 p.m.
Thursday	9:30 a.m. - 9:00 p.m.
Friday	9:30 a.m. - 6:00 p.m.
Saturday	9:30 a.m. - 6:00 p.m.
Sunday*	2:00 p.m. - 5:00 p.m.

*Sunday closing - effective May 18, 2003

LIBRARY CLOSURES
January to July 2003

New Year's Day   ◆ Wed., Jan. 1, 2003
Good Friday   ◆ Fri., Apr. 18, 2003
Easter Sunday   ◆ Sun., Apr. 20, 2003
Easter Monday   ◆ Mon., Apr. 21, 2003
Victoria Day   ◆ Mon., May 19, 2003
Canada Day   ◆ Tues., July 1, 2003

RENEWALS may be made in person, by telephone, or using our website.

For Hours of Operation contact:
Perth East Public Library   519-595-8395
www.pertheast.library.on.ca
West Perth Public Library   519-348-9234
www.westperth.library.on.ca

JANUARY - JULY 2003 @ your library

SPL

The first issue of Splash, January 2003

The Perth County Information Network

In 1997, Jane Kirkpatrick and other library heads in Perth County began to discuss ways of sharing services and cutting costs, especially where book-buying was involved. Within two years those talks had resulted in the formation of the Perth County Information Network, a voluntary, non-profit co-operative that provides a common automation system for all members and allows the patrons of each library access to the Internet.

Founding members of the PCIN were the SPL, the Perth East Public Library (Milverton) and the West Perth Public Library (Mitchell).

Because of what they felt was prohibitive cost, the libraries in St. Marys and the Township of North Perth (Listowel), elected to set up their own computer systems and withdrew from the PCIN initiative. So, when Stratford officials began to charge people in those municipalities a non-resident fee of $70 a year for membership with the SPL, in some quarters it was thought to be retaliation for St. Marys' refusal to pay a $4,000 bill for computer services rendered at that library by the SPL systems administrator David Harvie.

Not so, says SPL director Jane Kirkpatrick. It was simply a case of St. Marys and North Perth no longer being entitled to the reciprocal

borrowing arrangement that had been in place under the PCIN agreement since January 2000. For St. Marys and North Perth, that arrangement officially ended on Oct. 15, 2001.

"It's obviously a bit disappointing we don't have all five (municipalities) now," said Dr. Susan Tamblyn, chair of the SPL board. "Our board and I believe all the partners are enjoying benefits such as sharing books and cataloguing."

"I hope it will eventually get resolved," said Kirkpatrick, "I think it will."

Incorporated in 2000, the PCIN is governed by a board comprising two

STRATFORD PUBLIC LIBRARY

PCIN Online Catalogue

www.stratford.library.on.ca

PERTH COUNTY INFORMATION NETWORK LIBRARY CATALOGUE

Now Available on the Internet!

www.stratford.library.on.ca

You can now search from home, place holds, and even renew your own books!

Catalogue includes the holdings of:
Stratford Public Library (STR)
West Perth Public Library (WPL)
Perth East Public Library (PEL)

If you have any questions about using the catalogue, **PLEASE ASK!**

STRATFORD PUBLIC LIBRARY

19 St. Andrew Street, Stratford ON N5A 1A2
(519) 271-0220
spl@pcin.on.ca

representatives from the trustees of each founding member. The SPL's reps at present are Michael Dale (PCIN vice-chair) and Marilyn Dimeo (PCIN secretary).

By logging on to www.pcin.on.ca, Net users can access information about community services and recreational resources, as well as the collections of all participating libraries. Members used software already in place at the SPL to catalogue and automate those collections with minimal cost.

As of Jan. 1, 2001, the resources available through the PCIN were 123,653 books (104,282 in Stratford), 4,869 video tapes (4,455 in Stratford), 2,315 compact disks (2,310 in Stratford) and 19 Internet stations (14 in Stratford).

It's estimated the partnership is saving each library close to 40 per cent in annual purchasing costs because of its central acquisition and processing functions. Further, the members now have a mechanism to collaborate in the areas of program planning, policy development, and training and collection development.

The Stratford-Perth Archives became the PCIN's fourth member in January 2002.

Get lost in a book

In the fall of 2000, on a suggestion from staffer Robin Godfrey, the SPL enlisted the voluntary services of film and stage actor Colm Feore, a city resident, in creating a limited-edition poster to raise money for its literacy initiatives.

Stratford photographer Terry Manzo had Feore pose with a book in Confederation Park. Heidi Holdsworth, also from Stratford, did the design work, and the library printed 1,000 posters, which went on sale in time for Christmas at $8 each, including tax ($13 with Feore's autograph).

In July 2001, the library launched the second installment in the series, featuring singer-actor Cynthia Dale.

In the following summer, actors Sheila McCarthy and Peter Donaldson dressed as trench-coated detectives for their photographic contribution to the fund-raiser.

The last stage and film celebrity in the four-poster set is Christopher Plummer, who posed for Manzo in November 2002. The fruit of their labour was unveiled at the SPL's first annual volunteers tea on May 1, 2003. It features Plummer reading a book amid leaves in the Chalmers room.

The first in the *Get lost . . . in a book* poster series

Manzo, Holdsworth and all of the actors donated their time and talents to the project.

Thus far, the Feore and Dale posters have netted more than $2,500 for the library, and the McCarthy-Donaldson edition is on the verge of showing a profit.

All are selling for $10 and $15 (signed). Because of exposure on the SPL's Web site, there have been sales across North America, and in Sweden, Germany and South Africa.

Sheila McCarthy and husband Peter Donaldson at the photo shoot for the third *Get Lost . . . in a Book* poster, June 2002. The location was the Huron Street bridge.

The SPL at night, 2002

Here's to "the best job in libraryland"

By Jane Kirkpatrick

In October 1982 I was visiting Stratford on the Thanksgiving Day weekend. My friend Leita and I walked down Ontario Street towards the courthouse. I remember standing on the corner and looking across the street to the library and saying to Leita, "Wouldn't that just be the best job in the world? To be chief librarian and able to live in Stratford year round?"

Lo and behold, when I attended the Ontario Library Association conference in November, *there* was the job posting.

I arrived in the middle of May 1983 and had two weeks overlap with my predecessor, Sue Bonsteel. By the end of the fortnight, I was thoroughly intimidated and ready to go back to Nepean. No way could I fill this woman's shoes!

Sue set an incredibly high standard of community service, and while I knew I had strong skills as an administrator, the public relations aspect of the job was not my forte. When I talked to Sue about it she just laughed and told me it was easy. And, in

Lorraine Greenberg (left) and Jane Kirkpatrick, July 2002

fact, the community involvement and public relations did become the best part of the job. I quickly grew to enjoy speaking to the Noon Hour Book Club, the service clubs and organizations such as Gallery Stratford. Of course, I was fortunate to have a really good programming co-ordinator on staff in the person of Lorraine Greenberg, and she helped me at first.

In the 1980s and well into the '90s we had a television show on Rogers Cable. Actually we had several, including "Your Card is the Key" and "Library Connections." As well, Rogers taped the weekly Noon Hour Book Club meetings. We worked with Ken Forrest, a really accommodating fellow, and had tremendous fun doing the shows. Almost all the staff got conscripted to come on the show at one time or another. Gail Poole and Kate Jacob were favourites with their storytelling episodes, and Katherine Seredynska was very comfortable in front of the camera. She could talk on just about anything to do with the library.

Unfortunately, it took a long time for us to get smart and tape the shows. In those days, Rogers filmed on ³/₄-inch tape, so we couldn't get copies from them.

I also had a lot of fun with my "Marion the librarian" column, wherein I answered patrons' questions about the library. (Marion the Librarian came from The Music Man.) A lot of the questions came from children, such as:

Dear Marion, Who are you and where do you live? Signed Curious.
Dear Curious, I'm Marion the Librarian and I live in the library of course!

Another thing I came to love was doing the radio spots on CJCS with the morning guy, first Mark Philbin and now Eddie Matthews. Mark and I would have a lot of fun kibitzing back and forth, and he always played Frankie Valli, Roy Orbison or early Beatles records on the morning I would be on air.

There are many appealing things about living in Stratford and working at the public library. I guess that is why my intended five-year stint has stretched to 20. By far, the most compelling reason for staying in Stratford has been the wonderful people with whom I work. The library staff is a second family. And yes, sometimes we have down times, just as any family does, but when you put those periods against the times we have supported each other through crises and celebrations, they become pretty insignificant. We are a staff who likes to party – birthdays, bridal showers, baby showers, retirements, farewells, welcomes, Christmas. For about 10 years I organized an SPL staff picnic around my birthday in August. We would go in shifts over to the Shakespearean Gardens and enjoy the park, some lunch and my birthday cake.

I like when we have projects that pull us together. Two stand out: the 1988 library automation project and the 1994 carpeting project. One of the things we had to do when we automated was place a bar code on every book and link it to a record in the database. With over 90,000 books, this was a massive undertaking. We decided that the fastest way to do it was to close the library and put everyone to work bar-coding. We called it the "week of the mums," because my mother, Helen, and Chris Wilson's mother, Joan, along with other volunteers, came in and checked in all the books being returned through the book drop. Every day someone would take responsibility for

SPL director Jane Kirkpatrick (left) with staffer Elizabeth McKay for a Rogers Cable TV taping of Your Card is the Key.

organizing lunch for us all. There were so many errors in the "smart" bar codes and the database that eventually all we could do was laugh. It was that or run screaming up Ontario Street. When I think back on it, I remember the fun we had. Oh yes, and how organized and efficient the project manager Christina Wilson was. I think our volunteers

Ask Marion the Librarian

If you have a question, a comment, a criticism or a compliment about library services, write it out below and place in Marion's box. Watch for Marion's answers in the Beacon-Herald.

This is what SPL patrons in the 1980s filled out to correspond with Marion the librarian. Marion (Jane Kirkpatrick) responded to their queries, comments or criticisms in the Beacon Herald.

The old and the new. This sample of the last version of SPL card before automation (top) belonged to George Graff. The first card issued after automation, No. 00000001, belongs to Jane Kirkpatrick.

changes when we had the whole floor cleared.

We hired two guys from the then-manpower office to help with moving the heavy furniture. Otherwise, the women of the SPL moved that floor. We had carts from a specialist mover in London, as well as boxes. There is a real art to taking books off the shelf and packing them so that they come back out in the correct order. All the books went upstairs to the auditorium, as did most of the furniture. The stacks were dismantled shelf by shelf and moved upstairs, too. I will never forget the three tech services ladies taking apart and moving the circulation desk. Everyone worked so hard that the floor was ready for carpeting a day and a half early, and we were pushing the contractor to get in and get working.

All the time this was going on, we were offering service on the lower floor and staff members were running to the top floor to try to find books from the storage. We saved enough money on the main floor that we were able to carpet the lower floor as well, so that it was a bit of a rush trying to get a tender out and things packed up so the project would be finished by September when school went back in. What a team and what fun we had.

One of the most rewarding aspects of my tenure as library director has been the opportunity to work with librarians as they start their career or take the next step. There have been excellent people come to work here, and it is quite exciting for me to see where they go. One is a senior systems administrator in a large library, one a chief librarian, one a senior manager in a regional system, one a head librarian, one heading up a government library, one a training librarian at an East Coast university. They are a credit to their profession and, I'm pleased to say, all good friends now. I was fortunate to inherit a couple of top-notch librarians who are with us still, and to hire

enjoyed their peek at what happens when the library is not open.

Recarpeting the main floor in 1994 was another mammoth job. We had been trying for several years to get the funding from city council but couldn't get approval. The big stumbling block was the cost of the movers and storage. I don't remember now which staff member suggested we do the moving ourselves, but when it was put to the staff, enough of them volunteered that we thought we could do it. With the project cost reduced by $30,000, we got the go-ahead from council. Our systems librarian at the time had been a planning librarian at the D. B. Weldon Library at the University of Western Ontario, and she was invaluable at creating diagrams and plotting how we would rearrange stacks and furniture. Naturally, we took the opportunity to make

"I Survived the Carpet Move of 1994!"

Artwork from the front of the T-shirts awarded to those who helped in the recarpeting project, summer 1994

them don't decline the appointment. No, they stay and work hard to learn the acronyms, the jargon, the issues. They care deeply about the library and its staff, and, while we don't always agree, we have a mutual respect and can deal with the differences. It is also interesting to me that in 20 years, in a city the size of Stratford, there have been only three people appointed that I knew beforehand – all from city council (Christopher Blake, Harry Nesbitt and Karen Haslam).

good people who opted to stay with the organization, providing us with stability.

I have also been incredibly fortunate in terms of the library boards I have worked for since 1983. Boards are an interesting phenomenon. Nine people come together every three years, charged with operating an organization that employs 24 people and has a budget well in excess of $1 million. They have legal responsibilities under the Public Libraries Act, the Municipal Conflict of Interest Act, the Municipal Freedom of Information/Protection to Privacy Act, and the Health and Safety Act, to name but a few. They get no compensation for what they do.

Every three years, after I've done the board orientation, I am amazed that most of

I don't think you can have a history of the library without mentioning the patrons – the citizens for whom we exist and who, in fact, own this place. I said earlier that the staff are like family. Well, so it is with our patrons. We have a significant number of registered users, about 70 per cent of the population, and that is high when you compare statistics in the library community. Many of those borrowers are, as I said, like family. They share in our joys and sorrows; they have helped us through the grief of losing staffers Gail Poole and Guy McKone. They adapt with good cheer to changes in

The reference desk

Few library services anywhere have been more warmly embraced by the public than the reference department, which in Stratford has gone from a desk to a room to a kiosk with a computer.

Libraries are considered to be repositories of information, and patrons expect the people who staff them to be able to put their fingers on just about all of that information.

It wasn't until the board hired Sue Bonsteel in 1970 that the Stratford Public Library had someone whose job title was "reference librarian." But all who had worked at the SPL before her, and all who have been there since her arrival, have been reference librarians, for it is generally held that all librarians are people in the know. It's not a matter of whether they are able to answer one's question, rather how long it will take.

Librarians tend to commit to memory one or two favourites from the hundreds of queries they have fielded. SPL staffer Anne Marie Heckman says one of hers was out of this world: "Somebody wanted to know when their interplanetary loan would be in. They had an inter-library loan request and they came in asking about their interplanetary loan."

Employees of the Stratford Festival have asked some of the most unusual questions, she says. "We spent hours on them. They used the library a lot. One of my most interesting was for the skull of a bear. They needed to know the bone structure of a bear for A Winter's Tale. I had to find the skeleton of a bear because they needed the face."

She also recalls the Festival wanting to know the design and colour of paper money from a specific country and time period. But the Festival doesn't call

Staffer Kate Jacob fields a question for a young patron in the children's department.

much anymore, because it has developed a sizeable database of its own, and most of what it still might need is available on the Internet.

When it comes to reference, the Internet has also revolutionized the way librarians do business. "The nature of work in the library has changed (because of technology)," says SPL director Jane Kirkpatrick. "We now spend much more time giving (Internet) instruction to patrons. We spend as much time selecting appropriate Internet sites as we do on choosing books to go in the collection.

"Selecting those sites is more critical in some respects. When children come in to use our Internet, they are directed to sites that have been vetted by the librarians. So we help create search paths for people now. The nature of the work has changed. It's still essentially the same work, but what's involved is different."

While some of the questions from patrons are novel, most are practical. These are some examples: Do you have the Employment Standards Act? Do you have any information about mutual funds? How do I go about conducting an employment interview? Can you give me an economic and demographic profile of Stratford? How do I develop a business plan? Can you give me a list of all the major newspapers in Australia? Where can I get a list of suppliers of straw hats?

Questions for the SPL reference desk in 2002 numbered about 90,000, the most yet for any one year.

SPL

A birthday cake for the boss, Jane Kirkpatrick, in August 1984.

routine, suggest new books for us and, most important, keep us well supplied with goodies. For example, we know the Christmas season is upon us when we receive our tray of exotic home-baking, dates, figs and nuts from one of our regulars.

We love it when someone takes the time to send a thank you note telling us that our reference assistance has helped them get a job, complete their General Educational Development courses, or deal with a health issue. We love to see the wonder on a child's face when she discovers she's reading by herself. We love to hear the laughter of the children in story time. We love the thrill of the hunt and being able to present a patron with the answer to his question. The neat thing about the library is that it is here for everyone, whether you are from the theatre, the education system, the home, the service sector, the factory or the farm. We cross all those sectors and thus have a wonderful opportunity to meet and help people with diverse interests. I love that part of the job.

All of this is not to say that we don't have situations in which dealing with a patron can be a challenge. Policies and rules can sometimes be frustrating for people, and they can react pretty strongly with staff. I think because 99 per cent of our borrowers are so great, when we do encounter the one per cent, the situation takes on epic proportions. Coming from an environment

where drug deals went down in the stacks, and where staff had to break up gang fights, I found Stratford to be a paradise, and it has continued that way.

When I joined Stratford Public Library in 1983, I planned to stay for five or six years and then move on to a larger library. By 1988, I had concluded that I already had the best job in "libraryland," so why move on? I have worked with and for great people. I've had lots of challenges to keep me engaged. And I live in a wonderful and unique city. Twenty years later, all my reasons for coming to Stratford – and staying in Stratford – have not changed.

Library 101 in "the city of the pork congress"
By Chris Wilson

Christina Wilson was the head of adult services at the Stratford Public Library from 1985 to 1988. During that time she headed the SPL's automation project. She is now manager, technical support services for Cambridge Libraries and Galleries.

I was here for a short time, but for me it was pivotal. It was a great place for me. Jane (Kirkpatrick) was a great person to work for. She gave me some good opportunities to succeed and to fail, and that's how you learn. And I learned so much from Marion (Gibb), Dorothy (Robinson), Lorraine (Greenberg), Gail (Poole), Billie (Kirkby), Anne Marie (Heckman), Theresa (Talsma), all those people.

I was one of those young things coming in out of library school with a lot of ideals. I had ideas and some practice, but things were reshaped here. I never, never had a problem coming to work here. I never had to drag myself out of bed. I loved walking across town to come to come to work. I lived over on Bay Street, and it was like being in Europe in a way. I'd walk to work, meet a lot of our patrons along the way, get

here, do my job, walk home at night, stop at Loblaws, buy a few fruits. The life and the job were great.

SPL

Christina Wilson, July 2002

With this job, because so much crossed your path, you knew so much about what was going on here – the politics, the business, the history, the agriculture. It's an inspiring community to serve. There were some days when I would open that door, step out, and the smell was overwhelming. You knew you were in the city of the pork congress. You just knew that somebody was spreading manure on their field. The neat thing about this town is that it's not pretentious, even though it's Stratford. You'd see all these people walking to the theatre in their finery, smelling that same smell. I used to like those kinds of contrasts.

When I was here we had 3.5 librarians, and we met every Wednesday morning in the auditorium for a management meeting. Jane really encouraged us to get involved in the profession. During the time I was here I was an executive member of the Ontario Library Association, and I participated in doing their conferences and everything, and that was really through Jane's leadership. That's a dangerous thing for a chief librarian to do, you know, because there's the possibility that you get to see other positions, other libraries, meet other chief librarians. But it really was good for people like Elizabeth (McKay) and me, to grow in the profession. I think it's Jane's contribution, to keep people like us in it, and positive and making a difference. And I think it really has made a difference. But Jane would say, 'That's my job.'

DEAN ROBINSON

Scenes from the mural of Disney characters created
by staffers Mary Lynn Cook and Norma Bissonnette
in the children's department, in time for Christmas
1981

"A really fine children's service"

Children have always been a part of the Stratford Public Library on St. Andrew Street. "To the left of the main entrance is another reading room, but of smaller dimensions," reads a newspaper's description of the newly constructed building in 1903. "This is set aside for the children and is called the children's reading room. Both rooms are in view of the librarian, who can thus see that order is preserved."

For the 100 years since, the SPL has been an exciting world for young minds, a place to play and a place to learn. While their styles have varied, the librarians charged with preserving the order of those children have spared little in their efforts to entertain and educate.

While Louise Johnston and her staff no doubt did their best to accommodate the youngsters who visited the SPL, and Jennie Daly introduced the ever-popular story hour, it was Lois Thompson who made the Stratford children's department among the best anywhere. You won't get an argument

on that point from Joyce Banks, who worked under Miss Thompson for more than a decade.

"Lois was a wonderful children's librarian," she says, "and she had a really good collection of children's literature in that library. She really knew children's literature. She was quite remarkable in that respect. I bracket her with people like Judith St. John at the Osborne collection (Osborne Collection of Early Children's Book, Toronto Public Library), and Margaret Maloney, also at the Osborne collection, and Irene Aubrey, who was founder of the children's literature service at the National Library of Canada.

"I trained to be a children's librarian, and I met a few of them in my time. I would look back at what was in our collection (in Stratford), and think, oh boy, she (Lois Thompson) was right on top of it; she knew what she was doing. She was smart, and she cared about it (the department). And I think she was respected outside of Stratford, too. She was the only one on staff when I was there to have had any formal library training. The rest of us learned by being there.

"We had a really fine children's service. Even though this was not a wealthy library, we managed to have a very fine collection. And, of course, Lois was a masterful storyteller. The kids loved her. When I went to the IODE with

Staffers Mary Lynn Cook (left) and Carol Robinson, puppet corner power, 1981

the Lois Thompson Memorial Essay Contest idea (in 2002), there were women in that room who remembered going to story hour or who took their children there. One of my closest friends is about 60, and she went regularly to story hour."

Stories are a time-proven essential in the children's department of the SPL. But so are puppets. For years, the staffers have been enticing young patrons with the promise of puppet appeal, paper puppetcraft, puppet performance, purely puppets, puppets with pizzazz, puppets on parade, and a puppet pageant.

In the summer of 1974, SPL employees Geraldine Cuerden and Janet Robertson presented a series of improvised puppet plays, after building a stage of chipboard and making curtains from crepe paper.

The library has also called upon professionals such as The Friendly Puppet People, Puppet Pandemonium, The TV Puppetree Company, The Playful Hands Puppet Theatre, The Pepi Puppet Theatre, The Purple Dragon Puppet Troupe, and Pea Pod Puppet Productions.

In August 1976, the SPL hired Cheryl Smith of Exeter to conduct two four-day workshops on puppeteering. She taught about 35 eager youngsters how to create puppets and how to make them perform. Previously, she had taken some of her puppets on rounds with the SPL bookmobile in an effort to encourage children to read.

Smith and her husband, Richard Keelan of the Perth County Conspiracy musical group, ran a business called No Strings Attached Puppeteers, and one of the dates on their performance calendar in 1976 was at the SPL. They entertained their wide-eyed audience with two shows, Jacques the Woodcutter and Winnie the Pooh.

Other puppeteers to bring their talents to the Stratford library have included Jeff Marontate, Marian Doucette and Pat Lewis.

Live theatre has drawn the same sort of favour among the SPL's younger crowd, particularly when the playbill has announced the likes of Aunt Betty's Rhubarb Pies children's theatre company, The Toy Town Troupers, The Port Stanley Players, Stratford Children's Theatre, The Erewhon Theatre of Canada, The

Enchanters Theatre Troupe, The Whirligig Children's Theatre, The Cascade Theatre Company, Performers for Literacy, Children's Trio Productions, Generic Theatre, and Turkey Rhubarb.

The various other children's performers who have played the SPL include Jill Carter, who starred in an environmental play called Mother Earth; Mr. P the talking screwdriver; Magpie Jim and Magpie Wayne; Captain Cam and Ben; a musical trio called Picks and Sticks; and magicians Mr. Oh! (Owen Anderson), Rick Rossini, Mert the Magnificent, Bill Van Gorder, John Henley, Abra, and The Great Gerard (Gerard Dietrich).

Entertainment has long been a conduit for learning, and nowhere more than at the SPL, where kids have been taught everything from juggling to oil painting to communicating with sign language to building and flying a kite. They have learned about working with plasticine and clay from Barbara Reid; clown performance, makeup and costumes from Nancy Musselman; art appreciation and skills from Ted Harrison of Porter Creek, Yukon; yo-yo tricks from world champion Fast Eddy MacDonald; flipbook animation from Patrick Jenkins; fencing from Paddy Crean; and physical fitness from Heather Thompson of the YMCA.

They have been sung to or read to by Bob Schneider, Robert Munsch, Eric Nagler, Robert Peck, Janet Foster, Jean Little, Peter Mennie, Celia Lottridge, Erick Traplin, Dean Griffiths, and Sharon, Lois and Bram. And they have done their share of reading and singing.

Not all of the special guests in the children's department have been people. In February 1981, Jim Lovisek of the Toronto Nature Centre was accompanied by 10 snakes, including an eight-foot Bimini boa constrictor from the Bahamas called Julius Squeezer II, and a ball python from Africa. About 100 children showed up for his

ANNE MARIE HECKMAN

Delsyn Stott makes a new friend during The Snake Lady's visit, March 2002. Bent over behind them is *Beacon Herald* photographer Scott Wishart.

Snakes Alive show, a hands-on experience.

In July 1992, Brad Brezina was at the SPL with his exotic pet show. In 1994, also in July, Ron Bauman of the Grand River Conservation Authority presented For the Birds, a wildlife program that featured a live wild turkey named Tom.

During the March-break week in 2002, The Snake Lady, Valerie Means of London, entertained about 120 children and adults with a 90-minute show that featured snakes, lizards, tarantulas and frogs.

The SPL has always been a busy and exciting place during the March school breaks. Through the years, those weeks have been enhanced with more story hours, more crafts, more puppets and more magicians.

Many have unfolded around themes,

Children's librarian Sally Hengeveld with Megan Callan (left) and Lisa Pryde during the Turn on the Sun events at the SPL, March 1982.

ranging from Turn on the Sun to The Greatest Show on Earth to Medieval Times, and they have included sand sculpting, a luau, hula lessons, a jungle, fruit punches, a limbo contest, sword-making, and underwater displays.

The numerous "book" and "library" weeks that have been observed through the years have also generated a flurry of children's events. In the 1940s and '50s there was Young Canada's Book Week, whose focus was rarely lost on the public. In November 1958, the week's patroness, Senator Muriel McQueen Fergusson, said, "Today in rural Canada, only 15 per cent of our children have access to public library services. Efforts should continue until these services are available to all Canadian children."

In October 1988 the SPL held a story-writing contest for children and young adults to help mark the fourth annual Ontario Public Library Week. The topic was "Why my library books are late," and the competition attracted 243 entries. The winners and honourable mentions were, in the five-to-seven-year-old division: Caroline Simpson and Stephanie Carlisle (Chelsea Clark, Brent Johnson, Matt Busigan); eight-to-11-year-old division: Sarah Falconer (Jordan Lemmon, Devon Searle, Kathy O'Connor, Geoff Whitlock); and the 12-to-17-year-old division: Kirsten Van Drunen (Tina Eidukaiis, Pat O'Reilly, Gregory Dack, John-Paul Bell).

In October 2002, in celebration of the same week, the library asked those up to 12 years of age to name the new pony in the youth section of the library. From between 80 and 100 entries, the pony became Paige, a friend for Dewey the dragon, who came on staff in October 2001. At one time the department also had a dog called Raggs, who liked to hang out near Midget Mountain.

Summers, too, have been jammed with children's activities, and often the students assigned to lead them have been hired by the SPL with the help of government grants.

In August 1979, they held a baking competition, for which the judges were Winnifred Henderson, former children's librarian; Rev. Fred Faist of St. John's United Church; Lorraine Greenberg of the library staff; Brian McKone, head of the SPL's audio-video department; and Ann Gagnon, the children's librarian. There was another such contest in 1980.

In July 1981, members of the children's reading club, in re-enacting the Peter Pan story, joined Captain Coat-hook (Stratford Information Centre co-ordinator Paul McKone) and his mates Linda Drennan and Carol Robinson (both from the children's department of the library) for a pirates

In 2000, the theme of the summer was wilderness, and the program featured Canada's national parks, wild animals and reptiles, the ocean, sports, the environment, travel, science and natural wonders, and weather. At the heart of the program was a children's reading kit developed and made available to public libraries in Ontario by the TD Bank Financial Group.

There was also a series of events planned around the release of the fourth book in the Harry Potter series.

In 2001 the TD kits supported a program called the Summer Sleuth Reading Challenge, for which children could register as senior sleuths (ages 9-11), clue catchers (ages 6-8) or top secret tots (ages 2-5)

There were also free Friday movies related to castaways, legends, heroes, Halloween, dinosaurs, science and meet an author.

The reading theme in 2002 was Exploring the Wonders of the World, which included oceans, safaris, rainforests, lost treasurers, science, and folklore and legends. The participants were divided into the touring team, the compass crew and the map munchkins.

Staffer Anne Marie Heckman and ???? sample entries in the children's cooking contest, November 1980.

cruise aboard the H. M. S. Pinafore on Lake Victoria.

In 1982, about 40 youngsters, members of the SPL's craft club, met through the month of August to make a quilt to commemorate the 150th anniversary of the settlement of Stratford, and the 80th anniversary of the founding of their library. Their huge effort was hung along a wall in the library through the autumn months.

In the early 1990s, there was a read-around-the-world program and a babysitter's club in the summer afternoons.

Stratford *Beacon Herald* photographer Lloyd Dark discusses picture possibilities with Captain Coat-hook (Paul McKone) and his pirate mate (SPL staffer) Carol Robinson during a children's outing in July 1981.

Bedford School, Mon. July 5-Aug. 23, 10-12 A.m. (except Aug.2)

St. Aloysius School, Fri. July 9 - Aug. 20 10-12 A.m.

Juliet School, Mon. July 5- Aug. 23, 2-4 P.m. (except Aug. 2)

Mystery, Mystery, and more Mystery at your SUMMER LIBRARY!

Shakespeare School,

St. Joseph's School, Thurs. July 8- Aug. 19, 10-12 A.m.

Tue. July 6-Aug. 17, 10-12 A.m.

Sponsored by the Stratford Public Library, the Perth County Board of Education, and the Perth County Roman Catholic Separate School Board.

The SPL's summer schedule for city schools, 1982

There was also a read-around-the-world game, a reading circle, a quest box (family history) workshop, a movie night with popcorn, a magic show, and a star-studded stories series. The latter, which ran on seven Tuesday evenings, brought children of all ages to the auditorium to hear half-hour readings by local "stars," namely Jim Chapryk, a city councillor; Kirsten Blaine, a pediatrician; Pat Stanley, Anne Hathaway Public School principal; Karen Haslam, Stratford mayor; Ken Nutt, children's book author and illustrator; Carol Smith, former children's programmer at the SPL; and Rob Neves, early literacy specialist.

As well as offering a full slate of activities in-house each summer, the SPL has often been part of an outreach program that involved city parks and the libraries and playgrounds of schools. Just as often, the leaders have been hired with the help of government funding.

Their offerings have included crafts, drama, games, music, films, stories, and, of course, puppet shows. Their aim was to stimulate an interest in books and libraries, and to keep children and adults reading through the summer months.

One year, they staged Highland games. On another occasion, at Dufferin Park, they used a parachute as the central object for two games. The Olympic Games were the theme one summer.

Usually, the leaders took their road show from school to school or park to park, and sometimes brought the program to a close with a barbecue on the last day at each location.

Not all of the SPL's outreach for children has been in the summer. Early in January 1988, for instance, staffers Linda Drennan and Elizabeth McKay dressed in medieval costumes to visit Shakespeare elementary school, where they helped to kick off a study unit on the Middle Ages with hour-long story and film sessions.

Seasonal events have always been a reason for special activities at the SPL, whether making cards for Mother's Day or masks for Halloween. At Easter one year,

A Halloween party in the children's department, October 1990

there was an egg hunt in the nearby Shakespearean Gardens, followed by the showing of two Easter films. The staff also set up an incubator and hatched some chicks.

Sometimes the library's special events have stood on their own, usually reflecting the interests of the day. In May 1975 there was a martial arts festival for school-age children.

In April 1979 there was a series of films to coincide with the International Year of the Child. There were also discussions for adults on child abuse, Big Brothers, Big Sisters, health and nutrition, children's aid, and children's rights.

In December 1987, a curator from the Waterloo Museum and Archive of Games used slides in showing the assembled how to play Inuit games.

In April 1988, Karen Stemmle, a member of Canada's national ski team, talked to the children of the SPL.

On a Saturday afternoon in May 1993, author and craftsperson Julie Ann Sadler was at the library for a doll-making program that was open to kids and their parents.

In April 2002, the library, the Upper Thames River Conservation Authority and the Civic Beautification and Environmental Awareness Committee combined their efforts in recognition of Earth Day. Events at the SPL included a craft night for families.

Films and videos have been as much a mainstay in the children's department as in other sections of the library. The fare has ranged from cycling to surfing, from Laurel and Hardy to Charlotte's Web and Mary Poppins. In March and April 1975, there was a Saturday fairy tale film festival that featured The Story of Cinderella, The Ugly Duckling, and Tom Thumb in King Arthur's Court.

In September 1985 the boys and girls department at the SPL became the youth

Stratford Public Library   19 St. Andrew Street, Stratford, Ontario

Dear Friend,

        You are most cordially invited to attend the Official Opening of the Stratford Public Library's newly renovated areas: the Audio-Visual Department and the new Teen Services Area.

        Opening ceremonies will take place at 2:30 during the afternoon of Sunday, February 9th on the lower floor of the Library.

        Bring your friends and family to attend the ribbon-cutting ceremony, to view the special display of art work and to tour our new and enhanced services.

                Hope to see you there!

                Jane Kirkpatrick

                N5A 1A2 Telephone (519) 271-0220

services department, and the library announced it was creating a teen services area, to be overseen by Carol-Todd Robinson.

On Feb. 9, 1986, Mayor Ted Blowes was on hand to help officially open the new teen

area, as well as the renovated audio-visual department. The former was given the name Young Adult Konnection – YAK for short, and was located in the A-V lounge area in the basement. It featured more than 2,000 teen-oriented books and a reading room, as well as listening posts for A-V equipment.

Programs in the teen area included a movie series called "hot-buttered flicks," the fun of photography with Scott Wishart, and fashion and beauty for teens with Paro Bickell.

SPL

Looking east in the children's room, on the south half of the second floor, 1973. Bookshelves were placed above the main beams of the building. The floor was carpeted in blue.

SPL

Kid's Internet Site

The SPL Kid's Website is now available from home!
www.stratford.library.on.ca/kids/home.htm
From this site you can find professionally selected websites for homework help, book stuff, fun and games, search engines for children, information regarding Internet safety, and much more!
Try it out today!

In February 1988, gifted Grade 6 students from across Perth County created maps of fantasy lands which were displayed in SPL's youth services department.

While changes in the physical space of the children's area have been far fewer than in the programs, they have been significant. From the main floor to the second floor to the basement, the kids have been shuffled about.

In January 1969 their second-floor quarters were re-carpeted in a bright green-blue, mostly to improve the soundproofing of their room.

When the addition was being built in 1974-75, the children's department moved with the rest of the library to the former A&P grocery store on Erie Street. There, librarian Jane Crozier invited her adaptable young charges to create a wall mural to help spruce up their temporary digs. The theme was "What would you like to see in the library's new addition?" The imaginative painters responded with lions, bears, a soft drink machine, a swimming pool, televisions, and books about pets and the making of airplanes.

Upon their return to St. Andrew Street, the children were relocated in the basement, where they have remained. In the fall of 1981, staffers Mary Lynn Cook (full time) and Norma Bissonnette (part time) enlivened the department by designing and creating a wall mural of Disney cartoon characters. They dedicated their four-by-16-foot work to the young and the young at heart.

They based their creations on material they dug up in the library.

The youth services department continues to be a beehive of activity, with a schedule that includes Babytime (six-18 months), Lambs' Tales for Twos ((19-36 months) and Storytime for Preschoolers (three to five years).

The library has published a series of flyers to help parents and caregivers select appropriate reading material for kids of all ages.

The department's most notable sign of the times is an interactive computer network available for kids up to 12. Comprising six stations, it is designed to provide Internet access and training.

When it was officially launched on the afternoon of Oct. 20, 2001, Dr. Susan Tamblyn, chair of the library board, said, "We have done our utmost to make this a safe computer experience for children. The search engines are designed specially for children." Librarian Sally Hengeveld said she and her colleagues spent about four months selecting child-appropriate sites and search engines – which don't include chat rooms and e-mail.

But amid all of the changes, some things have stayed the same. Winnifred Henderson probably said it best for all children's librarians at the SPL when she talked about making it a happy place.

From culture club to creepy crawlers

Through the years, those in the children's department of the Stratford Public Library have had little trouble drawing a crowd, in part because of the titles they have given their many programs and special events. Who wouldn't want to show up for Pinocchio's big bad lie contest, or Emmet Otter's jug-band Christmas?

Some of the other catchy handles include kids kapers, culture club, wacky Wednesdays, mad hatter mix, monster mania, the big snooze, the art of stampooning, play dough day, laughs unlimited, turkey talk, Jack-o-who-who, mad scientists' day, make merry music, tittle tattle . . . tell a tale, buckskins and buckboards, make way for ducklings, practically people, Peter Pan and other favourites, bunny tales, juggling jesters in January, pipecleanosaurus, clothespin creatures, the land of leprechauns and lucky charms, one tough turkey, penguins on parade, dinosaur daze, make magnificent masks, flick Friday, who done it Wednesday, wishful Wednesday, wordy Wednesday, way back when Wednesday, Garfield in disguise, fabulous frogs, discover Columbus, discover science, discover music, skeletons in the closet, scarecrows, cornzapoppin', old-fashioned Christmas, adventures through the reading glass, king for a day reading club, knights and legends, 'twas in the moon of wintertime, whale watching at the library, playdough party, and creepy crawlers.

Some titles have been in the form of pronouncements or questions: It's a hodgepodge harvest, Here's your chance to go hog wild on lucky Friday the 13th, Birds of a feather stick together, Make a kite fly on a windy day, Time flies with Rip Van Winkle, I never saw a purple cow, Want to get to know a great dane? What will you get if your sheep studies karate? Where's Waldo?

Then, there have been: hop, hop, hoppy Easter; homburg, astrakhan, tuque and sombrero; little people, gnomes, leprechauns and Martians; nitwits, numbskulls and knuckleheads; gobble, gobble, gobble; frogs a jumpin', frogs a leapin', frogs, frogs everywhere; Willy Nilly, Jelly Belly; and films, fiddles and whimmydiddles.

The SPL's children's/youth services department heads

Lois Thompson 1921-1954

Winnifred Henderson 1954-1974

Jane Crozier 1974-1978

Ann Gagnon 1978-1979

Valerie Clarke 1980-1981

Sally Hengeveld 1981-1986

Warren James 1986-1987

Sally Hengeveld and Anne Marie Heckman 1987-1989

Lesley Beckett 1989-1990

Katherine Seredynska 1990-1995

Sally Hengeveld 1995-

Making the library a happy place

Winnifred Henderson's work at the Stratford Public Library dates back to her high school years. In the spring of 1930 she was on the Stratford Public Library's staff list as supply help. In September of that year she was appointed circulation assistant, upon the retirement of Doreen Bishop. In 1954, when Lois Thompson replaced Jennie Daly as head librarian, Miss Henderson became the children's librarian, the position she held until her retirement at the end of 1974.

In July 2002 she penned the following reminiscences of her days at the SPL:

"City schools and some country schools patronized the library, and their students arrived by bus or car. They sat on the floor in front of my circular desk. I told them about our library, and how books were arranged on the shelves with the Dewey Decimal numbers. One time I purchased artificial daffodils and gave one to each child as they left. It was quite a sight.

"There was a small display table for special days (Christmas, Easter, Valentine's, etc.), and many interesting things to look at. There was a big ship in a glass case at the end of the room. It was made by a Mr. Davis. The (stuffed) squirrels in a glass case drew a lot of attention. 'Are they real? They are not moving.' I replied, 'No, they are resting.'

"There were some big tables for children to sit down and read, and there were tables for tots, so they could look at picture books. One little girl used to say, 'Always wear that dress when I come to the library.'

"The children liked to play with the toys kept on a shelf near my desk. Sometimes, if the weather was hot and humid, I decorated those shelves with glass icicles and used cotton batting for snow.

"I always gave a little talk as to why the children should join the library – for information, to improve their reading, or just for fun. Usually, I showed a picture book or told a short story. Then they were free to browse or choose a book to read. I never had any behavior problems. My ambition was to make the library a happy place.

"The story hour was held Saturday mornings in the auditorium. We were very lucky to have a stage – and a blackboard. The auditorium was also a schoolroom for a while.

"There were treats for special days – candy canes and apples and oranges for Christmas, and coloured eggs at Easter. If a child wanted to recite a verse or do something, they were welcome to do so at story hour.

"When the Shakespearean Festival was on, we had visitors from the vicinity and the United States, too, who were intrigued with our library.

"We worked four nights one week and three nights the next week, and all day on Saturday. We repaired some books, and sent others to Albert Taylor in the city, or to Ridgetown.

"At one point, some of the staff were Jennie Daly, chief librarian; and Lois Thompson, children's librarian; and Kay Arnold, Jean MacDougall, and Margaret Rosamond were supply.

"When I was in Toronto visiting relatives, a librarian invited me to her home. She also invited a class of teenagers. I was happy to give them a talk on Stratford and our library. They were very interested and planned to come that summer to the Festival.

"I certainly enjoyed myself when I was children's librarian. Our library will celebrate 100 years in 2003. That is something to look forward to."

Story hour in a storied place

If one were looking for pillars of the children's department at the Stratford Public Library, the short list would have to include story hour, the innovation introduced on a weekly basis by Jennie Daly, soon after she became the SPL's head librarian in 1911.

It started at 10:30, and for decades it attracted as many as 200 inquisitive young minds to the library each Saturday morning from September to Easter. Regularly, there was a lineup of juvenile patrons awaiting the opening of the library on those mornings. Once inside, they raced to the children's room or auditorium, where they would squat on the floor, scramble onto radiators and squeeze into the windowsills.

The hour usually featured three stories, but on occasion some of the attendees would be recruited for the presentation of a play. Or there were special guests, such as James Reaney, who in November 1943 told the story of Cinderella by using puppets. At the end of such mornings it was common for many of the children to sign out books from which the stories had been drawn.

The longest serving of the SPL storytellers has been Lois Thompson, who headed the children's department for more than 30 years, before becoming chief librarian in 1954. There were 26 children's story hours at the library that year.

Miss Thompson's ability to hold audiences spellbound was due, in part at least, to her skills as an elocutionist. Comfortable on the stage, she enjoyed reading stories. "I get a chuckle when someone meets me on the street and says 'You used to tell me

stories,'" she said in 1969, her last year before retirement. By then, the popularity of television was making it harder to attract older children to help with story hour.

As interesting as her stories, was the children's room at the library, which Miss Thompson decorated to reflect each special day or season – Halloween, Christmas, Easter.

On its shelves were books in the Little Cousin series and the ever-popular animal tales of Thornton Burgess and Beatrix Potter. They were joined by the stories of Rudyard Kipling, Walter De la Mare, Hugh Lofting and Lewis Carroll. At the other end of the room were volumes for older children and a reference section that included "books of knowledge" and a four-volume set of The Boy Mechanic. There were illustrated works, such as Peter Pan, Black Beauty and The Book of Indian Braves, which could not be taken from the children's room unless requested by a parent.

Book fare for the SPL's younger patrons ranged from fantasy to far-off places, from mediaeval to mystery, from adventure to

SPL

Librarian Sally Hengeveld and friends in the summer reading program, August 1999

astral. To encourage reading, Miss Thompson was not above contests and competition. In 1940, for instance, she built a miniature cardboard house whose walls were covered with scenes from storybooks. On each of the roof shingles she wrote the name of a Stratford boy or girl as he or she completed the reading of six suggested books. The goal was to determine which city school had the best-read students. The winner was Avon, followed by Romeo, St. Joseph's, Hamlet and Shakespeare (tied), Falstaff, Juliet and Anne Hathaway. The shingles also bore the names of four out-of-town schoolchildren who had heard of the challenge while visiting Stratford in the summer. Two were from Toledo, Ohio, one from Great Neck, N.Y., and the other from Ottawa.

Stories and books were not the only appeal in the children's room. For many years there was, under glass on a table, An Anciente Mappe of Fairyland, which was donated by the John MacDonald chapter of the Imperial Order Daughters of the Empire. In a corner sat a small glass case of stuffed squirrels, compliments of Catherine Murr, wife of the library's janitor.

"I visited the library only three or four times as a child," says Sally Hengeveld, who now heads the SPL's youth services department, "but I remember coming and talking to those squirrels, and being told by one of the staff members that I was being too loud. I'm sure they told me very nicely, and I probably was being loud. I tended to go to the Bayfield Public Library after that. My parents had a cottage up there. I guess I was pretty embarrassed that day (at the SPL). Maybe I was embarrassed because I thought the squirrels were real."

Below the squirrels was a similar box of stuffed Muskoka birds, a gift from Agnes (Mrs. Edward) Sydney-Smith. There was also a stuffed baby seal, which had come from Newfoundland and was a gift from Bessie (Mrs. Thomas) Ballantyne.

Our library

The following was written by Marion Illman, 10, on Jan. 30, 1937, during story hour at the SPL.

Row upon row,
Wherever one looks,
On our libra'y shelves,
Are books and books.

Books for little ones,
With pictures bright,
Books for older ones,
Tales that delight.

Stories of Fairyland,
Nature and hist'ry,
Tales of adventure,
With thrills and myst'ry.

Once every week,
For an hour or so,
Stories are told,
And we like to go.

The room's eye-catcher for many years was a model of a fully rigged 1860s English sailing ship called The Emperor, built by William Thomas Davis in 1895. He had been a shipbuilder in England, until he immigrated to Stratford in the 1870s to work in the Grand Trunk Railway repair shops. The Emperor had been used to bring immigrants to Canada.

W. T. Davis eventually moved to St. Ignace, Mich. His model was given to the library in 1923 through his brother O. W. Davis, and it was exhibited in a glass cabinet measuring more than five feet in length, $4^1/_2$ feet in height and 15 inches deep.

The Emperor became part of a collection

of artifacts whose stewardship was assumed by the Perth County Historical Association. She was eventually moved from the library and, for a while, was on display in the Perth County courthouse. Some of that collection is now owned jointly by the county and the City of Stratford, and The Emperor has found a home in the Stratford-Perth Museum.

The stuffed squirrels and birds that once shared library space with The Emperor also became part of the historical association collection, but, for the most part, their future was snuffed several years ago by vandals who broke into the building that housed some of the museum's collection.

Amid the changes that have transformed the children's department, story hour has remained a constant, albeit repackaged, rescheduled and renamed. After the children's area was moved from the second floor to the basement, when the library was enlarged in 1975, story hour became children's hour.

Children's hour retained the Saturday morning time slot, but the SPL introduced other activities for children from Monday through Friday, beginning at 4:30 p.m.

A preschool story time was also added to the weekly program, and in 1977 it was running at 10:30 a.m. and 2:30 p.m. on Thursdays, for kids 3 to 5. "We introduce the children to books, records, films, games and creative play," said librarian Jane Crozier.

While children listened to stories, their parents or caregivers were invited to the auditorium, to learn finger painting and other crafts, all designed to help them amuse their kids at home.

DEAN ROBINSON

The Emperor, now on display at the Stratford-Perth Museum

By 1977, Anne Marie Heckman was in charge of the mother's program, and the areas of discussion included pets for preschoolers, choosing good toys, indoor gardening, nutrition for children and selecting a music teacher.

In the spring of that year the SPL had an eight-week session for new mothers and children only.

In January 1982 the library began offering bedtime story sessions, called Wynken, Blynken and Nod, on Wednesdays beginning at 7 p.m. Each half-hour session included stories, songs and finger plays. Admission was free, and children were invited to wear pyjamas and bring along their teddy bears.

A decade later, the bedtime series was being advertised as "a lively drop-in story time for children 2 to 5," and it was at 7 p.m. on Mondays.

During the summer months, it wasn't uncommon to find the story-time crowd on the front lawn of the library.

Mostly, the tellers of the stories were members of the SPL staff, but through the years the library has brought in a number of professionals, among them Beverly Matson, Mary-Eileen (Mickie) McClear, Marilyn

Malton, and the Second Story Workshop Storytelling Guild. Tweedledum (Keith Dinicol) has made an appearance, as has Madeline, a character in Ludwig Bemelman's stories.

Since 1998, the library's story time for toddlers and preschoolers has been sponsored by the Friends of the Library and the Stratford Rotary Club. In light of reduced government funding, their financial support has allowed the SPL to continue offering this part of its children's program without charging user fees.

The Stratford Community Toy Library

For more than two decades, there has been a library within the Stratford Public Library.

Specifically, it's the Stratford Community Toy Library, and it operates from 9:30 to 11 on Wednesday mornings on the second floor.

From September to December and from January to June, parents and caregivers gather with their preschool children for some play, some crafts, a snack and a singsong.

They also sign out toys for a two-week period, which, says Cathy Petryna, "is great at Christmas time, to see if the kids like them or not."

A member of the toy library for about eight years, she is winding up a three-year stint as its one-person executive and manager. (The youngest of her four children is soon bound for kindergarten.) There used to be a more formal organization.

There also used to be about 20 kids showing up each Wednesday. But the numbers have fallen off since the Early Years program began in the Falstaff Family Centre on Waterloo Street North.

"We pay a fee, and they don't," says Petryna, "so it (the number of SCTL participants) has gone down." The fee for each fall or spring session at the library is $20 per parent or caregiver, regardless of the number of children that accompanies each.

"We have a membership (fee) because we have to cover our insurance, and we supply the craft supplies and juice and stuff," says Petryna. "We have a craft every week. We used to pay less than $100 a year for insurance, but now we pay $278, all because of 9-11. At Christmas time we have a Christmas party. We have Santa come in, and everyone buys presents for their own, but Santa distributes them. We replace some of the toys each year with whatever money we have left."

It was early in 1980 that the Children's Aid Society and the Festival City Nursery approached the SPL about some space for a toy library. Both organizations had set aside some money for such an endeavour, and they were talking about getting additional funding from a women's service club in the city.

While she didn't oppose the proposal, chief librarian Sue Bonsteel said she did have concerns about how much room the toy library would require. Her board subsequently decided to explore the possibility of a toy library as a pilot project.

Within a month or so, there was a group of parents talking about forming a club to buy the necessary toys and run a toy library, but the SPL was still first choice as a location.

SPL records indicate the toy library began operation in October 1980. A number of organizations provided the non-profit group with guidance. The CAS also donated some funds for the initial purchase of toys, as did the Stratford Optimist Club.

Barb Montgomery was the parents' charter president, and Anne Orr was in charge of programming. "It was a very informal group," says Orr, "but the 15 to 20 women who were part of it were pretty committed. It was a wonderful program. We bought plastic containers in which we could store the toys, and we got some shelves made by inmates at a provincial jail."

In 1981 the group enlisted the help of Louise McColl, who, for about the next five years, was the toy library's volunteer co-ordinator. She ensured that the toys were set out and packed away, and that the snacks were served. "She's the one who really held it together for those years," says Orr.

The second president of the toy library was Karen Lefrancois Hill.

The SPL has never charged the SCTL for the use its auditorium. For a few years that use was on Tuesday and Thursday mornings. Thursdays became a problem because of the Noon Hour Book Club's need for the space, so the toy library was eventually moved to Wednesdays only.

Despite the slide in membership, Petryna is confident about the toy library's future, confident there will always be people who think it worthwhile. "It's good for the parents or caregivers to be able to chat with each other while the kids play. It's an outing for everybody."

SPL

Friends of the Stratford Public Library

In October 1995, library administrator Jane Kirkpatrick talked to the Noon Hour Book Club about the provincial legislation that governs the financing of public institutions. "That's when Reg (White) stood up and said, 'It looks like the library needs some help and I'm prepared to do it,'" she recalls. "So, with his support, I went to the board, gave them Mr. White's name, and after a couple of months of study they (the board members) decided to take him up on his offer."

Such was the conception of the Friends of the Stratford Public Library, though formal organization didn't take place until their inaugural meeting on June 13, 1996.

Describing themselves as "a group of concerned citizens who love the library," they drew up bylaws and a constitution.

They also named an executive and directors: Reg White, president; Heather Pryde, vice-president; Carol Lease, secretary; Allan Waddingham, treasurer; and Jane Boyce, Elaine Riehl and Ann Rigler, officers.

Then they turned their attention to

supporting the library by taking responsibility for some services and events, by introducing some new programs, and by raising money.

One of their earliest tasks was to get businesses and individuals to become donors of the SPL's 120 or so magazine subscriptions, so they started an adopt-a-magazine program. Government cutbacks to funding for the library had at least some of those

Friends president Reg White (left), SPL board chair Pat Stanley and Perth-Middlesex MPP Bert Johnson at the ceremony celebrating 150 years of library service in Stratford, November 1996.

the formation of a mechanics institute in Stratford by donating to the SPL a copy of the lavishly illustrated Canada's Living Heritage. They also had Perth-Wellington-Waterloo MP John Richardson arrange to have the book signed by Gov.-Gen. Romeo Leblanc. As well, they gave the SPL a commemorative plaque.

In July 1997 the Friends sponsored a garden tour in Quebec and stops at the National Library of Canada and Rideau Hall in Ottawa. They filled a 40-passenger bus for the seven-day fund-raiser.

In November of that year, they held their first gingerbread house exhibition and raffle, for which they were successful in getting the chefs at five Stratford and St. Marys eateries to make and donate the colourful, candied prizes.

Tickets were priced at $2 each and three for $5, and the Friends used the $500 they raised to build a toy box in the children's department.

The gingerbread project has become an annual event, and the ticket prices have not

magazines on the endangered list. By June 1999 they had sponsors for 50 magazines and an anonymous donor paid the subscriptions for three newspapers, the *Toronto Star*, the *Globe and Mail*, and the *Guardian* out of England. In 2000 they raised $1,554 for the sponsorship of 40 of the library's magazines, which numbered close to 130.

The Friends also took an interest in reviving the library's literacy program and help those unable to read or write, or able to do so only at an elementary level.

They brought new energy to book delivery for the homebound, a service whereby volunteers drop off and pick up books and other materials for those unable to travel to the SPL. And they took over the library's annual book sale.

In November 1996 the Friends helped the library celebrate the 150th anniversary of

Five-year-old Reicza Ham and her creation at the Friends' gingerbread cookie-making day at the SPL in December 2002.

No. 2   Summer 1998

AMONG FRIENDS

A Publication of the Friends of the Stratford Public Library

Message from the President

This publication is the second of the newsletters to our members and friends. It is July, we are halfway through the year and we are now working on our involvement with the Library's annual book sale. Our efforts in this event support the staff of the Library who are able to use their time elsewhere. In late Fall we will be holding our second annual Gingerbread House Exhibit and Raffle.

Beginning this month we are embarking on a more aggressive Magazine Subscription Campaign. For those who are not sure what that means, we are asking individuals and businesses to donate the cost of an annual periodical subscription. A sticker is pasted to the front of the publication with the name of the sponsor. This effort last year received the support of a number of Friends, however we would like to greatly expand this effort. The cost to the library to purchase magazines, newspapers and professional periodicals is $8000 annually.

If you would like to support this campaign please contact myself at 273-0952 or Burnie Laws at 272-2845.

You have no doubt noticed that this publication includes a questionnaire. We are somewhat in doubt as to the value of the monthly open meetings which have not attracted sufficient attendance. We have therefore put together some questions which, if you would kindly respond to, may help the executive decide the direction we should take with regard to future meetings.

Finally, this month the Friends have set up and information desk in the Library which will be attended to during the afternoons fro 2:00- 4:00 in order to answer questions about our group, enrol new member and accept magazine subscription sponsors.

Reg White, President

In This Issue	Page
Publishing Forum	2
Book Review	2
Canada Book Day	3
Book Sale	3
Committees	4
Executive Members	4
Questionnaire	insert

changed.

"We just wanted to create a little Christmas magic," said White. "Gingerbread homes are something people can relate to, especially children. They have a real sense of awe when they look at something like this."

It was also in 1997 that the group published its first newsletter Among Friends.

In March those Friends took to the City Hall auditorium to hold a public workshop on writing and publishing, Get it Write and Get it Published. The panelists were Noel Hudson, an editor with Boston Mills Press in Erin; Bob Newland of Fanfare Books in Stratford; Jane Kirkpatrick of the SPL; and Mary Hoy Schmidt and Dean Robinson, Stratford writers. Geoff Hancock, editor of Canadian Fiction Magazine and Reveal Ontario, chaired the workshop.

In November 1998 the Friends channelled a $2,400 donation from the Stratford Rotary Club to the SPL, which meant the library for at least a year could suspend the user fees it was planning to attach to its children's programs because of a lack of government funding.

In November 1999 they ($800) and the Rotarians ($1,800) again teamed up to sponsor the library's toddler and preschool story time programs. That has become an ongoing sponsorship for the Friends and the Rotarians, which now covers Babytime, Lambs' Tales for Twos, and Storytime for Preschoolers. Reduced government funding had the SPL talking user fees for those programs when the Friends and Rotarians stepped in.

Also in November 1999, the Friends announced plans for a bus trip in March 2000 to Boston and Philadelphia, a six-day excursion that included the Philadelphia and New England flower shows, a performance of the Boston Symphony and a tour of the Boston Public Library. But the response was not sufficient, and the fund-

You can
help your
Library

JOIN
THE
FRIENDS
**OF THE STRATFORD
PUBLIC LIBRARY**

raiser was scrapped.

In June 2001 the group held an evening
with Canadian actor, author and playwright
Timothy Findley, who had agreed to be the
Friends' honorary patron. The proceeds
from that night have been directed to the
purchase of a series of books to be used in a
literacy program for adults.

Other money raised has been used to
install a sound system in the auditorium of
the library ($1,500), build a bookshelf,
reupholster chairs in the children's area, buy
a book trolley, take out ads to promote
special days and programs, and donate
special books to the SPL.

Membership categories and annual fees
for the Friends are individual $10, family
$20, senior or student $5, sustaining $35-$99,
patron $100 and up, corporate $250.

The group now has 40-45 paid-up
members.

SPL

Bookmarking the future

By Sharon Malvern

Sharon Malvern chaired the Stratford Public library foundation from 2000 to 2002.

By 1998 it was clear to the Stratford Public Library board that the core funding provided by the province and the city was sufficient for basic services, but not for the changing needs of its patrons. The ever-growing use of the Internet for research, the demand for children's programs, the need to provide post-secondary educational support in a community without a university or college, and the ongoing necessity to promote literacy initiatives all meant that the library had to look elsewhere for money.

The library did not want to charge user fees for any of those programs and services. Equal access to library resources is a fundamental principle of public libraries; the people who most need library services are often those who can least afford to pay.

So members of the library board took the initial steps to acquire a charitable registration number and set up a foundation to raise funds. This endeavour marked the first time in its history that the library had appealed to the public for money. In fact, there are few library foundations in existence in the province, and of those, most have been established to invest monies received from bequests.

In April 2000, the Stratford Public Library Foundation board held its inaugural meeting. The charter members included Tom Orr (honorary chair), Sharon Malvern (chair), Marilyn Dimeo (secretary), Steve Mitchell (treasurer), Reg White (Friends of the Library liaison), Chuck Dingman, Heather Pryde, Terry Marklevitz, Jennie Warus, Libby Miller and Jane Kirkpatrick (SPL director). They were charged with raising an endowment fund of $500,000, which would generate sufficient annual

revenue in future years to meet the needs of library patrons, from toddlers to seniors.

The foundation board invited Lloyd Robertson, Stratford native and CTV news

BOOK MARK

The Future

Invest in the future – of the Library, of literacy, of Stratford by making a donation to the

Stratford Public Library Endowment Fund

SPL

anchor to be its honorary patron.

City council agreed to a request for "seed money" to produce a brochure and other materials, and the board members began the long process of learning about the library's needs, about fundraising, and about managing a campaign.

The library board held focus groups to identify the public's needs with respect to library services, and subsequently prepared a strategic plan which the foundation board used as a basis for its work.

The slogan "Bookmark the Future" was chosen, and Sharon Malvern (freelance writer), with new members Tony Carter (graphic designer) and Michelle Purdy (development officer with the Stratford Festival) produced a brochure and pledge form.

The foundation board members developed a campaign plan, kits, a donor recognition piece, requests to foundations, and lists of potential donors. Guest speakers advised them on various aspects of fundraising. Several donations resulted.

However, in 2001-02, Stratford was saturated with fundraising campaigns for several major community projects. An appeal to the public to give money for a long-term endowment fund for the library, without a specific identifiable

project, proved to be a hard sell.

Another obstacle was the privacy issue; though the library has more than 20,000 active patrons, the foundation board could not access those names and addresses for fundraising purposes.

Therefore, in the spring of 2002, the foundation board, in co-operation with the library board, changed its focus to a planned giving (bequests) campaign, led by vice-chair Terry Marklevitz. It also identified a specific fundraising initiative, namely an early literacy outreach program.

In addition to that campaign, the foundation has received funds from the library's celebrity poster series and from the Stratford Book Festival, all in support of the proposed literacy program.

The library's newsletter, SPL@sh!, first produced in January 2003, has given the foundation a means of communicating information about its efforts to library patrons, as has the SPL's Web site.

GIFT PLANNING

Your public library is one of your community's most trusted and treasured institutions.

What better way to secure its future than making a planned gift to your library.

Planned gifts can mean making a gift today, or planning now to make a gift in the future.

Gift planning is the best way to ensure your library benefits from your generosity, while you achieve your personal, financial and philanthropic goals.

Thank you to the volunteers and staff from Brantford and Burlington Public Libraries for their help with this brochure.

SUPPORTING YOUR WISHES

Making a planned gift will benefit and support your wishes. These could include special programs and services, support for branch libraries, capital projects, endowments, or you can designate gifts to two or more areas.

Your giving options include:

• wills and bequests
• memorial and celebration gifts
• annuities
• life insurance
• trusts
• gifts of property or securities

☐ YES, I am interested in further information on making a lasting gift to my library.

☐ I want my public library to know that I intend to include them in my will.

☐ I want my public library to know that I've already included them in my will.

Name

Address

Postal Code

Telephone

Please return this form in confidence to:

Steve Mitchell, Treasurer
Stratford Public Library Foundation
19 St. Andrew St.,
Stratford, ON
N5A 1A2
(519) 273-4145

Registered Charitable Business #87245 9334 RR0001

The planned giving brochure used by the SPL

Stratford Public Library employees

Following is a list of people who have worked for or are now on staff at the SPL. It includes full-time and part-time employees, as well as summer help. Compiled from a number of sources, it is only as complete and accurate as those sources. Where only one year is listed, it could be the first year of employment, the only year of employment, or one of the years of employment.

When it comes to unbroken service, Jennie Daly, Winnifred Henderson, Lois Thompson and Jean (MacDougall) Bain are the class of the league, all with more than four decades.

The longest-serving current staff member is technician Theresa Talsma. In September 2000, she received a 25-year award from Mayor Dave Hunt at a meeting of city council. "She's like a rock," said SPL director Jane Kirkpatrick. "She's the type of person you can depend on. It's employees like Theresa that give an organization its strength."

SPL

From left, Theresa Talsma, Jeane Ferguson and Irma Sass work on the SPL's card catalogue in the late 1970s.

Carolyn Abercrombie	1991-1992	Judith Calixto	2002-present
Elizabeth Ainslie	1999-present	Lois Chippa	1988
Jim Anderson	1972-1975	Larry Chu	1972-1974
Wendy Anderson	1992-1997	Ken Clarke	1973-1975
Margaret Andrea	1971-1972	Valerie Clarke	1980-1981
Samuel Andrews	1924	Dan Cole	2001
Kathleen Arnold	1931-1937	Elise Cole	1997-1998
William Ashmore	circa 1897-1900	Jim Commerford	1976
Cindy Atchison	1988-present	Ryan Connor	1992-1993
Mary Ellen Attard	1989	Gertrude Cook	1900
Chetan Bahri	1979-1983	Mary Lynn Cook	1980-1987
Janet Baker	1988-1997	May Cook	1902
Jean (MacDougall) Bain	1931-1972	Nancy Cook	1983-1985
Maureen Baldry	1984-1988	Tanya (Daum) Cook	1987-1990
Joyce Banks	1954-1965	Fred C. Crerar	1929-1957
Ingrid (Schock) Bassett	1971-1972	Jane Crozier	1974-1978
Leslie Beckett	1989-1990	Geraldine Cuerden	1971-1976
Betty Jo Belton	2002-present	Marilyn Cunningham	1977-1981,
Gordon Bertrand	1999		1987-1988
Wayne Billo	1975	Jennie Daly	1911-1953
Doreen Bishop	1930	Scott Davis	1978-1981
Norma Bissonnette	1980-1983		1984-1985
Melissa Black	1990-1995	Rebecca Deckert	2000-2002
Mary Kay Blatchford	1969	Jo Deslippe	2002-present
Phil Bonner	1996-1999	E. Addie Dingman	1904-1912
Beth Bonsteel	1973	Linda Drennan	1979-present
Jane Bonsteel	1976	Allan Drown	1983
Sue Bonsteel	1969-1983	Don Drown	1981-1988
Beverly Boogerman	1966	Michelle Ducharme	1984
Susan Boshart	1978-1985	Ruth Dunlop	1968
Marie Bourret	1971-1973	Eric Falconer	1996-1999
Margaret Bowers	1995	Cindy Farmer	1998-2002
Kenny Brien	1976-1981	Megan Faulds	1986-1988
		Jeane Ferguson	1975-1983
		Sonya (Geisler) Fischer	1988-present
		Carolynne Fleischauer	1969
		Anne Marie Fleischauer	1969-1970
		Stuart Foley	1990-1994
		Marlene Forrest	1973
		Ann Gagnon	1978-1979
		Susan Gearing	1975-1976
		Marion Gibb	1978-1992
		Kate Gibbings	1995-1996
		Robyn Godfrey	1999-present
		Nuala Goldberg	1977-1981
		Lorraine Gordon	1987-present
		Becky Grant	1992

Ken Clarke, July 2002

SPL

SPL staff 1974. Back row, from left: caretaker Russ Marlow, Ken Clarke, Brian McKone and chief librarian Sue Bonsteel. Front, from left: Dorothy Robinson, Billie Kirkby and Janet Robertson.

Kathy Grant	1990-present
Lorraine Greenberg	1979-1988
Kara Gregory	1987
Ron Gregory	1994-present
Sheila Grandison	1951-1952
John Groothuizen	1976-1983
Robert Groothuizen	1984
Margaret Hackney	1986-1988
Susie J. Hamilton	1910
Jordan Hardy	1994-1996
Todd Hart	1987-1989
David Harvie	1999-present
Christopher Hatch	1990
Elizabeth Hay	1910-1911
Anne Marie Heckman	1975-1985,
	1987-1998,
	2000-present
Sari Heiber-McLenaghan	1999-2000
Janice Henderson	1970-1971
Winnifred Henderson	1930-1974
John Heney	1977
Sally (Lightfoot) Hengeveld	1980-present
Florence Henry	1975-1979
John Henry	1977
Miss C. Hepburn	1908

Jacqueline Herold	1981
Miss ???? Hess	1922
Wendy Hicks	2002-present
Christopher Hiemstra	1992-1993
Michael Hiemstra	1987-1992
Jennifer Hoke	1990-1994
Karen (Bailey) Higgins	1980-1981
	1985-present
Patti Hoytink	1980-1983
Andrew Hulbert	2000-present
Cathie Huras	1967
Kate Jacob	1982-1999
Warren James	1986-1987
Jackie Jarrett	1982-1985
Paula Janveau	1995-2002
Nicole Janzen	1992
Reta Jeffries	1911
Florinda Johnson	1975
Louise Johnston	circa 1897-1931
Miss ???? Kappelle	1923
Walter P. [Butch] Kelterborn	1957-1971
Chander (Bahri) Khullar	1977-1982
Marilyn Kicks	2000-2002
Melanie Kindrachuk	2002-present
Jessie [Billie] Kirkby	1967-1992
William Kirkham	1928-1929
Jane Kirkpatrick	1983-present
Kim Knechtel	circa 1984
Kasia Kocot	1996-present

Florinda Johnson puts labels on the spines of newly arrived books in the late 1970s.

Kelly Ann Kooy	1979-1981
Barbara Kuepfer	1964
Tom Kidd	1977
Linda Lawrence	1955
Edna Leckie	1920
Janet Linden	1995-2000
Gary Lindsay	1971
Beatrice Lithgow	1986-1988
Jan Louch-Rycroft	1983-present
Elizabeth Lotz	1978-1980
Walt Lupsor	1990-1992
Margaret Macklin	1908-1910
Kathleen MacNicol	1954
Natalie MacPherson	1992-2002
David Marlow	1990
Russell Marlow	1971-1993
Cathy Matyas	1989-1991
Celia McConville	1995-present
Donald Blake McDougall	1969-1971
Scott McEachern	1975-1976
Lorraine McGovern	1973
Elizabeth McKay	1987-1991
Brian McKone	1971-1990
Guy McKone	1976-1999
Paul McKone	1974-1979

Some of the SPL staff in the Halloween spirit, Oct. 31, 2002. From left: Sally Hengeveld, Anne Marie Heckman, Cathy Perreault, Perry Wilson and Krista Sutherland.

Albert Murr	1903-1924
Betty Murray	1960
Roxy Murray	1966-1967
Brent Nancekivell	1995-present
Kathy Newman	1972-1973
Matthew Ort	1985-1986
Ed Pass	1986
Cathy (Jezard) Perreault	1984-present
Gail Poole	1982-1994
Nancy Poppe	1990-1995
Deborah Purcell	1993-1995
Robert Reid	1978-1983
Bea Renton	1984
Grace Reynolds	1975-1979

Staffer Guy McKone, audiovisual services

Hugh and Annie McMillan	1927-1928
Ruth McNaught	1970-1971
Janice McPherson	2002-present
Jean McTavish	1916-1917
Mary Moffet	1978-1980
Jennie Montgomery	1976
Ruth Morris	1919-1920

Irmgard (Irma) Sass, July 2002. She worked at the SPL from 1976 to 1982.

Marilyn Reynolds	1949-1953	Kate Thomson	2000-2002
Ruth Richards	1980	Robert Thrasher	1983-1984
Miss ???? Ridgedale	1902	Valerie Todd	1919
Colin Ripley	1978-1979	Gord Vandervliet	1976-1977
Catherine Robertson	1975-1983	Tina van Heyningen	1981
Mrs. J. W. Robertson	1???-1908	Kim Wagner	1988-1990
Janet Robertson	1972-1976	Catherine Wake	1985
Dorothy Robinson	1959-1986	Eleanor Waldie	1975-1979
Krista (Sutherland) Robinson	2001-present	Catherine Walker	1986-1987
Shirley Robinson	1970	Deanna Weber	1953-1954
Carol Robinson-Todd	1979-1987	Sandra [Sam] Webster	1998-1999
Astrid Roch-Russell	1985-1996	Marlene Weiss	1988-1991
Becky Rogers	1991-1997		
Margaret Rosamond	19??-1946		
Wanda Roth	1990		
Cathy Rothwell	1976-1980		
Ann Ryan	1952		
Fred Rynor	1975-1977		
Irmgard [Irma] Sass	1976-1982		
Margaret Seguin	1954		
Marilyn Seguin	1954		
Julie Schaefer	1985-1986		
Chris Schmidt	1992		
Barb Scholz	1983		
Ron Schram	1977-1978		
Gloria Schumacher	1975-1980		
Leslie Scott	1979-1983		
Miss ???? Scott	1922-1923		
Amardeep Sehra	1988-1991		
Manjeet Sehra	1984-1991		
Katherine Seredynska	1990-1995		
Naomi Shore	1964		

SPL

When it comes to entertaining children, SPL staff members have often had as much fun as their patrons. Dressed for the circus theme of the 1983 March break are, from left, ringmaster Carol Robinson-Todd with clowns Mary Lynn Cook, Linda Drennan (kneeling), Kate Jacob, Norma Bissonnette and Sally Hengeveld.

Eileen Sillito	1968-1969	Alison West	1953-1954
Joel Silver	1989-1990	Richard Wilton	1900-1903
Fred Sinko	1984	Sue Wickenheiser	1980-1982
Samantha Skowby	1995-1996	Edna Widenmaier	1965
Brad Smith	1996-1999	Erlyn Wilker	1977-1983
Carol (Bailey) Smith	1981-1996	Barbra Williams	1988-1998
Joan Smythe	1977-1980	Christina Wilson	1985-1988
Guy Sonier	1994	Perry Wilson	1992-present
Verna Spera	1966	Natalie Wownuk	1990
Pam Spencer	1992-1993	Faye (Huras) Wreford	1977-1982
June Steckley	1982-1983		1984-1989
Shannon Sword	1999-2001	Rae Young	1995-1998
Theresa Talsma	1975-present	Andrea Zucca	1995-1998
Lois Thompson	1921-1971	Isobelle Zurbrigg	1965-1966
Ron Thompson	1975-1982	Kirk Zurell	1985-1987

The Stratford Public Library staff, January 2003. On staircase, from the top: Jo Deslippe, Sally Hengeveld, Judith Calixto, Jan Louch-Rycroft, Kathy Grant, Theresa Talsma, Wendy Hicks, Krista Robinson and Kasia Kocot. Middle level, from left: Elizabeth Ainslie, Cindy Atchison, Ron Gregory, David Harvie and Sonya Fischer. Lower level, standing from left: Perry Wilson, Janice McPherson, Karen Higgins, Melanie Kindrachuk, Robyn Godfrey, Lorraine Gordon and Jane Kirkpatrick. Front row, seated from left: Linda Drennan, Cathy Perreault and Anne Marie Heckman. Absent: Betty Jo Belton, Brent Nancekivell, Celia McConville and Andrew Hulbert.

Volunteering on its behalf

By Sharon Malvern

When my husband and I moved to Stratford in 1970 to take up teaching positions at Stratford Central Seconday School, I was delighted to find that the public library was just across St. Andrew Street. An avid reader, I craved new books, and, in the pre-computer circulation era, I could check if I'd taken out a book previously by looking for my library card number on the book card.

I took my English students there over the next 20 years to explore the collection and do research. The National Film Board films encased in those huge flat tin cans were treasured resources for teachers in the days before videos.

After I retired briefly to have my children, I was asked to serve as one of the Perth County Board of Education representatives on the board of the library, which I did, from 1974 through 1982.

Although I had spent my teenage years working after school and during the summers in the children's department of the Sarnia Public Library, I was fascinated to be part of the behind-the-scenes operations of a library. In those days, the library board was much more involved in the day-to-day operations of the library than it is today.

Besides setting the budget, hiring staff, making policies, dealing with the building and personnel, the board was preoccupied (as it is today) with the issue of space for materials and patrons. Then, the library really only used the main floor; the basement was an apartment for the custodian, and the top floor, as I recall, was full of glass cases containing stuffed birds and squirrels.

We spent many meetings debating the advantages of building a new facility outside the downtown area, how to resolve the parking problem at the site, and eventually the plans for an addition. When construction began, the library moved to the old A&P building on Erie Street. The grand climax came with the opening day for the new addition. I'll never forget standing on the library steps, under a bright blue sky, amazed at what had been accomplished and proud to be part of the library.

My children were young during that period, and I remember several occasions sitting in chief librarian Sue Bonsteel's office, with Matthew on my knee, as we went over library business. The children's programs with Jane Crozier were big hits with both boys, and we lugged home great

STRATFORD PUBLIC LIBRARY

Celebrating our past Building for our future

The Carnegie Library, 1903-2003

In recognition of the generosity of your commitment to the
Stratford Public Library,
the Board of Directors
invites you to attend our first annual

Volunteer Appreciation Tea

Thursday, May 1, 2003
3:00-5:00 P.M.
Library Auditorium

Regrets only
by April 25, 2003
to Cindy Atchison
at 271-0220 ext. 47
catchison@city.stratford.on.ca

19 St. Andrew Street, Stratford, ON N5A 1A2
(519) 271-0220   www.stratford.library.on.ca   spl@pcin.on.ca

SPL

armfuls of children's books.

Another innovation was the introduction of videos to the library loan collection, after much discussion over the respective merits of Beta or VHS formats. (We almost gambled on Beta.)

Libraries are frequently targets for people who would like to restrict what others read. The board received letters on this topic, and I remember arguing passionately for a policy on it, one premise of which HAD to be that the complainant had read the whole book before passing judgement on it. One suggestion was that library board members should read all the books purchased – an idea that was quickly dismissed. Even for a book lover, that was too much to ask.

After all three floors of the library were open to the public, we had to address the question of accessibility. Hence the elevator, built with a Wintario grant. An earlier experiment with a ramp at the back of the building proved disastrous. We had someone in a wheelchair try it out, but the grade was so steep he practically flew over the parking lot.

Those years on the board fuelled my lifelong passion for books and libraries. After I stepped down, I took the school librarian courses and worked for a short time in the library at Stratford Northwestern Secondary School. And after I retired as an educator, I served from 2000-2002 as chair of the SPL foundation board, and wrote the Library Lines column for the *Beacon Herald* (which I continue to do).

The Stratford Public Library has been an integral part of my life for more than 30 years, and I am happy that I have been able to volunteer my time on its behalf.

A view from the northeast, New Year's Day 2003. A lintel facing St. Andrew Street and bearing the words PUBLIC LIBRARY continues to indicate where the main entrance was from 1903 to 1926, the year in which the new front was added.

The guiding hands

For about 75 years, the mayor of Stratford was automatically named a member of the city's public library board. Some of those mayors showed more enthusiasm for the role than others, but the city has always had a well-placed voice – and ear – on the board.

From the late 1960s until recently, the city's seat on the SPL board was warmed by councillors. At present, the rep is again the mayor.

In addition to a member of council, the city has always had citizens at large on the library board. Currently, the number of those is set at five.

The rest of the SPL board has long comprised representatives from the public and separate school boards of Huron and Perth counties. On today's board there are two trustees from the public board, one from the separate.

These days, time served on the library board is limited to two full consecutive terms, totalling six years. Trustees are named after each municipal election.

Since 1971 the SPL's chief librarian has been the board's secretary-treasurer.

DEAN ROBINSON

189

1906	Howard A. Barker	J. Davis Barnett	Dr. James A. Devlin, Dr. Joseph A. Corcoran, R. Thomas Orr, J. Russell Stuart, Howard A. Barker, William J. Hanley, Mayor William J. Ferguson
1907	William J. Hanley	J. Davis Barnett	Howard A. Barker, Dr. James A. Devlin, John Ridgedale, James Steele, J. Russell Stuart, Mayor William Gordon, James H. Smith
1908	John Ridgedale	J. Davis Barnett	Howard A. Barker, William J. Hanley, James H. Smith, Dr. James A. Devlin, R. Thomas Orr, Dr. Fred J. R. Forster, Mayor William Gordon
1909	James H. Smith	J. Davis Barnett	Howard A. Barker, John Ridgedale, Dr. James A. Devlin, Dr. Fred J. R. Forster, George Rennie, Rev. D. J. Egan, Rev. T. J. Thompson, Mayor William S. Dingman
1910	Dr. Fred J. R. Forster	J. Davis Barnett	George Rennie, Dr. James A. Devlin, Rev. D. J. Egan, Mayor William S. Dingman, James H. Smith, Rev. T. J. Thompson, John M. McCutcheon, Howard A. Barker
1911	George Rennie	J. Davis Barnett	Howard A. Barker, William S. Dingman, James H. Smith, John M. McCutcheon, Dr. Peter F. Quinlan, Mayor Thomas Brown, Dr. James A. Devlin
1912	William S. Dingman	J. Davis Barnett	Howard A. Barker, John M. McCutcheon, Dr. Peter F. Quinlan, James H. Smith, George Rennie, Dr. James A. Devlin, Mayor Thomas Brown
1913	John M. McCutcheon	J. Davis Barnett	Lydia C. Dent, Dr. James A. Devlin, W. G. Owens, Dr. Peter F. Quinlan, George Rennie, James H. Smith, Mayor Chalmers N. Greenwood
1914	Dr. Peter F. Quinlan	J. Davis Barnett	Lydia C. Dent, Dr. James A. Devlin, James H. Smith, John M. McCutcheon, W. G. Owens, George Rennie, Mayor John Stevenson, Leon A. Duggan
1915	W. G. Owens	J. Davis Barnett	Lydia C. Dent, Leon A. Duggan, Samuel R. McConkey, George Rennie, Dr. Peter F. Quinlan, James H. Smith, Mayor Ezekiel K. Barnsdale
1916	Lydia C. Dent	J. Davis Barnett	W. G. Owens, Leon A. Duggan, Samuel R. McConkey, George Rennie, Dr. Peter F. Quinlan, James Steele, Mayor Ezekiel K. Barnsdale, James H. Smith
1917	Leon A. Duggan	J. Davis Barnett	Lydia C. Dent, James H. Smith, James Steele, Edwin Tobin, Mayor Joseph D. Monteith, W. G. Owens, George Rennie, Dr. J. W. Emery

1918	Dr. J. W. Emery	J. Davis Barnett	Lydia C. Dent, Leon A. Duggan,Walter H. Gregory, James. H. Smith, Edwin W. Tobin, James Steele, Mayor Joseph D. Monteith
1919	Edwin W. Tobin	James H. Smith	Dr. J. W. Emery, Leon A. Duggan, Lydia C. Dent, James H. Smith, John C. Garden, Walter Miller, James Steele, Mayor John L. Youngs
1920	John C. Garden	Dr. J. W. Emery	Leon A. Duggan, James Steele, Edwin W. Tobin, James H. Smith, Lydia C. Dent, Mayor John Stevenson
1921	James Steele	Dr. J. W. Emery	Edwin W. Tobin, William Preston, R. Thomas Orr, Leon A. Duggan, James H. Smith, Lydia C. Dent, Mayor Walter H. Gregory
1922	William Preston	Dr. J. W. Emery	Edwin W. Tobin, William E. Goodwin, R. Thomas Orr, James H. Smith, Lydia C. Dent, Walter H. Gregory, James Steele, Mayor Tom Brown
1923	William E. Goodwin	Dr. J. W. Emery	Edwin W. Tobin, William Preston, R. Thomas Orr, James H. Smith, Lydia C. Dent, James Steele, Mayor Tom Brown
1924	R. Thomas Orr	Dr. J. W. Emery	Edwin W. Tobin, William Preston, William E. Goodwin, James H. Smith, Lydia C. Dent, James Steele, Mayor Tom Brown
1925	James H. Smith	William E. Goodwin	Lydia C. Dent, R. Thomas Orr, James Steele, Edwin W. Tobin, William Preston, Dr. J. W. Emery, Mayor Tom Brown
1926	A. Hayward Alexander	William E. Goodwin	Lydia C. Dent, R. Thomas Orr, James Steele, Edwin W. Tobin, William Preston, James H. Smith, Mayor David R. Marshall, Leon J. Long
1927	Leon J. Long	William E. Goodwin	A. Hayward Alexander, James Steele, R. Thomas Orr, James H. Smith, B. William Preston, Mayor David R. Marshall, Lydia C. Dent
1928	Leon J. Long	William E. Goodwin	James Steele, William Preston, William J. Blakeston, Lydia C. Dent, R. Thomas Orr, Mayor John A. Andrew, James H. Smith
1929	William J. Blakeston	A. Hayward Alexander	James Steele, James H. Smith, Leon J. Long, William E. Goodwin, Mayor John A. Andrew, Alex W. Fisher, Lydia C. Dent
1930	Alex W. Fisher	A. Hayward Alexander	William J. Blakeston, Rev Leo J. Kelly, James H. Smith, Harold W. Strudley, Lydia C. Dent, Leon J. Long, Mayor Charles E. Moore
1931	Harold W. Strudley	A. Hayward Alexander	Lydia C. Dent, Alex W. Fisher, Rev. Leo J. Kelly, James H. Smith, William J. Blakeston, Mayor George I. Graff, Leon J. Long

Year			Members
1932	Harold W. Strudley	A. Hayward Alexander	William J. Blakeston, Rev. J. H. Chisholm, Mayor George I. Graff, James H. Smith, Daisy L. Lightfoot, Leon J. Long, Alex W. Fisher
1933	Rev. J. H. Chisholm Daisy L. Lightfoot as of May 16	A. Hayward Alexander	Alex W. Fisher, James H. Smith, William J. Blakeston, Harold W. Strudley, Leon J. Long, Mayor George I. Graff
1934	Daisy L. Lightfoot	A. Hayward Alexander	William J. Blakeston, Alex W. Fisher, Rev. J. T.Gibbons, James H. Smith, Harold W. Strudley, Mayor Oliver J. Kerr, Leon J. Long
1935	Rev. J. T. Gibbons	A. Hayward Alexander	Daisy L. Lightfoot, William J. Blakeston, Alex W.Fisher, Leon J. Long, James H. Smith, Harold W. Strudley, Mayor Oliver J. Kerr
1936	Rev. J. T. Gibbons	William J. Blakeston	Daisy L. Lightfoot, Harold W. Strudley, James H. Smith, Mayor Walter H. Gregory, Alex W. Fisher, Rev. Francis G. Lightbourn, Leon J. Long, Charles McDonald
1937	Rev. J. T. Gibbons	Charles McDonald	Daisy L. Lightfoot, Alex W. Fisher, James H. Smith, Harold W. Strudley, Leon J. Long, John Anderson, Mayor Thomas E. Henry, Rev. Francis G. Lightbourn
1938	Alex W. Fisher	Charles McDonald	Daisy L. Lightfoot, Rev. J. T. Gibbons, John Anderson, Chris J. McKeough, George N. Edwards, James H. Smith, Mayor Thomas E. Henry, Rose J. McQueen
1939	Alex W. Fisher	Charles McDonald	Rose J. McQueen, Daisy L. Lightfoot, John Anderson, George N. Edwards, Chris J. McKeough, Rev. J. T. Gibbons, Mayor Thomas E. Henry
1940	Alex W. Fisher	Charles McDonald	George N. Edwards, Rose J. McQueen, Daisy L. Lightfoot, John Anderson, Chris J. McKeough, Wilfred Firth, Mayor Thomas E. Henry
1941 1942	Alex W. Fisher	Charles McDonald	John Anderson, Daisy L. Lightfoot, George N. Edwards, Mayor Thomas E. Henry, Chris J. McKeough, Newman M. O'Leary, Wilfred Firth, Rose J. McQueen,
1943	Alex W. Fisher	Charles McDonald	Rose J. McQueen, Daisy L. Lightfoot, George N. Edwards, Chris J. McKeough, John Anderson, Newman M. O'Leary, Mayor Thomas E. Henry
1944	Alex W. Fisher	Charles McDonald	Rose J. McQueen, Daisy L. Lightfoot, George N. Edwards, Jean Gordon, Chris J. McKeough, Newman M. O'Leary, Mayor J. Waldo Monteith

Year	Chair	Vice-chair	Secretary-Treasurer	Board Members
1945	Alex W. Fisher		Charles McDonald	Rev. E. R. Glavin, Daisy L. Lightfoot, Jean Gordon, Chris J. McKeough, George N. Edwards, Rose J. McQueen, Mayor J. Waldo Monteith
1946	Alex W. Fisher		Charles McDonald	Dr. James G. McDermott, Daisy L. Lightfoot, Jean Gordon, Rose J. McQueen, George N. EdwardsChris J. McKeough, Cecilia Dorland, Rev. E. R. Glavin, Mayor J. Maurice King
1947	Alex W. Fisher		Charles McDonald	Rev. E. R. Glavin, Daisy L. Lightfoot, Jean Gordon, Rose J. McQueen, Chris J. McKeough, George N. Edwards, Mayor J. Maurice King
1948	Alex W. Fisher Daisy L. Lightfoot (March) George N. Edwards (April)		Charles McDonald	Daisy L. Lightfoot, Rose J. McQueen, Cecilia Dorland, George N. Edwards, Dr. Joseph A. Boyd, Jean Gordon, Mayor Thomas E. Henry
1949 1950	George N. Edwards	Dr. Joseph A. Boyd	Charles McDonald	E. Raeburn Crawford, Daisy L. Lightfoot, Jean Gordon, Cecilia Dorland, Rose J. McQueen,Mayor Thomas E. Henry
1951	George N. Edwards		Jean Gordon	E. Raeburn Crawford, Dr. Joseph A. Boyd, Daisy L. Lightfoot, Cecilia Dorland, Rose J. McQueen, Charles McDonald, Mayor A. David Simpson
1952	George N. Edwards		Jean Gordon	E. Raeburn Crawford, Dr. Joseph A. Boyd, Daisy L. Lightfoot, Cecilia Dorland, Rose J. McQueen, Mayor A. David Simpson
1953 1954	George N. Edwards		Jean Gordon	E. Raeburn Crawford, Daisy L. Lightfoot, Rose J. McQueen, Cecilia Dorland, Dr. Joseph A. Boyd, Mayor Lawrence Feick
1955	George N. Edwards		Jean Gordon	E. Raeburn Crawford, Dr. Joseph A. Boyd, Daisy L. Lightfoot, Rose J. McQueen, Cecilia Dorland, Charles McDonald, Mayor Wilfrid P. Gregory

Year	Chair and [Vice-chair]	Secretary	Treasurer	Board Members
1956	George N. Edwards	Jean Gordon	Charles McDonald	E. Raeburn Crawford, Dr. Joseph A. Boyd, Daisy L. Lightfoot, Rose J. McQueen, Cecilia Dorland, Mayor Wilfrid P. Gregory
1957 1958	George N. Edwards	Jean Gordon	Charles McDonald	E. Raeburn Crawford, Daisy L. Lightfoot, Rose J. McQueen, Cecilia Dorland, Dr. Joseph A. Boyd, Mayor Fred W. Cox
1959	George N. Edwards	Jean Gordon	Charles McDonald	E. Raeburn Crawford, Daisy L. Lightfoot, Rose J. McQueen, Cecilia Dorland, Dr. Joseph A. Boyd, Mayor Robert Mountain
1960	George N. Edwards	Jean Gordon	Charles McDonald (illness) Gladys Eickmeier (acting treasurer)	Daisy L. Lightfoot, Rose J. McQueen, E. Raeburn Crawford, Cecilia Dorland, Dr. Joseph A. Boyd, Robert I. Cathcart, L. Victor Lindsay, Mayor C. H. Meier
1961	George N. Edwards	Robert I. Cathcart	Gladys Eickmeier	Hope Bowra, E. Raeburn Crawford, Cecilia Dorland, Harold Treen, Jean Gordon, L. Victor Lindsay, Mayor C. H. Meier
1962	George N. Edwards	Robert I. Cathcart	Gladys Eickmeier	Hope Bowra, L. Victor Lindsay, E. Raeburn Crawford, Glen Bain, John A. McCrudden, Mayor C. H. Meier
1963	George N. Edwards	L. Victor Lindsay	Gladys Eickmeier	Hope Bowra, Emerson J. Williams, E. Claude Harvey, Foster Graham, E. Raeburn Crawford, James Morgan Riddell, Mayor C. H. Meier
1964	George N. Edwards (until December)	L. Victor Lindsay	Gladys Eickmeier	Hope Bowra, Emerson J. Williams, E. Claude Harvey, Foster Graham, E. Raeburn Crawford, James Morgan Riddell, Mayor C. H. Meier
1965	Chris B. Swanston	L. Victor Lindsay	Gladys Eickmeier	James Morgan Riddell, Foster Graham, E. Claude Harvey, Grant Kropf, John J. Quirt, Mayor C. H. Meier
1966 1967	Chris B. Swanston	L. Victor Lindsay	Gladys Eickmeier	Foster Graham, E. Claude Harvey, William H. Pollard, John J. Quirt, Lorne W. Brothers, Grant Kropf, Mayor C. H. Meier
1968	Chris B. Swanston	L. Victor Lindsay	Gladys Eickmeier	Foster Graham, Grant Kropf, John J. Quirt, Lorne W. Brothers,

Year	Chair	Vice-chair	Secretary-Treasurer	Board Members
				E. Claude Harvey, Gerry Cullen, Mayor John V. Killer
1969	Chris B. Swanston [Gerry Cullen]	L. Victor Lindsay	Gladys Eickmeier	Foster Graham, John J. Quirt, Grant Kropf, E. Claude Harvey, Lorne W. Brothers, Mayor John V. Killer
1970	Chris B. Swanston [Lorne W. Brothers]	L. Victor Lindsay	Gladys Eickmeier	Foster Graham, E. Claude Harvey, John J. Quirt, Gerry Cullen, Grant Kropf, Ald. Betty McMillan
1971	Chris B. Swanston [Lorne W. Brothers]	L. Victor Lindsay Blake McDougall (May-October) then Sue Bonsteel	Gladys Eickmeier	E. Claude Harvey, Grant Kropf, John J. Quirt, Gerry Cullen, Daniel J. Devlin, Ald. Bob Smith
1972	Chris B. Swanston [John J. Quirt]	Sue Bonsteel	Gladys Eickmeier	George Smith, L. Victor Lindsay, Daniel J. Devlin, Grant Kropf, Gerry Cullen, Ald. Bob Smith
1973	Chris B. Swanston [John J. Quirt]	Sue Bonsteel	Sue Bonsteel	Fred Bergsma, Daniel J. Devlin, John Devlin, Joe Cassone, George Smith, Jim Morris, Gerald Cullen, Ald. Gar Landers
1974	George Smith [Daniel J. Devlin]	Sue Bonsteel	Sue Bonsteel	Fred Bergsma, Gerald Cullen, Sharon Malvern, Ald. Gar Landers, John Devlin, Joe Cassone, Joan Smith
1975	George Smith [Fred Bergsma]	Sue Bonsteel	Sue Bonsteel	Joan Smith, Sharon Malvern, Joe Cassone, John Devlin, Dan Devlin, Gerald Cullen, Ald. John Skinner
Year	**Chair**	**Vice-chair**	**Secretary-Treasurer**	**Board Members**
1976	Fred Bergsma	Dan Devlin	Sue Bonsteel	George Smith, Sharon Malvern, Joan Smith, John Devlin, Joe Cassone, Fred Bergsma, Ald. John Skinner
1977	Sharon Malvern	Fred Bergsma	Sue Bonsteel	John Devlin, Dan Devlin, George Smith, Ed Neigh, Joe Cassone, John McCarroll, Ald. Colleen Misener
1978	John Devlin	Fred Bergsma	Sue Bonsteel	Wayne Billo, Sharon Malvern, Dan Devlin, John McCarroll, John Heney, Ed Neigh, Joe Cassone, Ald. Colleen Misener
1979	John Devlin	Sharon Malvern	Sue Bonsteel	Fred Bergsma, Ed Neigh, Joanne Jackson,

				Elizabeth Heney, Wayne Billo, Joe Cassone, Dan Devlin, Ald. Betty McMillan
1980	Fred Bergsma	Sharon Malvern	Sue Bonsteel	John Devlin, Wayne Billo, Elizabeth Heney, Ed Neigh, Ald. Betty McMillan, Dan Devlin, Joanne Jackson
1981	Sharon Malvern	Wayne Billo	Sue Bonsteel	Dan Devlin, Fred Bergsma, Elizabeth Heney, Ken Varley, Ed Neigh, Delmar Smythe, Ald. (Rev.) Fred Faist
1982	Sharon Malvern	Wayne Billo	Sue Bonsteel	Joan Smith, Elizabeth Heney, Fred Bergsma, Larry McKay, Dan Devlin, Joe Cassone, Ald. Bruce Gibson
1983 1984	Ken Varley	Wayne Billo	Jane E. Kirkpatrick	Anne Orr, Fred Bergsma, Dan Devlin, Larry McKay, Joan Smith, Ald. Delmar Smythe, Joe Cassone
1985	Ken Varley	Anne Orr	Jane E. Kirkpatrick	Dan Devlin, Ald. Delmar Smythe, Joe Cassone, Joan Smith, Alice Herbert, Marianne Huitema
1986	Joe Cassone	Alice Herbert	Jane E. Kirkpatrick	Ald. Richard Linley, Donna Bousher, Nigel Gough, Joan Smith, Dan Devlin, Harry Nesbitt, Marianne Huitema, Alice Herbert, Burt Reid
1987 1988	Joe Cassone	Alice Herbert	Jane E. Kirkpatrick	Joan Smith, Harry Nesbitt, Burt Reid, Ald. Richard Linley, Dan Devlin, Bob Neely, Donna Bousher
1989	Burt Reid	Doris Stewart	Jane E. Kirkpatrick	Ald. Harry Nesbitt, Deedee Herman, Grant Bowers, Margie Leushuis, Jack Hamilton, Harry Fisher, Laura Beckner, Irene Dutchak
1990	Burt Reid	Grant Bowers	Jane E. Kirkpatrick	Ald. Harry Nesbitt, Deedee Herman, Donna Sherratt, Margie McCarthy Leushuis, Margaret Steel, Irene Dutchak, Laura Beckner, John Hayes
1991	Burt Reid	Irene Dutchak	Jane E. Kirkpatrick	Ald. Harry Nesbitt, Deedee Herman, Donna Sherratt, Margie McCarthy Leushuis, Margaret Steel, Laura Beckner, John Hayes
1992	Irene Dutchak	Harry Nesbitt	Jane E. Kirkpatrick	Eric Ferguson, John Hayes, Ald. Chris Blake, Margie McCarthy, Shirley Weitzel, E. Joan Smith

1993	Irene Dutchak	Harry Nesbitt	Jane E. Kirkpatrick	Eric Ferguson, John Hayes, Patricia Stanley, Shirley Weitzel, Margie McCarthy, E. Joan Smith, Ald. Chris Blake
1994	Harry Nesbitt	Irene Dutchak	Jane E. Kirkpatrick	Margie McCarthy, Charles Mountford, Ald. Chris Blake, Eric Ferguson, Shirley Weitzel, E. Joan Smith, Patricia Stanley
1995	Ald. Harry Nesbitt	Patricia Stanley	Jane E. Kirkpatrick	Joyce Jantos, Lester Wilker, E. Joan Smith, Ramona Million, Charles Mountford, Joan G. Smith, Debbie Rabidoux
1996 1997	Patricia Stanley	Joyce Jantos	Jane E. Kirkpatrick	Ald. Harry Nesbitt, Ramona Million, Michael Dale, Jane Taylor, Burt Reid, Debbie Rabidoux
1998	Patricia Stanley	Marilyn Dimeo	Jane E. Kirkpatrick	Ald. Michael Dale, Betty Jorna, Ramona Million, Burt Reid, Bonnie Butcher, Merton Proctor, Mary Jane Karkheck
1999	Marilyn Dimeo	Dr. Susan Tamblyn	Jane E. Kirkpatrick	Bonnie Butcher, Ald. Michael Dale, Mary Jane Karkheck, Ramona Million, Merton Proctor, Betty Jorna, Perry Hill, Patricia Stanley
2000	Ald. Michael Dale	Dr. Susan Tamblyn	Jane E. Kirkpatrick	Patricia Stanley, Bonnie Butcher, Mary Jane Karkheck, Perry Hill, Ramona Million, Marilyn Dimeo, Betty Jorna
2001	Dr. Susan Tamblyn	Perry Hill	Jane E. Kirkpatrick	Michael Dale, Marilyn Dimeo, Darren Redfern, Mike Dewan, Doug Pratley, Sheila Clarke, Ruth Lovell, Mayor Karen Haslam
2002 2003	Dr. Susan Tamblyn	Perry Hill	Jane E. Kirkpatrick	Craig Burtch, Marilyn Dimeo, Darren Redfern, Mike Dewan, Sheila Clarke, Ruth Lovell, Mayor Karen Haslam

Chief librarian Sue Bonsteel and board chair George Smith go through some Canadiana stored in the SPL basement, 1974. The room they are in was in the northwest corner of the building and was accessed from the main floor by a staircase that was built in the 1960s.

Public School and Court House, Stratford, Ont.

The double chimney of the Stratford Public Library is visible between the Perth County courthouse (right) and the bell-towered Central School.

About Dean Robinson

Dean Robinson grew up in Mitchell, Ont., but since 1969 has lived in Stratford.

As a high school student, he contributed stories to the *Mitchell Advocate* and became hooked on journalism.

He joined the *London Free Press* in 1965, and from then through 1982 worked on newspapers and magazines, and at radio and television stations in Seaforth, Stratford, London and Kitchener.

His first of more than 15 books, a biography of hockey legend Howie Morenz, was the outgrowth of a project he completed for his master of arts degree in journalism at the University of Western Ontario. It was published in 1982.

Since then his work has included books on hell driver Lucky Lott, the towns of Mitchell and Seaforth, his high school, the Stratford Agricultural Society, the Stratford YMCA, the Stratford Rotary Club, the Stratford Cullitons, Stratford General Hospital and the history of the railway in Stratford. He has also edited five township histories, and produced the photographs for a book on daytripping in southwestern Ontario.

From 1989 to 2001 he taught journalism at the Doon campus of Conestoga College.

His other interests include kayaking, sailing, travel and the Montreal Canadiens.

For more than 20 years, he and his wife Judy have lived within a short walk of the Stratford Public Library.